Manannan's Cloak

An anthology of Manx Literature

Manannan's Cloak

An Anthology of Manx Literature

Selected by
Robert Corteen Carswell

Francis Boutle Publishers

First published by Francis Boutle Publishers
272 Alexandra Park Road
London N22 7BG
Tel/Fax: (020) 8889 7744
Email: info@francisboutle.co.uk
www.francisboutle.co.uk

This selection © Robert Corteen Carswell 2010
All rights reserved.
No part of this book may be reproduced, stored
in a retrieval system, or transmitted, in any form
or by any means, electronic, mechanical
photocopying or otherwise without the prior permission of the publishers.

ISBN 978 1 903427 49 1

Acknowledgments

Grateful thanks are extended to the Manx Heritage Foundation (Undinys Eiraght Vannin) for its support in making this publication possible. The Manx Heritage Foundation has also been instrumental in publishing or in making possible the publication of a number of the books referenced and quoted herein.

Yn Cheshaght Ghailckagh (The Manx Gaelic Society) continues to produce a wide range of publications in and about Manx, and I am grateful to the Secretary for permission to quote and reference works which it has published.

Publications in Manx have been labours of love by the authors and translators themselves, to whom a huge debt of gratitude is owed. Thanks are extended to present-day authors for their permission to quote from their works. Their details will be found throughout the text and in the attached bibliography.

Some older works quoted here are not generally available, such as those which appeared in the volumes of the Manx Society in the nineteenth century, for all their faults. However, Manx National Heritage (Eiraght Ashoonagh Vannin) provides an excellent reference library facility which makes books and manuscripts available to the interested reader. A piece by J J Kneen is also included which was published in the former *Journal of the Manx Museum*.

Not least amongst these acknowledgments is that to Clive Boutle, who proposed the project. He also set the text in the first place, then had to cope with numerous revisions. These were caused not by Clive but by the author who not only switched his policy on how to deal with some texts, but also changed his mind about which text to use when there was a choice. Grateful thanks and sincere apologies to Clive for making his task that much more difficult.

Contents

- 9 Foreword by Dr Breesha Maddrell
- 11 The Manx Language

From Under the Cloak
- 17 The Traditionary Ballad – Coontey Jeh Ellan Vannin Ayns Arrane/An Account of the Isle of Man in a Song *Anonymous*

Sacred and Secular
- 22 The Litany *Lioar Padjer (Bishop John Phillips)*
- 23 Creggyn Scarleode/Scarlet Rocks *Samuel Rutter*
- 25 Eubonia Soilshagh/Eubonia Bright *Samuel Rutter*
- 27 Trimshey Baiht 'Sy Jough Lajer/Sorrow Drowned in the Strong Drink *Samuel Rutter*
- 29 Shee As Maynrys Ny Manninee/The Peace and Happiness of the Manx People *Samuel Rutter*

The Eighteenth Century
- 33 Baase Illiam Dhone/The Death of Illiam Dhone *Anonymous*
- 40 Ny Kirree Fo Niaghtey/The Sheep Under the Snow *Anonymous*
- 42 Coyrle Sodjeh/Principles and Duties of Christianity *Thomas Wilson*
- 45 Carval Noa/A New Carval *Anonymous*
- 49 Carval Ny Drogh Vraane/Carval of the Bad Women *Anonymous*
- 59 Yn Sushtal Scruit Liorish Yn Noo Mian/The Gospel According to St Matthew *Translated by William Walker*
- 62 Tra Ta Mish Jeeaghyn Er Yn Yrjid Heose/When I am Looking on the Height Above *Thomas Allen*
- 66 A Sorrowful Ditty on the Death of Her Two Sons *Widow Teare of Ballaugh*
- 72 Coontey-Ghiare Jeh Ellan Vannin/A Short Account of the Isle of Man *Joseph Bridson*
- 75 Thurot as Elliot/Thurot and Elliot *Anonymous*
- 80 Psalm XC *Robert Radcliff and Matthias Curghey*

CONTENTS

84   Fin as Oshin/Fin and Oshin *Anonymous*
86   Yn Fer-rauee Creestee/The Christian Monitor *Paul Crebbin*
88   Coayl Jeh Ny Baatyn-Skeddan/The Loss of the Herring Boats *Quayle Vessie*
94   Marrinys Yn Tiger/The Voyage of the Tiger *John Moore*
102 Lhig Da'n Slane Seihll Cur Clashtyn/ Let the Whole World Give Hearing *Attributed to William Kinrade*
106 Roish My Row Flaunys Er Ny Chroo/Before the Heavens Were Created *Attributed to Thomas Christian*
115 Pargys Caillit/ Paradise Lost *Thomas Christian*

The Nineteenth Century

121 Mylecharaine *Anonymous*
123 Yn Chied Homily Jeh Agglish Hostyn/The First Homily of the Church of England *Translation attributed to John Thomas Clarke*
124 Coontey Jeh Saggyrt William Tyndall/An Account of the Priest William Tyndall *Anonymous*
126 Hymn 150 *Anonymous*
128 My Chaarjyn, Gow Shiu Tastey/My Friends, Take You Notice *Attributed to John Lewin*
132 Pingyn Yn Ommidan/The Fool's Pence *John Lewin and Evan Christian*
137 Dobberan Chengey Ny Mayrey Ellan Vannin/Lamenting the Mother Tongue of the Isle of Man *William Kennish*
143 Eam Er Y Theay/A Call to the Populace *Proclamation*
144 Acts Which Have Received Royal Assent *Official Document*
147 Loayrtys Yn Arr T Caine, Caarliagh/Speech of the Rev T Caine, Chairman *Rev T Caine*
148 Screeuyn Yn Arr J T Clarke/Letter of the Rev J T Clarke *Rev John Thomas Clarke*
151 Early Years *Neddy Beg Hom Ruy (Edward Faragher/Farquar)*
153 Yn Moddey-Oaldey As Yn Eayn/The Wolf and the Lamb *Neddy Beg Hom Ruy (Edward Faragher/Farquar)*
153 Vannin Veg Veen/Dear Little Mannin *Neddy Beg Hom Ruy (Edward Faragher/Farquar)*

The Twentieth Century

156 Yn Arrane Ashoonagh/The National Anthem *Translated by John Joseph Kneen*
161 Rubaiyat of Omar Khayyam *Translated by John Joseph Kneen*
165 Cheer Nyn Aeg/The Land of the Young *John Joseph Kneen*
166 Arrane Lhong-Liauyr Ny Lochlinnee/The Song of the Vikings' Long-Boat *Juan Comish*
168 Yn Edd Ec Jac/ Jac's Hat *A S B Davies*
172 Yn Brack T'Ayns Yn Awin Mooar/ The Trout That's in the Big River *Frank Bell Kelly*

174	Yn Whallag/The Whallag *John Gell*
175	Aalican/Tranquility *John Gell*
176	Morte D'Arthur *John Gell*
179	Skeeal Auddyn Veih'n Neear/The Story of Auddyn from the West *Robert L Thomson*
181	Bardoonys Son Archibald Cregeen/Elegy for Archibald Cregeen *Mona Douglas*
182	Bardoonys Son Illiam Dhone/Elegy for Illiam Dhone *Mona Douglas*
185	Skeealaght – Raa-Toshee/Story-telling – Foreword *Shorus y Creayrie (George Broderick)*
186	Ny Three Muckyn Beggey/The Three Little Pigs *Colin y Jerree (Colin Jerry)*
189	Gynsaghey Gaelg/Learning Manx *Doug Fargher*
191	Harry Kelly *Mark Braide*
194	Phillie Mac Y Phaill/Phillie Quayle *Chalse y Craayne (Charles Craine)*
196	Caesar Cashin *Leslie Quirk*
197	Pooar Veih Chesh-Vean Vreneen: Cre Cho Gaueagh?/Power From an Atom's Nucleus: Just How Dangerous? *Brian Stowell*
199	Ersooyl Myr Scadoo/Away Like a Shadow *Robard y Charsalagh (Robert Corteen Carswell)*
206	Bible Chasherick Yn Lught Thie/The Family Holy Bible *Robert Thomson*
206	Preface to English-Manx Dictionary *Doug Fargher*
208	Ny Tree Reayrtyn S'Aaley/The Three Most Beautiful Sights *Robard y Charsalagh (Robert Corteen Carswell)*
209	Arrane Mysh Aile Y Ghrianane/ A Song About the Summerland Fire *Shorus y Creayrie (George Broderick)*
215	Faaie-Croquet Y Venrein/The Queen's Croquet-Ground *Brian Stowell*
217	Er y Cheer 'Sy Cheeiragh/ In the Countryside in the Gloaming *Robard y Charsalagh (Robert Corteen Carswell)*
217	Foillycan Ec Yn Uinnag/Butterfly at the Window *Robard y Charsalagh (Robert Corteen Carswell)*
219	Irree Ny Greiney/ Sunrise *Robard y Charsalagh (Robert Corteen Carswell)*
220	Dunverys er Traen-Tappee yn Niar/Murder on the Orient Express *Joan Caine*
224	Dunveryssyn Yn Tooder-Folley/The Vampire Murders *Brian Stowell*
226	Goll Er Oai/Going Ahead *Graham Naylor*
228	Jough-Laanee Aegid/ Elixir of Youth *Christopher Lewin*
230	Yuki Onna *R W K Teare*
231	Creeaght/ Courage *R W K Teare*
233	Brann Foillycan/ A Butterfly's Dream *Graham Naylor*
235	Manannan Mac Y Leirr/ Manannan Son of Leirr *Peddyr Shimmin and Chris Sheard*
237	Bibliography

Foreword

This anthology would have surprised and delighted the late R L Thomson, who noted in 1988 that the audience for Manx literature had been 'too small and too poor and its authors too lacking in patrons …for us to expect a rich harvest of literary works…' In gathering together such a rich and wide variety of texts, Robert Carswell clearly demonstrates that this is no longer the case. *Manannan's Cloak* is a celebration of Manx literature from its earliest publication to the present day and, as such, is a great gift not only to the Manx speech community but also to those around the world interested in minority languages and traditional song.

The collection brings together original texts and translations which have lain hidden away in archives or have disappeared from sight in the rather ephemeral pamphlets and scripts which have long been part of the Manx language movement. Alongside the more familiar religious texts of the 18th and 19th centuries are translations of Aesop's Fables, Tennyson and the Rubaiyat. It is, however, the collection of songs and stories of the late 20th century that shows a new confidence in celebration of the language.

There could have been no better choice as compiler and editor than Robert Carswell, a fine poet, songwriter and translator, someone who understands the beauty of the Manx language, someone who appreciates its intricacies and intimacies. He has been involved in writing and broadcasting in Manx since the 1970s and in providing books and rhymes for Manx medium playgroups from 1983. Since 2006 he has been working to develop Manx language resources for the Bunscoill Ghaelgagh (Manx medium primary school) and the Manx language team for the Isle of Man Department of Education. A talented singer, musician and Gaelgeyr, he presents a bilingual programme, Claare ny Gael, on Manx Radio and has long been involved in organising festivals such as Yn Chruinnaght and the Cooish Inter-Gaelic festival.

Manannan's Cloak is framed with images of the sea-god Manannan, the legendary first ruler of the Isle of Man and inspiration for many writers. With the author's deep and detailed understanding of the texts and their context in Manx history, shared here with the reader so generously, this collection will refresh and revitalise the language movement in the Isle of Man whilst revealing the treasures of its literature to readers around the world.

Dr Breesha Maddrell
Manx Heritage Foundation, 2010

The Manx language

The Isle of Man is, in its Gaelic form, Ellan Vannin or simply Mannin. The Manx Gaelic language is now generally referred to as 'Manx', though the earlier spelling, in general use until the mid-nineteenth century, is 'Manks'. Since about 1970, use has again been made by some people of 'Manks' for language and other cultural matters, as Manx itself does not make use of the letter *x*.

Manx is a member of the Celtic group of Indo-European languages. The Celtic group now comprises six languages, divided into two branches: the Brythonic (Welsh, Breton and Cornish) and the Goidelic (Irish, Scottish and Manx Gaelic).

Manx has developed from Irish Gaelic, which arrived in the Island probably in the fourth or fifth century AD. The oldest inscriptions in the Island are in Ogam characters from the end of the fifth or beginning of the sixth century. These inscriptions attest the Gaelic language, with MAQ representing the later 'mac', meaning 'son', and include the name MAQLEOG, an early appearance of a still widespread Manx surname, Clague (127 entries in the Manx Telecom Phone Book 2009).

The appearance of Scandinavian influence in the Irish Sea from about 800 AD led to raids and later settlement in the Isle of Man. Was Gaelic ousted by Scandinavian influences? Might it have continued on an equal basis, as the language of a minority, as the language of a subordinate group? This has been a topic of considerable academic debate. However, the most famous of the Scandinavian Kings of Man and the Isles and founder of a 200-year dynasty, Godred (ruled 1079-1095), already had a Gaelic soubriquet, Crovan.

A stone from about the middle of the tenth century contains ogams, though one set is illegible, and the other is a complete ogam alphabet. In addition to these indications of Gaelic, the stone also has an inscription in Scandinavian runes, yet these include references to MAL LUMKUN, MAL MURU AND TUFKALS. These are Gaelic names, but in Scandinavian runes. The word given as MAL is now 'meayl' in modern Manx, defined partly as 'bald, without hair'. The prefix of 'meayl' refers to the shaving of part of a man's head as a mark of his religious vocation. The subsequent part of the name refers to the saint to whom they have dedicated themselves. The name MAL MURU developed into the later Manx surname, Mylevoirrey, subsequently anglicised as Morrison.

The Mal Lumkun stone is not alone in showing Gaelic names amongst Scandinavian runes from the tenth and eleventh centuries. Amongst them is MAIL BRIKTI, the Gaelic Mael Brighde, later Mylevreeshey, a follower of Breeshey, Bride or Bridget. This was anglicised into another common Manx surname, Bridson (pronounced Bride-son – 71 entries in the 2009 phone book). The appearance of Gaelic names in a Scandinavian context suggests continuation of Gaelic to some degree. It also suggests that some Gaels made up not just a lower level of society, but enjoyed sufficient status to be honoured in death on the same basis as their Scandinavian neighbours.

After the Scandinavian period, Manx was the majority language of the populace. Those who consider that Gaelic died out during the Scandinavian period have suggested that its re-emergence and subsequent dominance arose through influence mainly from Scotland, though also from Ireland, from the mid-thirteenth century AD. However, Latin and English were the languages of administration. After a few early indications of its presence, Gaelic becomes hidden from view for some time, apart from contemporary names recorded amongst the Latin and English of officialdom.

The Bishop of Sodor and Man from 1577 to 1599 was John Meryk. He wrote of the Island in a letter dated 22 October 1577 to William Camden. Camden reprinted Bishop Meryk's letter in 'Britannia', which was first published in 1586. Amongst Meryk's observations, he writes that

> whereas the whole isle is divided into two parts, south and north, the inhabitants of this speak like the Scots, and those of the other like the Irish.

This point is echoed by D B Gregor in his 'Celtic – A Comparative Study', published in 1980:

> One might suppose that an island as diminutive as Man was from the first a natural unit, but even geographically this is not quite so. There is a watershed which divides the island into two parts, and the differences between those who live north and south of it were once sufficiently marked for each to give its allegiance to a different contender for the Manx throne ... , and even to fight a battle on opposite sides ... It is even the reason why there are still today two Deemsters (Judges).

If a work is to be put into writing, a literate audience is required large enough to make the production of books worth while for copyists, printers or publishers, and rich enough to pay for books produced. As the Isle of Man could not meet these criteria, the Gaelic language of the Island was developing within an oral tradition. Without the conservativism of a written tradition, it developed characteristics of its own in choice of words and preferred verb forms. It became Manx. Manx finally emerges in written form in the early seventeenth century. By this time it had grown away from its Old Irish, common Gaelic roots. As D B Gregor observes in a note to a description of the Isle of Man, 'What emerges from the present study is the extraordinary independence of Manx'.

When a written form of Manx developed, some texts from an earlier oral tradition were committed to writing. Internal evidence suggests that the earliest composition is from the early fifteenth century. However, before we can go back to that early work, we have first to see how written Manx arose.

The catalyst for creating Manx literature was the church. The church realised that it could not reach its congregation in the Isle of Man without Manx. A translation into Manx of the 1604 Anglican Book of Common Prayer was in manuscript form from about 1610. The orthography was based on both Welsh and English letter values, devised by Bishop John Phillips (Bishop of Sodor and Man 1605–1633), a native of Hawarden in North Wales. The first known publication including Manx was by Thomas Wilson (Bishop of Sodor and Man 1698–1755). The orthography used in Wilson's book of 1707 was different to that of the manuscript of one hundred years earlier, and was to set a general basis for later writing in Manx, though not by any means an absolute standard. The orthography makes written Manx quite different in appearance from Irish and Scottish orthography. However, it probably reflects the changes in Manx, including the alteration and loss of some sounds compared with its Gaelic neighbours, over a period of something like 1,300 years. As Jennifer Kewley Draskau describes it:

> For various reasons, its [Manx's] present spelling system differs radically from traditional Goidelic spelling, but in other respects Manx displays many similarities with related languages and is to some degree intelligible to speakers of Irish and Scots Gaelic, once they have recovered from the initial shock of its orthography.

Phillips made use of a number of accents over the letters [a], [e], [i], [o] and [y]. Some texts in 'standard' Manx also use marks:

(a) a cedilla under a c in 'ch' when denoting the sound as in English 'church' to differentiate it from the gutteral 'ch' as in Scottish 'loch';

(b) a circumflex over an [a] to denote a wide pronunciation as in English 'dare' as compared with a short [a] in 'dab';

(c) diareses over a vowel to indicate that it is pronounced, not lost in an adjoining vowel.

However, most texts do not use them, and they have not been included in this collection. The use of an apostrophe to indicate missing letters is common in the case of 'sy and 'syn for ayns y and ayns yn, but more variable in the case of a lenited f-, so that 'syn 'aasagh and syn aasagh are both found. In relation to lenition of f-, Robert Thomson has referred to it as 'the immutable f' as the letter is commonly retained rather than being either replaced by an apostrophe or omitted. This is not to say that its silent, lenited form would not have been observed in reading aloud. However, all three usages – the retained f-, the apostrophe and the omitted letter – are all found in Manx texts, and a single text may have all three. Jennifer Kewley Draskau again sums up the situation like this:

> The system itself is riddled with exceptions and some inconsistencies. Hyphenation is variable in Manx as in most languages. The hyphens and apostrophes used throughout this book represent one option ... but it is not the intention to present a prescriptive system.

In the preface to the 'Coyrle Sodjeh', Wilson refers to 'the Liberty which every Man take of 'Writing after his own Way' ...' This continues to be a feature of Manx, where spelling still displays flexibility. The Manx name for the language itself is either Gailck or Gaelg. The name of the god Manannan is found as Mannanan or Manninan, with emphasis on the first syllable, whilst the anglicised version tends to put emphasis on the second syllable. Wilson's reference is perhaps to attempts by his clergy to find a way of writing the Manx part of his book, or possibly for their own notes and translations of the Bible when preaching to their Manx-speaking congregation. It is not known by whom the chosen orthography was developed, but Wilson's remark suggests that it was one of several possible forms.

The eighteenth century saw a number of religious tracts translated into Manx. It also saw a native tradition of writing religious songs in Manx called 'carvals'. The name is related to 'carol', and the carvals became associated with a unique service, the Oiel Verree, on 24 December. The carvals deal with a wide range of religious subjects, though some include reference to the nativity. Carval writing continued into the early nineteenth century. The 'Mona's Herald' newspaper printed carvals and their translations in its columns in the late nineteenth century, and this was issued as 'Carvalyn Gailckagh' with a short introduction by A W Moore in 1891.

The Manx Society volumes edited by William Harrison and A W Moore's 'A Manx Note Book', 'Manx Ballads & Music' and 'Carvalyn Gailckagh' contain many songs and rhymes from manuscript copies, but their spelling has already been amended ('corrected') by the editors or their assistants. Lack of familiarity with Manx and with the hand-writing styles of earlier periods have allowed misspellings to come in. There is occasional confusion between: 'f' and the old-style 's', as in 'seme' for 'feme'; 'u' and 'n', as in 'yusagh' for 'ynsagh'; 'c' and 'e', as in 'sereenee' for 'screeuee'. The Manx content was further compromised by being set by compositors and proof readers without knowledge of Manx; obvious misreadings are, therefore, silently amended. Erratic punctuation may be at odds with the content and is generally omitted from these texts.

By the mid- to late-nineteenth century Manx was beginning to lose ground to the more widespread adoption of English. Manx came to be regarded as an encumbrance which would hold people back in the English speaking world of the British Empire. Though Manx was to remain a community language in the southern village of Cregneash until the 1920s, the period from 1870 saw a particularly determined move away from Manx. In the twentieth century, some of those who were known to be able to speak Manx would not admit to it. A small number of native speakers were, however, willing to pass the language on to enthusiasts. There are a number of recordings of Manx, including some from the early twentieth century, but most from 1948 onwards. The emphasis was on spoken Manx, though in some cases this was supported by use of the Bible in Manx. Though the last of the reputed native speakers of Manx, Ned Maddrell, died in 1974, a number of language enthusiasts had learned Manx from him and from other of the native speakers who had survived into the second half of the twentieth century. There has, therefore, been a continuation of spoken Manx.

A UNESCO report in 2009 declared the Manx language to be extinct, having died in 1974 with Ned Maddrell. However, Manx has attained increased status and use since Ned Maddrell's death. Officials have admitted that a separate category may have to be created to express the situation. George Broderick gave a technical analysis of the situation under the title, 'Language Death in the Isle of Man – An investigation into the decline and extinction of Manx Gaelic as a community language in the Isle of Man' (1999). He had earlier described the situation in a footnote in 'A Handbook of Late Spoken Manx' (1984): 'The Manx spoken today, though based on native Manx speech, is revived Manx and is usually classified as Neo-Manx.' Manx is not the only language in such a situation. The classic example of an 'extinct' language which has attained wide modern usage is Hebrew.

In 1899 Yn Cheshaght Ghailckagh (The Manx Gaelic Society) had been founded. Yn Cheshaght Ghailckagh made, and continues to make, dictionaries, primers and other texts of interest available, though only a limited amount of original work was produced until about 1970. Following interest aroused by a Manx column in the 'Manx Star' newspaper, a commercial book of Manx short stories, 'Skeealaght', was published in 1976. This led on to other, smaller-scale publications, largely photocopied from typed originals.

Since 1982 the Isle of Man Government has supported the language through the work of the Manx Heritage Foundation, which has made grants and loans available for the production of commercial publications. The number of Manx literary texts is increasing. Manx was given further impetus in 1992, when it was offered as an optional subject by the Department of Education to primary school children. The resultant numbers were too great to be accommodated. Since then there has been the establishment of the Bunscoill Ghaelgagh, a primary school where the medium of education is Manx. Four subjects at secondary level are now also being given in Manx, whilst a GCSE and A-level equivalent in Manx can also be taken.

From the arrival of Old Irish from about the fourth century AD, to the time of its first being written down some 1,300 years later in 1610, the language had become Manx. It had developed more flexibly as an oral language away from Irish, where change was slower owing to the conservative effect of an existing literature. From the first printed book using Manx in 1707, Manx literature remained largely religious over the next 200 years, with a flowering of vernacular writing in the carvals from the eighteenth and into the nineteenth century. It is ironic that the language had come into written form just as it was starting to come under pressure from the growth of English, a situation which became more intense throughout the nineteenth century and led to a strongly adverse reaction to the language right up to the 1970s.

There was an emphasis on preservation and safeguarding the language for much of the twentieth century. Since about 1970, the attitude to Manx has become increasingly positive. This has led to further translation, anecdote and memoir, but also to more original writing. A more broadly-based Manx literature is arising and is continuing to develop.

From Under the Cloak

Manannan's Cloak is a mist that protects the Island from outsiders. Reference to it may be more light-hearted than earnest these days, but it remains a well-known image in the Island. The earliest known composition in Manx opens with reference to Manannan and his cloak. Composition is thought to date to between 1490 and 1530, though not known in written form until about 1770. It includes the appointment as Kings of Man and some early actions of the Stanley family, who later became the Earls of Derby. The composition is 'Coontey jeh Ellan Vannin ayns Arrane' ('An Account of Ellan Vannin in a Song'), also known as 'The Traditionary Ballad'.

These are the first twelve verses out of the 57 thought to make up the older part of the song. A further five verses were added later, though prior to 1770. This Manx text is a 'best reading' by Robert Thomson.

Anonymous
Coontey Jeh Ellan Vannin Ayns Arrane (The Traditionary Ballad) *c.1490–1530*

Dy neaishtagh shiu agh rish my Skeayll
As dy ving lhieu ayns my Chant
Myr share dy voddyms lesh my Veeall
Yinnin diu geill da'n Ellan Sheeant

Quoi yn chied er ec row rieau ee
Ny kys eisht myr haghyr da
Ny kys hug Patrick ayn Creestee
Ny kys myr haink ee gys Stanlaa

Mannanan beg va Mac y Leirr
Shen yn chied er ec row rieau ee
Agh myr share oddym's cur-my-ner
Cha row eh hene agh Anchreestee

Cha nee lesh e Chliwe ren eh ee reayll
Cha nee lesh e Hideyn, ny lesh e Vhow
Agh tra aikagh eh Lhuingys troailt
Oallagh eh ee mygeayrt lesh Keaue

Yinnagh eh Dooinney ny hassoo er Brooghe
Er-lhieu shen hene dy beagh ayn Keead
As shen myr dreill Mannanan keoie
Yn Ellan shoh'n-ayn lesh cosney Bwoid

Yn Mayll deeck dagh unnane ass e Cheer
Va bart dy Leoagher-ghlass dagh blein
As eisht shen orroo d'eeck myr Keesh
Trooid magh ny Cheerey dagh Oie-Lhoine

Paart ragh lesh y Leoagher seose
Gys yn Slieau mooar ta heose Barrool
Paart elley aagagh yn Leoagher wass
Ec Mannanan erskyn Keamool

Myr shen eisht ren adsyn beaghey
O er-lhiam pene dy by-veg nyn Geesh
Gyn kiarail as gyn Imnea
Ny doggyr dy lhiggey er nyn Skeeys

Eisht haink ayn Parick nyn meayn
She Dooinney-noo v'eh lane dy Artue
Dimman eh Mannanan er y Tonn
As e ghrogh Vooinjer dy lieh-chiart

Nagh Deiyr E ad's chur E dy baase
Dagh unnane jeusyn hass ree-rout
As orroosyn cha ren E graase
Dy row Sluight ny Mutch ny Grout

Vannee eh'n Cheer veih Kione dy Kione
As rieau cha daag eh Boght ayn-jee
Dy row jeh yrjid Lhiannoo-beg

From Under the Cloak

Dy dob rieau dy ve ny Chreestee

Shen myr haink y chied Chredjue Mannin
Ec Parick Noo er ny chur ayn
As Creest dy niartagh aynin eh
As neesht myrgeddin ayns nyn Gloan

Translation

An Account of the Isle of Man in a Song (The Traditionary Ballad) *c.1490–1530*

If you would listen but to my Story
And to harmonise with them in my Song
As best as I can with my Mouth
I would have you pay attention to the Blessed Isle.

Who was the first person who ever had it
Or what then happened to him
Or how Patrick brought in Christianity
Or how it was that it came to Stanley.

Little Mannanan was the Son of Leirr [the sea]
That's the first person who ever had it
But as best as I can behold
He himself was nothing but a Heathen

It was not with a Sword that he kept it
It was not with his Arrows, or with his Bow
But when he would see a Fleet travelling
He would conjure it around with a Mist

He would put a Man standing on the Broogh
Those ones would think that there were a Hundred there
And that's how wild Mannanan kept
This very Island with a gain of Booty

The rent each individual paid from his Country [Land]
Was a bundle of green Rushes each year
And then they had to pay that as a Tax
Throughout the Country each St John's Eve

Some would go with the Rushes up
To the great Mountain that's up at Barrule

Some others would leave the Rushes below
For Mannanan above Keamool [lost place name]

Like that then those ones were living
O I myself think that their Tax was small
Without care and without Concern
Or dint of labour to bring Tiredness on them

Then came in Patrick amongst them
A saintly Man was he, full of Virtue
He drove Mannanan on the Wave
And his wicked Kinsmen roughly

Did He not Drive them and He put to death
Each individual of those who stood [warned beforehand?]
And to those He gave no grace
That were of the seed of the Conjuror of Cunning

He blessed the Country from End to End
And he never left a Wretched thing in it
That was of the height of a little Baby
That ever refused to be a Christian

That's how the first Faith came to Mannin
Having been brought in by Saintly Patrick
And may Christ strengthen it in us
And also as well in our Children

By the time the known versions of 'The Traditionary Ballad' were committed to writing, a form of 'standard' Manx had been baptised by Bishop Thomas Wilson (episcopacy 1698–1755) and confirmed under the hand of Bishop Mark Hildesley (episcopacy 1755–1772). What emerged in writing from under Mannanan's cloak was strongly Christian.

Sacred and Secular

An attempt had been made to capture Manx in writing about 100 years after composition of 'The Traditionary Ballad'. This was a translation of the Book of Common Prayer which was in manuscript form from about 1610. It was written using an orthography said to be devised by Bishop John Phillips (also Philips), a native of Hawarden in North Wales. Phillips was Bishop from 1605 to 1633. Parts of the Epistles and Gospels had to be translated to provide appropriate readings in the Book of Common Prayer. James Chaloner was a commissioner appointed in 1652 to assess the Island, and was later Governor of the Island from 1658 to 1660. In a short treatise, he refers to Manx and to Bishop Phillips's translation, though referring to the Bible rather than the Book of Common Prayer.

> Doutblesse this Island was first peopled from the Hebrides, or Highlands of Scotland, their Language being the very same with that of the Scottish-Irish; which is the same with that of Ireland; though spoken in a different Dialect: yet as the Isle is named Man; so are the People style Manksmen, and their Speech, Manks; And although the same hath great affinity with the Welsh or Brittish, (which that singularly Learned, Hospitable, painfull, and pious Prelate, Doctor Philips, late Bishop of Man, and a Native of North-Wales, well experimented; who out of Zeal, to the propagating of the Gospel in these parts, attained the knowledge thereof so exactly, that he did ordinarily preach in it, and undertook that most laborious, most difficult, but most useful Work, of the Translation of the Bible into Manks, taking to his assistance some of the Islanders ... perfected the said Work ...) yet he observed he could not have been able to have gone through with it, but for the helps he found in his own Native Tongue...

Chalenor also observed that 'Few speak the English Tongue.' John Speed described the Isle of Man as part of 'The Theatre of the Empire of Great Britaine', published in 1627, and notes that 'the common sort of people, both in their language and manners, come nighest unto the Irish'.

Phillips uses an emphatic form of the demonstrative, 'shen', ('that') – 'shenenni'. Elsewhere he also uses 'shononi', a demonstrative of 'shoh' ('this'). Spelling of these words is not invariable. These demonstrative forms are not generally found in later texts. However, it occurs in 'The Traditional Ballad' – see above, 'Yn Ellan shoh'n-ayn'. 'The Traditional Ballad' also has examples of a construction which is described by Robert Thomson in his 'Lessoonyn Sodjey 'sy Ghailck Vanninagh':

> ... when the verb is formed with jannoo as an auxiliary, or with foddym or another modal auxiliary such as saillym 'I wish', the object is placed after the auxiliary and the vbn. [verbal noun] follows it preceded by y (leniting); this may be termed the included object construction ..."

In the above extract from 'The Traditional Ballad' is 'ren eh ee reayll' (for 'ren eh ee y reayll'). An extract from Phillips' version of the Book of Common Prayer in his orthography is here followed by the same passage in 'standard' orthography, with an English translation. In this extract is 'gy vod shuiniyn tdy hervayntyn ... buias y hoyrt duit', and in Wilson's orthography, 'dy vod shinyn dty harvaantyn ... booise y chur dhyts'. This is from The Litany:

> O Iíh áer myghinagh nagh vell siaghy begg dy osny kri î vrist, na agháyn leid-shyn as ta layn dy hrimsey: gy myghinagh kúin lesh nan badjraghyn ta shuin dy ianu royds, ayns ully nan saghan, as nan ymmyrts, kre erbi yn trá ni î ayd tryn láys oruin: as gy grásoil klast ruiniyn gy vod ny holkyn shenneni ta kroutyn, as kalgyn ny jeoul, na duyne dy obraghey nan yei shuin, vé erna hoyrt gys gyn veg, as liórish fackyn rói dy vêyis gy vod aydsyn vé er an skeley, gy vod shuiniyn tdy hervayntyn gyn gortaghy liórish trynláys erbi, gybrágh buias y hoyrt duit ayns tdy ghi íll ghasserick, tryid Iesy kriist nan jarn.

The orthography of Bishop Phillips's manuscript did not come into general use. The first printed volume containing Manx was Bishop Thomas Wilson's 'Duties and Principles of Christianity', known to Manx speakers as the 'Coyrle Sodjeh'. The orthography used for Wilson's Manx in his book of 1707 was different to the text of one hundred years earlier. Here is the passage from the 1842 version of the Book of Common Prayer, which was largely a copy of the 1765 version with a few differences.

> O Yee, Ayr vyghinagh, nagh vel soiaghey beg jeh osney cree arryssagh, n'yn yeearree ocsyn ta lane dy hrimshey; Dy myghinagh niartee lesh nyn badjeryn ta shin dy yannoo hood's ayns ooilley nyn seaghyn as nyn ymmyrch cre-erbee yn traa ta shin laadit lhieu; as dy graysoil clasht rooin dy vod ny huilk shen ta croutyn as kialgys y drogh-spyrryd ny dooinney gobbraghey nyn 'oi, ve er ny choyrt gys veg, as liorish ard-chiarail dty vieys dy vod ad v'er nyn skeayley; dy vod shinyn dty harvaantyn, gyn skielley gheddyn liorish tranlaase erbee, dy bragh booise y chur dhyts ayns dty Agglish casherick, trooid Yeesey Creest nyn Jiarn.

Sacred and Secular

Despite the different orthography, much of the structure can be seen to be similar, with alternative lexical choices here and there. Finally, the same extract in English.

> O God, merciful Father, who does not despise the sighing of a repentant heart, nor the petitions of those who are full of sorrow; mercifully help our prayers which we make before you in all our affliction and need, whenever we are burdened with them; and graciously hear us, so that those evils which the craftinesses and deceit of the evil spirit or of man work against us, can be brought to nothing, and that by the great care of your goodness they can be scattered; so that we your servants can, without receiving harm from any oppression, forever give thanks to you in the holy Church, through Jesus Christ our Lord.

The work of Archdeacon and later Bishop Samuel Rutter (episcopacy 1661–1663) is in rather a different vein. He wrote pieces for his patron, James Stanley ('Yn Stanlagh Mooar', 'the Great Stanley'), Seventh Earl of Derby. Stanley was a staunch Royalist and held the Island for the King. He and his friends withdrew to the Island as a secure fortress, and continued to hold entertainments. Rutter refers to the political events surrounding them. It is not known whether Rutter himself made the Manx versions. However, a manuscript containing both English and Manx versions of Rutter's work was noted by A W Moore at Knowsley Hall as being marked '1648'. In 1663 Rutter's successor, Bishop Isaac Barrow, unaware of Bishop Phillips's efforts and of any Manx versions of Rutter's work, wrote of the Manx people that:

> There is nothing either written or printed in their language ... neither can they who speak it best write to one another in it, having no character or letter of it among them.

The translated work of Samuel Rutter was published by Moore in the later 'standard' Manx. This first piece is, in one copy, entitled: 'Threnodia, or Elegaic Song on the direful effects of the grand rebellion, with a prophetic view of the downfall and catastrophe thereof, composed by the Reverend author on Scarlet Rocks, near Castletown.'

Samuel Rutter

Creggyn Scarleode, *c.1648*

My chree lesh seaghyn tooillit
My aigney trimshey lane
My kione jeh cadley spooillit
Gyn saveen cheet er m'ayrn
My lhie er ynnyd cheddin
Yeearree aash ayns fardail

Son naght myr ta ny tonnyn
Ta m'aigney foast rouail

Yn muir lesh goanlys caggey
Ta craa ny creggyn foym
As sneih lurg sneih er m'aigney
Cur eh my chree ve trome
Ny brooinyn syrjey lhaggit
Lesh tonnyn sheer chleih foue
T'an cheeayll ain mennick mollit
As mooads nyn jerkal mow

My ta yn sterrym troggal
'Sny bodjalyn dyn seiyt
T'an aer gaase dhoo as gobhal
Yn soilshey hed neese veih
Myr bleayst goll fo ny lhongyn
Ga t'ad jeh darragh jeant
Ta'n seihll as mooads ny croneeyn
Cur er my chree ve faiynt

Myr shoh er chroshyn smooinaght
Jeh'n chreg cloaie [ta] mee skee
Foast er my lhong veg smooinaght
Te aker ayns my chree
Son cheeayll mee red myr sonnish
Dy bee ain laa caghlaa
Bee'n sterrym dew'l shoh harrish
As voue mayd sollys hraa

Translation

Scarlet Rocks, *c.1648*

My heart with trouble fatigued
My mind [with] sorrow full
My head robbed of sleep
Without slumber coming as my portion
Lying in the same place
Desiring ease in vain
For in the [same] way as are the waves
My mind is still wandering

The sea with malice striving

Is shaking the rocks below me
And vexation upon vexation on my mind
Makes my heart to be heavy
The highest brooghs are loosened
With waves that dig to a great extent beneath them
Our sense is often deceived
And the extent of our expectation destroyed

If the storm arises
And the clouds are not agitated
The air grows black and denies
The light that will come down from it
As a shell going under [are] our boats
Though they are made from oak
The world and extent of [its] faults
Makes my heart to be faint

Like this thinking on [the] crosses [i.e. that I have to bear]
Of the stony rock I am tired
Still thinking of my small ship
It is an anchor in my heart
For I heard something like a whisper
That we will have a day of change
This cruel storm will be over
And we will find a bright[er] time

Bishop or no, Rutter was also the author of some spirited drinking songs. The surrounding political events of the Civil War period will no doubt have influenced his calls for merriment. The name 'Eubonia' is a Latinized form of the Gaelic name 'Emhain Abhlach', an 'other world' which came to be identified with the Island.

Samuel Rutter
Eubonia Soilshagh, *c.1648*

Jeeagh, jeeagh yn ghrian ta reill yn oie
Son soilshey daue ta gennal soie
Jeh'n billey-feeney s'moyrnagh troo
Mysh shoh, ta jeh yn coontey smoo

Chorus
Moyllee-jee maryms, Vanninee
Yn lune vie lajer as y vraih

Dagh seaghyn as dagh kiarail t'ayn
Ta gholl ersooyl lesh bree yn oarn

Dy beagh y staghyl nagh gow coyrle
Er n'iu jeh shoh, ga losht yn seihll
Yn ooir as aer mygeayrt-y-mysh
Veagh eh cho sauchey's ta shin nish

O heshey, gow yn ghless shoh hood
Cre'n aght hee'yms dty stroin ny hrooid
Myr ta'n gholl twoaie jeh cooyl yn aile
Myr shen ta shoh lesh soilshey'n chainle

Agh myr t'an ghrian fo bodjal still
Dasyn ta doal ny doon y hooill
Eshyn nagh n'iu jough tra t'eh paa
She shoh ta jannoo 'n oie jeh laa

O boyaghyn, ny cur-jee geill
Da eddin aalin nee falleil
Dooghys cha dug dooin ny share vie
Na shoh lesh eash ta gaase ny spooie

Translation
Eubonia Bright, *c.1648*

Look, look [upon] the sun that rules the night
For light to them that are cheerfully sitting
The envy of the proudest grapevine
Is about this, that it is considered best

Chorus
Praise with me, Manx people
The good strong ale and the malt
Each trouble, and each care that exists
Goes away with the vigour of the barley

If each awkward person who will not take advice
Had drunk of this, though burnt was the world,
The soil and the air about him
He would be as safe as we are now

O comrade, take this glass to yourself

In such a way that I will see your nose through it
As is the rainbow from the fire surround
Like that is this by the light of a candle

But as the sun is still under a cloud
To him that is blind or closes the eye
He that does not take drink when he is thirsty
It's this that makes the night of a day

O boys, don't give attention
To a beautiful face that will fail
Nature didn't give us any better good
Than this that with age grows more gladsome

Rutter would surely have approved of a beer named 'Eubonia Bright'. A W Moore's 'Manx Ballads and Music' (1896) shows that the following Manx piece derives from Rutter's lyric in English under the title, 'Mellancolly Drown'd in a Glass of Eubonia' – meaning, of course, a glass from Eubonia.

Samuel Rutter

Trimshey Bait 'Sy Jough Lajer, *c. 1648*

Ny bee-jee groamagh arragh
Cur-jee kiarail ergooyl
Eh ta smooinaght er mairagh
Te cheau laa mie ersooyl
Cha vel eh agh lhome
Cha nel eh agh lhome
Nagh vel giu as ceau seaghyn ersooyl.

Te dooinney dangeyragh dy akin
'Sy cheer ta shin nish ayn,
Tra ny naboonyn troggal y cappan
Ta boirit foast ayns e chione
As ooilley yn vea shoh
Goaill doot ny choud bio
Dy n'aase e argid ro-ghoan

She t'an eirinagh 'screeney nagh vel girree
Choud as ta'n cheeaght traaue
Lhig da'n boddagh dy moghey girree
Son doccar myr ta'n traa cheau

Choud's ta famlagh 'sy traie
Bec oarn ayns yn 'aaie
Ver orrin arrane y ghoaill daue

Tra hig yn oarn hooin 'sy vagher
Nee mayd jerkal son chaart y chione
Eisht, ven-y-thie, jeeagh nagh dagh 'er
Rouyr jeh yn ushtey y hoyrt ayn
Veih'n s'ooasle farrane
Ta cheet yn oarn vane
Te chur er sleih creeney ve goan

Nish ayns y thie lieen dooin
As lhig da'n lhin ve lane
Son she shen nee cur dooin
Chreenaght ayns nyn goan
Te ooashley da'n ree
Te ooashley da'n ree
Dy chur er e kione lheid y crooin

Translation

Sorrow Drowned in the Strong Drink, *c.1648*

Don't be gloomy ever
Put care behind
He who thinks on tomorrow
He throws a good day away
He's not but empty
He's not but empty
That isn't drinking and throwing affliction away

It's a man dangerous to see
In the country that we are now in
When the neighbours raise the cup
He's troubled still in his head
And all this life
Doubting as long as he lives
That his money will grow too scarce

It's the wisest farmer who doesn't arise
Whilst the ploughshare is ploughing
Let the peasant labourer arise early
For the exertion of labour as the time passes

Whilst there is seaweed on the shore
There'll be barley in the homefield
That'll make us raise a song to them

When the barley comes to us in the field
We will expect a quart per head
Then, woman of the house, look that each one doesn't
Put too much of the water in it
From the worthiest spring
Comes the white barley
It makes wise people to be scarce

Now in the house fill us up
And let the vessel be full
For it's that that will give to us
Wisdom in our speech
It's reverence to the king
It's reverence to the king
To place on his head the like of [such a] crown

The following was written as a prologue to a masque held at Castle Rushen in 1643.

Samuel Rutter

Shee As Maynrys Ny Manninee, *c.1648*

Chorus
Lhig da'n seihll chyndaa mygeayrt
Lhig da'n seihll chyndaa mygeayrt
Nagh nhione da fea, ny aash erbee
Choud as ta shee dooin er ny reayll
Fud ashoon beg ny Manninee

Ee mayd as iu mayd, gow mayd arrane
As lhig da'n seihll goll bun-ry-skyn
Yn veeal's y feddan kiaull smoo t'ain
Gyn geill da cloie, ny schlei, ny guin

As nish, my nee drogh hengey erbee
Er y cloie gyn-loght ain drogh imraa
Lhig baase y vooghey y ghooinney keoie
Choud as vees shin dy gennal soie

Ga dy vel yn shee ain mooarit dooin
Cha lhias dooin ve ayns dooyt erbee
Hee mayd dagh cheer mygeayrt-y-mooin
Ayns caggey streeu dy chosney shee

Myr shoh veih noidyn ta shin seyr
Eddrym as aer nyn kione as cree
Gyn laadyt lesh y verchys vooar
Agh wheesh shen shickyr ta nyn shee

Airh as y seaghyn geiyrt er airh
Cha dug rieau crosh ny trimshey dooin
Cha vel nyn coamrey deyr ny feayr
T'eh coodagh shin, as t'eh lhien hene

Cha vel shin shirrey reamys smoo
Dy hayrn fo bondiaght shin hene
Myr eeanlee feayslit trooid yn aer
Gys ta nyn skeanyn goit 'sy lieen

Nyn bochilyn er y feddan cloie
Cleaynagh nyn graih as nyn shioltane
Veg jiu cha jed er shaghryn voue
Un woaillee as un vochil t'ain

Ta ec dagh cree e heshey hene
Nagh vod ve er ny violagh veih
Ta shin ennoil, foast dooinney as ben
Agh glen veih'n loght ta noi yn leih

Eh ta booiagh nyn sheshaght coayl
(Dy ve berchagh nagh vel fys ain)
Lhig da smooinaght er cheer ny Gaul
Cre'n leih as keeshyn dewil t'ayns shen

Mainshter yn aitt ta harrin reill
E chree rieau firrinagh da'n ree
T'eh goaill er-hene ooilley'n charail
As lhiggal dooin ve gennal cloie

Shoh hoods eisht slaynt nyn mainshter mie
As eh nagh giu yn cappan ass

Lhig da ve eebrit ass y thie
Dy castey-paays 'syn awin Dhoo-Ghlass

Translation
The Peace and Happiness of the Manx People, *c.1648*

Chorus
Let the world turn around
Let the world turn around
That knows not rest, or any ease at all
Whilst peace is kept for us
Throughout the little nation of the Manx people

We'll eat, and we'll drink, we'll have a song
And let the world go topsy-turvy
The mouth is the greatest musical whistle we have
Without need of playing, or skill, or pain.

And now, if any bad tongue
Speaks ill of our innocent play
Let death extinguish the mad man
Whilst we may be pleasantly seated.

Though our peace is begrudged to us
We need not be in any doubt
We'll see each country about us
Fighting in battle to gain peace.

Thus from enemies we are free
Light as air our head and heart
Not burdened with the great wealth
But just as certain as that is our peace.

Gold and the woe consequent on gold
Never gave us a cross [to bear] or sadness to us
Our clothing is not expensive or cold
It covers us, and it's our own.

We're not seeking a greater space
To draw ourselves under bondage
Like birds released through the air
Until their wings are caught in a net.

Our shepherds play on a pipe
Attracting their love and their flock
None of them will go astray from them
One fold and one shepherd we have.

Each heart has its companion
That can't be tempted from it
We are beloved, still man and woman
But clean from sin that's against the law.

He that's satisfied to lose our company
(We don't know how to be rich)
Let him think of the country of Gaul
What harsh law and taxes are there.

The master of the revel that rules over us
His heart was ever true to the king
He takes upon himself all the care
And allows us to be merry playing.

Here to you then is the health of our good master
And he that doesn't drink out of the cup
Let him be banished out of the house
To slake thirst in the Douglas river.

In the absence of James Stanley the Seventh Earl of Derby from the Island to fight for the Royalist cause, the Island was under the command of his wife, the Countess Charlotte. With the approach of a Parliamentary force in 1651, there was concern that the Manx people would be disadvantaged because the Countess was secretly seeking terms favourable to the Stanleys, but thought to be at the Manx people's expense. William Christian, the Receiver-General of the Island and Captain of the Militia, was the leader of a popular rising which wrested control from the Countess and dealt directly with the Parliamentarians to preserve the rights and privileges of the Island, some of which the Stanley family had already attacked.

Despite the Act of Indemnity following the Restoration, Charles Stanley the Eighth Earl of Derby decided that it did not apply to the Island, and subsequently William Christian was arrested and tried for treason in having led the popular rising of 1651. On 2 January 1663 he was executed by firing squad. William Christian is still better known today by his Manx soubriquet, 'Illiam Dhone' (Brown William). A song about the event refers to the subsequent fate of people involved in the execution, so was written later than 1663. It later became popular as a political warning about the repercussions of mistreating the Manx people. John Murray the Second Duke of Atholl became Lord of Man in 1736. The Third Duke had been pressurised into selling the regalities of the Lord of Man to the British Crown in 1765. John Murray, the Fourth Duke of Atholl, demanded further money for this transaction. However, his actions led to the popular description of the family in the Island as 'the grasping Murrays'. Verses added to this song are a warning to him after he had connived to introduce a bill in the Westminster Parliament in 1787 to improve his family's position without advising the House of Keys of his intentions. The Manx people felt that he was going behind their backs to feather his own nest to their detriment. This compilation is from five manuscript versions of the song ranging from 14 to 21 stanzas.

Anonymous
Baase Illiam Dhone, *c. 1663*

Quoi yinnagh e hreishteil ayns ooashley ny pooar
Ayns aegid ny aalid ny ayns kynney mooar
Son troo farg as goanlys ver mow dooinney erbee
As ta dty vaase Illiam Dhone brishey nyn gree

V'ou dty Resour Vannin, ard-ghooinney ny cheerey
V'ou gowit son dooinney seyr as dooinney creeney
As she jeh dty gellal vie cha row shin skee
Agh ta dty vaase Illiam Mooar brishey nyn gree

V'ou laue yesh yn eearley as sooill yesh yn theay
Shen hug da dty noidyn gatt wheesh dt'oi ayns feah
She troo farg as goanlys ver mow dooinney erbee
As ta dty vaase Illiam Mooar brishey nyn gree

B'aalin dty state thallooin ec Runnsyvie
B'eunyssagh dty gharaghyn, b'ooasle dty hie
She troo farg as goanlys ver mow dooinney erbee
Agh ta dty vaase Illiam Dhone brishey nyn gree

Vadyr gra dy daink screeunyn dy choyrt oo dy baase
Lesh feanishyn foalsey va follym dyn grayse
Yn ving v'er ny h-agglagh dy beign dt'aagail mooie
As ta [dty] vaase Illiam Mooar brishey nyn gree

Lhigg fer ayns y thalloo, fer elley syn air
Agh Illiam M'Cowle lhigg sy voayl chair
Illiam M'Cowle sluight ny ba buee
She dty vaase Illiam Dhone ren brishey nyn gree

Nagh dhere clein Colcad keoi nyn aigney hene
Tra hooar ad dy lhie syn floor Chlein Christeen?
She troo farg as goanlys ver mow dooinney erbee
As ta dty vaase Illiam Dhone brishey nyn gree

She oo va dty vaaderagh as dty ghooinney foalley
Hug saynt da Runnysvie, myr roie da Logh Molley
Er garey-feeyney Naboth va'n geantagh cloie
As ta dty vaase Illiam Mooar brishey nyn gree

Nagh byrrys enn dooinyn nagh hoill eshyn baase
Son fer hug laue ayns dt' uill cha ren rieau grayse
Agh feoghey as creenagh myr yn vaskad wuigh
As ta dty vaase Illiam Dhone brishey nyn gree

Gow uss dys manishter ny caillaghyn doo
As eie son clein Colcad der' vrishys dty ghoo
Ta'n ennym shen caillt veuish Manninee chooie
As ta dty vaase Illiam Mooar brishey nyn gree

Son bleeantyn ny martar va Robin ny lhie
She bwoirey ny cruinney v'eh choud's ve dy mie
E chaarjyn 's naboonyn jehsyn va skee
As ta dty vaase Illiam Dhone brishey nyn gree

Ghow Dickey lhuingys as dt'uill er e laue
Agh she fer ny cairagh kiart hug meeiteil daue
Yn tonn cha dymmyrk ee'n laad, sink eh aynjee
As ta dty vaase Illiam Dhone brishey nyn gree

As nish raad ta rass ny cass jeusyn er-mayrn
T'ad myr y dress gonnagh, ny myr yn onnane
Er cleiy fo nyn naboonyn v'adsyn sheer cloie
Agh ta dty vaase [Illiam Dhone brishey nyn gree]

Dy shooyllagh oo Mannin cha geayll oo fer gaccan
Ny keayney yn ennym va keayrt ayns Bemackan
Agh keeadyn dy voghtyn still goltagh as gwee
Dy vel dty vaase Illiam Mooar brishey nyn gree

Gow dys ny Cregganyn ny dys Balla-Lough
As cha now fer jeh'n ennym shen jir rhyt cheet stiagh
Ec joarreeyn ta nyn thieyn nyn thalloo as nhee

As ta dty vaase Illiam Dhone brishey nyn gree

Scarleod vooar verchagh ta heese ec y traie
T'ee ny steggyn Ronney ec mooinjer ny Faaie
Yn eirey boght tarnit sheese dys greim dy vee
As ta dty vaase Illiam Mooar brishey nyn gree

Ny dunveryn folley ren Caesar y stroie
V'ad shelgit lesh noidyn dewil seihltagh as shee
Son cha row fer jeusyn hooar rieau yn baase cooie
Agh she dty vaase [Illiam Dhone vrishys nyn gree]

Myrgeddin ny dunveryn hug Illiam mow
Nyn dhieyn as nyn dhalloo 's nyn ennym ren loau
Son lheie ad ersooyl myr lieh-rio ny hoie
As ta dty vaase [Illiam Dhone brishey nyn gree]

Neem's mee hene y gherjag lesh mooadys treishteil
Dy vaikins banglane my ghraih ny hoie sy whaiyl
Coyrt sneih er e noidyn lesh order y ree
Ga ta dty vaase [Illiam Dhone brishey nyn gree]

Dreamal ren mish er y chreg chreoi ny lhie
Dy beagh sluight Illiam Dhone ayns Runnysvie
E noidyn dewil castit as eh hene ec shee
As Clein Christeen gennal as slane ec y chree

Da fir-choyrlee foalsey ayns agglish ny theay
Ver cummaltee Vannin slane dwoaieys as feoh
Coyrt naboonyn bun ry skyn 's brishey nyn shee
Myr ta dty vaase Illiam Dhone brishey nyn gree

Chiarn ooasle yn Ellan eer Athol graysoil,
T'ad dolley as molley lesh foalsaght nyn goyrle
Yn ard-chlagh chorneilagh e hie mooar y stroie
Nyn noidyn da Mannin yn Chiarn as y Ree

Translation

The Death of Illiam Dhone, *c.1663*

Who would put his trust in honour or power
In youth or beauty, or in great kindred?
For envy, spite and malice will destroy any man

And your death, Illiam Dhone, breaks our hearts

You were the Receiver of Man, the leader of the country
You were held to be a gentleman and a wise man
And of your good dealing we were not tired
But your death, Illiam Dhone, breaks our hearts

You were the right hand of the earl, and the right eye of the people
Which caused your enemies to swell so much against you in loathing
It's envy, spite and malice that will destroy any man
And your death, Great Illiam, breaks our hearts

Beautiful was your estate at Ronaldsway
Delightful was your garden and noble your house
It's envy, spite and malice that will destroy any man
But your death, Illiam Dhone, breaks our hearts

They were saying that letters came to put you to death
With false testimonies that were empty of grace.
The jury had been intimidated so that it would be forced to leave you outside (i.e. to condemn you)
And your death, Great Illiam, breaks our hearts

One fired into the ground, another into the air
But Illiam M'Cowle shot in the right place
Illiam M'Cowle is the seed of the yellow cow
It's your death, Illiam Dhone, that breaks our hearts

Did the Colcatt clan not gain their evil will
When they got in the earth the glory of the Christian clan
It's envy, spite and malice that will destroy any man
But your death, Illiam Dhone, breaks our hearts

It's you who was a whoremonger and man of the flesh
You coveted Ronaldsway, as Logh Molley [Mallow] before
On Naboth's vineyard the [evil] doer was always playing
And your death, Great Illiam, breaks our hearts

Was it not well-known to us that he didn't deserve death
For anyone who put a hand in your blood never obtained grace
But withering and faded like the corn marigold
And your death, Illiam Dhone, breaks our hearts

Go you to the monastery of the nuns
And call for Clan Colcatt until your voice breaks
That name is lost from you, true Manxmen
And your death, Great Illiam, breaks our hearts

For years as a cripple Robin was lying
It's a troublemaker he was whilst he was well
His friends and his neighbours were tired of him
And your death, Illiam Dhone, breaks our hearts

Dickey took ship when your blood was on his hand
But it was a just avenger who met them
The wave didn't bear the load, he sank in it
And your death, Illiam Dhone, breaks our hearts

And now where is any trace of them remaining
They're like the injurious briar or like the thistle
At undermining their neighbours they were constantly playing
But your death, Illiam Dhone, breaks our hearts

If you were to walk throughout Man you will not hear anybody
   complaining
Or bewailing the name that was once in Beemaken
But hundreds of poor people still saluting and praying
That your death, Great Illiam, breaks our hearts

Go to the Creggans or to Ballalough
And you won't find anyone of that name that will say to you,
   'Come in'
Strangers own their houses, land and chatels
And your death, Illiam Dhone, breaks our hearts

Great wealthy Scarlett down at the shore
It is the staked out portion(?) owned by the people of the Flat
The poor heir dragged down to a morsel of food
And your death, Great Illiam, breaks our hearts

The bloody murderers who destroyed Caesar
They were hunted by cruel enemies of this world and of the
   supernatural
For there wasn't one of them who ever died a natural death
But it's your death, Illiam Dhone, which breaks our hearts

> In the same way the murderers who destroyed Illiam
> Their houses and their land and their names rotted
> For they melted away like the hoar-frost of the night
> And your death, Illiam Dhone, breaks our hearts
>
> I'll comfort myself with the extent of hope
> That I may see my love's branch sitting in the court
> Causing vexation to his enemies by order of the king
> Though your death, Illiam Dhone, breaks our hearts
>
> I dreamed when lying on the hard rock
> That the seed of Illiam Dhone would be in Ronaldsway
> His cruel enemies defeated and himself at peace
> And Clan Christian content and whole at the heart
>
> To the false advisers in the church or state
> The inhabitants of Man will give complete hate and loathing
> Putting neighbours topsy-turvy and shattering their peace
> Just like your death, Illiam Dhone, breaks our hearts
>
> The noble lord of the Island even gracious Athol
> They blind and deceive with the falsity of their advice
> To destroy the key corner-stone of his house
> They're the enemies to Man, the Lord and the King.

However, we return from the 1780s of the final verses of 'Illiam Dhone' to the seventeenth century again. William Sacheverell was Governor of the Isle of Man in 1693–4. In writing about Manx, he refers to Phillips' version of the Book of Common Prayer.

> As for the Manks language, according to the best information I could get, it differs no more from Irish than Scotch from English, and both of them different idioms of the Erse, or Highland, though Bishop Philips, a native of North Wales, who translated the Common Prayer into the Manks tongue, observes most of the radixes to be Welch, and pretends he had never been able to perfect the work but by the assistance of his native language ... Bishop Philips's attempt is scarce intelligible by the clergy themselves, who translate it off hand more to the understanding of the people ... In the northern part of the Island they speak a deeper Manks, as they call it, than in the south, which is nearer to the original Highland, as being least corrupted with English.

This reported attitude of the clergy may be more 'sour grapes' than incomprehension, because the orthography had been dictated by an 'outsider', albeit the appointed Bishop of Sodor and Man.

The Eighteenth Century

A well-known and still very popular song tells of events from about 1700. It concerns the loss of sheep on Raby farm, almost certainly by William Qualtrough (c.1660–c.1707). A continuing practice is for a farmer to be referred to by the farm name, or by a combination of personal name and farm name. Some versions of this song refer to 'Qualtrough Raby' or 'Colcheragh Raby' (a phonetic spelling of the name as then pronounced), whilst others refer to 'Nicholas Raby'. The successor to Raby was William Qualtrough's nephew Nicholas Kelly (c.1695–1783), which may have led to this uncertainty.

Anonymous
Ny Kirree Fo Niaghtey, *c.1707*

> Lurg geurey dy niaghtey as arragh dy rio
> Va ny shenn chirree marroo as n' eayin beggey bio
>
> *Chorus*
> 'Oh irree shiu boch'llyn, as gow shiu da'n chlieau
> Ta ny kirree fo niaghtey cha dowin as v'ad rieau
>
> Shoh dooyrt Nicholas, Raby, as eh 'sy thie ching
> "Ta ny kirree fo niaghtey ayns Braaid-farrane-fing"
>
> Shoh dooyrt Nicholas, Raby, goll seose er y lout
> "Dy row my shiaght vannaght er my ghaa housane muilt
>
> Kirree t'ayms ayns y laggan, Kirree-goair 'sy Chlieau-rea
> Kirree keoi Coan-ny-chishtey nagh jig dy bragh veih"

Dirree mooinjer Skeeyll Lonan as hie ad er y chooyll
Hooar ad ny kirree marroo ayns laggan Varoole

Dirree mooinjer Skeeyll Lonan as Skeeylley-Chreesht neesht
Hooar ad ny kirree beggey ayns laggan Agneash

Ny muilt ayns y toshiaght, ny reaghyn 'sy vean
As ny kirree trome-eayin cheet geiyrt orroo shen

Ta mohlt aym son Ollick as jees son y Chaisht
As ghaa ny tree elley son yn traa yioym's baase

Translation
The Sheep Under the Snow, *c.1707*

After a winter of snow and a spring of frost
The old sheep were dead and the little lambs alive

Chorus
O arise you, my shepherds, and betake you to the mountain
The sheep are under snow as deep as ever they were

This said Nicholas Raby as he was in the house ill
'The sheep are under snow in Braaid Farrane Fing'

This said Nicholas Raby going up to the loft
'May my seven-fold blessing be on my two thousand wethers'

'I have sheep in the hollow and goats in Slieau Ruy
The wild sheep of Coan y Chishtey that will never come from it alive'

The people of Kirk Lonan arose and they went by and by
They found the sheep dead in Laggan Barrule

The people of Kirk Lonan arose and of Kirk Christ [Lezayre] too
They found the little sheep in Laggan Agneash

The wethers in the front, the tups in the middle
And the sheep heavy with lambs coming following after them

'I have a wether for Christmas and two for Easter
And one or two others for the time I will die'

During Thomas Wilson's long episcopacy (1698–1755), Wilson wrote of 'the inhabitants, whose language is the Erse, or a dialect of that spoken in the Highlands of Scotland ...' He goes on to note that:

> It has been often said that the Holy Bible was, by Bishop Phillips's care, translated in to the Manks language ; but, upon the best enquiry that can be made, there was no more attempted by him than a translation of the Common Prayer, which is still extant, but of no use to the present generation.

In order to reach 'the present generation', Wilson published his Principles and Duties of Christianity (the Coyrle Sodjeh) in a bilingual edition in 1707, with an English text in a column alongside the respective text in Manx. The source of the Manx orthography is not known, but subsequent printed Manx adopted the basis of it in large measure as a standard – perhaps merely because it was the first printed Manx, but also perhaps because it was by a recognised symbol of authority, the Church, and from the pen, albeit in translation, of a much revered figure, Bishop Thomas Wilson.

The Manx of the Coyrle Sodjeh has been praised as a clear yet idiomatic rendering of the English. The Manx column retains Q. and A., as in the English, as it deals with the Catechism.

Thomas Wilson
Coyrle Sodjeh, *1707*

Q. Ta currym aym meehene y yanoo aarloo, dy ghol fo laue Aspick, ta mee gearee'n cooney eauish dy vod fys ve aym cre ta mee gol mish as cre ta er ny hirrey orrym?

A. Nee'm shen dy harryltagh as my tow dy jarroo shirrey dt'annym y hau-ail, ynsym oo ayns aght cha ashagh dy ve toiggit nagh lias dhyt cherraghtyn son laccal tushtey.

Q. Guee ym erriu eisht, insh jee dou cre'n fa ta mee er m'earnagh [sic, for 'eamagh'] dy ghol fo laue Aspick?

A. Dy vod fys ve ec yn Aglish dy vel oo dy Chreestee liorish dy reih hene, as cha nee ny lomarcan son dy rug oo ayns cheer Chreestee.

Q. Cre fa shegin fys ve ec yn Aglish er shoh?

A. Son dy vel yn Aglish sheshaght dy phersoonyn goal rish dy ve beaghey ayns aggle Yee, as jeaghyn son briwnyssyn Yee my ta veg jeh'n cheshaght cheddyn beaghey fegooish biallys y choyrt gys e Leihaghyn as adsyn gyn oghsyn y chur daue.

As shen-y-fa son shickerys share ta dagh Olt jeh'n cheshaght soilshagh magh dy vel ad kairit dy veaghey cordail rish Sushtal Chreest, yn leigh t'ad dy ve reilt liorish.

Q. Vel vondeish erbee sodjeh oddym jeaghyn er y hon, liorish gol fo laue Aspick?
A. Ta veih'n tra shen foddee oo treshteil dy bishee Jee e ghrayse aynyd dy choolley laa, my hirrys oo eh lesh dty chree. Son t'an Aspick marish ta laue Yee ayns ooilley ny te dy yanoo ayns ennym Chreest goal padjer er dy hon as liorish e laue y chur ort te shickeragh dhyt dy vou foar as aigney mie Yee.
As eisht my ta fys ayd, dy vel yn cliagtey crauee shoh. Gol fo laue Aspick er jeet veih Ostylyn Yeesey Creest, bee resoon ayd dy hreshteil son ymmodee foas veih; as dy ve meerioosagh jeh, raad oddys eh v.'er ny gheddyn ta shen soi-agh beg jeh myghyn as foar Yee.
Q. Ballym eisht mee hene y yanoo aarloo son gol fo laue Aspick, cha nee ny lomarcan son dy vel yn Aglish dy harey eh, agh son dy bee eh vondeishagh dou shoh y yannoo.
A. Bee eh dy jarroo, son y Credjue Creestee tow gol dy ghoal ort yn yn red oddys oo y yanoo ashagh ayns shoh as sauchey ny Yei shoh.
Son te gynsagh dooin ga dy vel shin nyn Greturyn treih, peccoil as fegooish cooney, ga dy vel ain Noidjin ymmodee as niartal, ny yei liorish foar Yee; foddee mad ve sauchey as bannit.
Ta shin gynsagh liorish, dy vel Jee shirrey nyn maynrys, as dy vod e ny smoo y yanoo er nyn son ny oddys shin hene y hirrey ny smooinaghtyn.
Te gynsagh dooin cre'n chirveish ta Jee dy hirrey orryn, cre'n aght oddys shin nyn shee y yanoo rish, tra ta shin liorish nyn beccaghyn er chur jummoose er; Cre cha dangeragh as ta bea vee-rioosagh. As cre'n vaynrys ver jee daue-syn ta gys y tushtey share oc dy hirveish e.

Translation

The Principles and Duties of Christianity, 1707

"Q. Having Notice to prepare my self for Confirmation, I beg your Assistance, that I may know what I am going about, and what is expected from me?
A. I will gladly assist you; and, if indeed you desire to save your Soul, I will instruct you after so plain a Manner, that you need not perish for want of Knowledge.
Q. I pray then let me know why I am called to Confirmation.
A. That the Church may be satisfied you are a Christian out of Choice, and not only because you was [sic] born in a Christian Country.
Q. Why must the Church be satisfied of this?
A. Because the Church is a Society of Persons professing to live in the Fear of God, and expecting God's Judgments, if any of their Body do live in an open Defiance of his Laws, without Rebuke.
And therefore, for better Security, all its Members are openly to declare

their full Purpose of Living as becometh the Gospel of Christ, which is the Law they are to be governed by.

Q. Is there any farther Benefit that I may hope for by going to be Confirmed?

A. Yes; you may expect, from that time, that God will daily increase his Graces in you, if you heartily desire them: For the Bishop, with whom is the hand of God in all that he doth in the name of Christ, prayeth for you, and by laying his Hand upon you, doth certifie you of God's Favour and good Will towards you.

And then, if you know that this solemn way of laying on of hands, was from the Apostles of Jesus Christ, you will have reason to hope for much Good from it, and to neglect it, where it may be had, is to despise God's Mercy and Favours.

Q. I would therefore prepare my self for Confirmation, not only because the Church requires it, but because it will be my Advantage to do so.

A. It will most certainly: for the Christian Profession, which you are going to take upon you, is the only Thing which can make you easie here, and safe hereafter.

For it teacheth us, that tho' we are miserable, sinful, helpless Creatures, tho' we have many and powerful Enemies, yet by the Favour of God, we may be Safe and Happy.

For by it we learn that God desireth our Welfare, and that he is able to do for us more than we can ask or think.

It teacheth us what Service God requires of us; How we may make our Peace when we have offended him by our Sins. How dangerous it is to lead a careless Life. And how happy God will make all such as serve him to the best of their Knowledge.

Following a visit to the Island in 1855, George Borrow wrote that:

> The Manx have a literature – a native vernacular Gaelic literature. This fact has been frequently denied, but it is now established beyond the possibility of doubt ... This literature consists of ballads on sacred subjects, which are called 'carvals', a corruption of the English word 'carol' ... Many of these songs have been handed down, by writing, to the present time. Some of them possess considerable merit, and a printed collection of them would be a curious addition to the literature of Europe ... The carvals are preserved in uncouth looking, smoke-stained, volumes, in low farm houses and cottages, situated in mountain gills and glens. They constitute the literature of Ellan Vannin.

The publication of 'Carvalyn Gailckagh' in 1891, with a preface by A W Moore, gave dates for the composition of some of its contents from 1720. Similar verse is found in Gaelic Scotland towards the end of the seventeenth century, and developed out of the ballad form which would have been well-known to the professional Gaelic poets of the medieval period. The existence of 'The Traditionary Ballad' and other material suggests that composition was taking place in the pre-literate Island. With the emergence of Manx in print, it may be that people were inspired to commit existing carvals to written form. The publication of the pieces in 'Carvalyn Gailckagh' followed their appearance in the 'Mona's Herald' newspaper. Others were also published in a newspaper by P W Caine in the 1920s, but his proposed printed collection failed to materialise.

Taking the dates given in 'Carvalyn Gailckagh' at face value, 'Carval Noa, or A New Carol' was written in 1720. This may be date of composition or perhaps the date on which it was written down from oral transmission. There are 45 verses in a Question and Answer format, perhaps based on that of Wilson's 'Coyrle Sodjeh'. The format is well realised in the following extract, starting at the fifteenth verse as printed in 'Carvalyn Gailckagh'.

Anonymous
Carval Noa

(Scruit ayns y vlein 1720)

Q. – Cha row me rieau fer breagagh
Loayrt olk jeh fer erbee
Na dellal dy molteyragh
Ny foalsagh ayns my chree
Agh tannaghtyn resoonagh
Da ooilley myr my vraar
T'eh dy mennick ayns my smooinagh
Dy vel mee yn dooinney share

A. – Shione da yn dooinney crauee
Quoi t'eh er credjal ayn
Ta feanish currit daasyn
T'eh feaysley as pardooin
Fegooish yn seal as cowrey
Ayns dorraghys tou shooyl
Dy hreish myr coau 'sy tourey
Ta'n gheay dy heebey ersooil

Q. – Cha row mee reau my vaarliagh
Ny gheid er dooinney erbee
Cur oyr dow veh angaaishagh
Dy vel mee vrasnagh Jee
Cordail rish slane my hushtey
Ta mee leeideil dy kiart

Cha vel my chredjue leaystey
Dy gaill ym foast yn mark

A. – Te caill't tra t'ayn, my charrey
Nagh moar yn trimshey eh
Dy bare lhiat lhiggey shaghey
Dyn shirrey tushtey jeh
Cha jig oo er yn doarlish
Cheet stiagh er raad neucair
Mac Yee te loayrit liorish
Tow maarliagh as roosteyr

Q. – Cha vel mee loo ny gweeaghyn
Cha beagh eh doaiagh dow
Ny doostey seose drogh cooishyn
Er chee unnane cur mow
Agh ta mee geek dy jeeragh
Da dagh unnane y cair
As baillym veh erreeishagh
Er moir as cloan gyn Ayr

A. – Dy bragh cha meet oo cooney
Shooyl ayns yn raad t'ou er
Ny d'obbyr oo pardooney
Myr ver oo eh my ner
Ta shin pointit myr kirree
Ta reih ve er ny strie
Dy heyrey shin ta Yeesey
Er nirree reesht veih 'n oaie.

Q. – Cha vel mee goll er meshtey
Lesh liggar ny lesh feeyn
Quoi honnick rieau neu-yesh mee
Fud yn lught-thie aym pene
Agh labaragh kiaralagh
Dy voddagh v'aym rolaue
Freill vowsyn va weastealagh
Nagh beeym my heshey daue

A. – Charrey, my vees oo brasnit
Cre'n roon vees ayns dy chree
Ymmodee noidyn tashtit
Ta girree magh n'oi Jee

My sailt yn chrosh y ymmyrk
Liorish dagh peccah chea
As roie dys Creest son kemmyrk –
Trooid credjue yiow livrey

Q. – Cha ren me poosey vrishey
Rish ben dooinney erbee
Cha row my aigney shirrey eh
T'eh dooiagh da my chree
Cha vel mee troo mysh dooinney
Son argid ny son airh
Ny fer erbee er chionney
Dy hirrey chooid neucair

A. – Eh hug my-ner ben aalin
Cur saynt j'ee ayns e chree
Ta'n ghoo dy hoilshagh dasyn
Dy vrish eh poosey r'ee
My vraar, cha neeu dhyt seyrey
T'ou foiljagh ayns dty chree
Cooinsheanse nee oo y geayrey
My ver oo cairys j'ee

Translation

A New Carval

(Written in the year 1720)

Q. – I was never a liar
Speaking ill of anybody
Or dealing deceitfully
Or false in my heart
But remaining reasonable
To all as my brother
It's often in my thinking
That I am the best man

A. – He knows the righteous man
Who he is that has believed in him
Witness is given to him
It releases and pardons
Without the seal and the sign
In darkness you are walking

Your trust like chaff in the summer
The wind blows you away

Q. – I was never a thief
Or stole from any man
That would give me reason to be anguished
That I am provoking God
According to my whole knowledge
I'm leading [life] properly
My faith is not wavering
That I will yet miss the mark

A. – It's already missed, my friend
Isn't it a great sorrow
That you prefer letting [life] go by
Without seeking knowledge from it
You will not come in at the narrow gap
Coming in on the unrighteous road
The Son of God, it's spoken by him
You are a thief and a robber

Q. – I don't curse or swear
It wouldn't be worthy of me
Or stirring up evil subjects
With the intention of destroying an individual
But I pay directly
To each individual his due
And I would like to be sympathetic
To a mother and children without a Father

A. – Never will you encounter help
Walking in the road you are on
Or your work pardon you
As you will behold
We are bidden like sheep
That choose to be destroyed
To free us Jesus
Has risen again from the grave

Q. – I'm not going getting drunk
With liquor or with wine
Who ever saw me improper
Throughout my own household

But labouring carefully
That what I had beforehand might
Keep from them that are wasteful
That I will not be of their company

A. – Friend, if you are provoked
What resentment may be in your heart
Many enemies stored up
That rebel against God
If you wish to bear the cross
Flee from each sin
And run to Christ for refuge –
Through belief you will receive deliverance

Q. – I didn't break marriage [commit adultery]
With the wife of any man
My inclination wasn't seeking it
It's hateful to my heart
I don't envy [any] man
For silver or for gold
Nor pressed anybody
To seek for unjust goods

A. – He who beholds a beautiful woman
Lusting after her in his heart
The word [Scripture] explains to him
That he committed adultery with her
My brother, it is not worth your justifying [it]
Conscience will condemn you
If you will give justice to it

G W Wood was a great bibliophile and collector of Manx publications. His view in 1911 was that 'The earliest "carval" (the date of which known) belongs to the year 1720, and perhaps one of the most striking of them is 'Yn Carval ny Drogh Vraane' (The Carval of the Bad Women) of the Scriptures'.

Anonymous

Carval Ny Drogh Vraane, *1720*

My chaarjyn deyr as graihagh
Ayns shoh jiu er veeiteil
My sailliu shaghney peccah

Fo mraane nagh jean jee reill
Ta'n reill oc feer neuchairagh
Ta'n Ostyl Phaul dy ghra
Tra haink y noid sy gharey
She'n ven s'leaie geill hug da

She ish va'n voir ain ooilley
Son v'ee da Adam ben
Ny-yeih ee chaill yn vaynrys
J'ee hene as da e cloan
She ish ren coayl yn vaynrys
Tra vrish ee sarey Yee
Tra ghow ee coyrle yn noid vroghe
She shen ren molley ee

O, ooilley shiuish chloan gheiney
Ta foast er-mayrn sy theihll
Nagh cur shiu saynt da aalid
Yn ven s'boiee ren rieau shooyl
Agh smooinnee shiu er David
As neesht er Solomon
Kys v'adsyn cleaynit lioroo –
Ny deiney s'creeney v'ayn

Ta shoh sampleyr diuish aegid
Gow shiu kiarail ayns traa
Nagh bee jee miolit lioroo
Naght myr ta'n Scriptyr gra
My ren shiu rieau agh lhaih jeh
Mychione yn dooinney aeg
Va shooyl dy feer almoragh
Tra veeit eh ben sy traid

As lesh e chengey veeley
She'n scollag violee lesh
Kiart myr yn voddey-oaldey
Yn vannin shooyl marish
Ny myr yn chretoor valloo
Yn butchoor shooyl ny chione
Ragh jeeragh gys yn traartys
My veg fys da cre hon

O, shimmey dooinney creeney

T'er hurranse liorish mraane
My lhaih shiu rieau j'eh Joseph?
Quoi hilg eh ayns pryssoon?
She olkys e ven-ainshtyr
Dreill eh fo boltyn-yiarn
Myr s'cairagh v'eh dy yannoo
Ayns fenish Jee as Chiarn

Dy gooinagh shiu er Samson
As smooinagh neesht er Job
Cre'n olkys v'ayns ny mraane oc
Er-chee dy violagh ad
Ny geayll shiu rieau j'eh Naboth
Kys hooar eh baase cha dewill?
She kyndagh rish ben Ahab
She ish va Jezebel

She ish ghow spooilley Naboth
As stroie Phadeyryn Yee
My cheayll shiu rieau jeh'n vaase eck
She moddee ren ee ee
Myrgeddin Athaliah
Yn olkys eck va dewill
Tra stroie ee pobble Yudah
As ghow ee hene yn reill

O quoi oo hene, my charrey
Veagh cleaynit liorish mraane?
T'ad soyllit ayns yn Scriptyr
Ny smessey na yn lion
T'ad soyllit dys y lion
As dys yn dragon neesht
Jeh'n olkys oc ny-sodjey
Ta nearey orrym ginsh

Ny-yeih te ayns y Scriptyr
Kiongoyrt rish dagh unnane
My ren shiu rieau agh lhaih jeh
Cre'n olkys ren rieau mraane?
Ta'n olkys oc dou trimshey
Dy smooinaght er Noo Ean
Dy row y dooinney vannee
Rieau tilgit ayns pryssoon

O, smooinnee jee, my chaarjyn
Er dooinney vannee Yee
Kys hooar ben-aeg son daunsyn
E yeearree voish yn Ree
Ean Bashtey va yn dooinney
My cheayll shiu jeh e vaase
E chione hooar ee son daunsey
Nagh bollagh v'ee dyn grayse?

Cha birrys da mac Sirach
Ve loayrt nyn oi cha dewill
Dy re drogh ven ny smessey
Jeh dagh cretoor sy theihll
Ta'n olkys oc reesht soyllit
Ny smessey na dagh nhee
Ta shen erskyn ny princeyn
Ta kerragh droghyantee

Nagh treih'n stayd, my chaarjyn
Dagh Creestee er yn oor
Dy beagh nyn yannoo soyllit
Ny smessey na'n cretoor
Son t'eshin as ny princeyn
Heese dooint ayns ooig dy aile
As adsyn ver rish peccah
Heese marish nee ad reill

She marish hene as Tubal
As Meshech as Elam
As maroo neesht ta Dives
Ayns sheshaght rish drogh vraane
As maroo hig oo, my charrey
As yn tutler vroghe ta shooyl
My ver oo raad da peccah
Roo shoh chyndaa dty chooyl

As jeeagh dy geyre sy Scriptyr
Dy chooilley oor yiow traa
Cre'n kerragh ta cour peccee
Ayns niurin heese dy braa
Ayns niurin heese ayns torchagh
Ayns aile nee oo geam dy geyre
Gra, "S'treih yn laa haink orrym

Tra reih mee yn laue chiare?"

Gra shoh va slane my haitnys
Tra ghow mee eh son reih
Ayns fiddleyryn as caartyn
Ayns feeyn as bwoalley sleih
Ayns streebeeys as daunsyn
V'aym taitnys oie as laa
As fark cre'n jerrey haink orrym
Tra ren y Chiarn rhym gra

"Nee shoh'n breearrey ren oo
Tra vow er dty ghaa ghlioon
Vow gee my eill myr arran
As giu my uill myr feeyn
Vow gialdyn neesht ve booisal
As bishaghey ayns grayse
Agh sleaie ren oo jarrood mee
As geiyrt er raad Yuaase?

"Ny-yeih ayns slane dty hurranse
Te ooilley'n foill ayd hene
Son va mish kinjagh sarey oo
Veih peccah as drogh vraane"
Te baghtal ayns y Scriptyr
Kiongoyrt rish cloan sheelnaue
Dy re drogh ven by-vessey
Jeh dagh cretoor va snaue

Cre'n sorch dy vraane, my chaarjyn
O, lhisagh shiu y ve
Ta geaishtagh rish ny goan shoh
Mysh olkys mraane cre te
Ny-yeih cre va nyn olkys
Cha row myr shen agh paart
Son she jeh ben v'eh ruggit
Yn charrey ghow nyn baart

She ish va'n Moirrey Vannee
As neesht Moirrey Malaine
As Deborah, ayns cairys
Ren bleeantyn reill yn rheim
As ymmodee mraane elley

Baghtal ta'n Scriptyr gra
Ren leeideil bea cha cairagh
As fer ren rieau chyndaa

Son te colaik, my chaarjyn
Da dooinney ny da ben
My nee ad treigeil peccah
As geiyrt er Creest nyn Jiarn
As geiyrt er lesh nyn aigney
Dagh Creestee meen yiow ayrn
Jeh miljid ainleyn flaunys
Trooid fuill deyr Creest nyn Jiarn

She trooid e uill, my chaarjyn
She eshyn hig nyn whail
As marish sheshaght dy ainleyn
Ayns bingys as ayns kiaull
Gra, "Gloyr hoods er yn Yrjid
As er y thalloo shee
As aigney mie gys deiney,"
Dy kinjagh myr shen guee

Translation

Carval of the Bad Women

My dear and loving friends
Who here today have met
If you wish to avoid sin
Under women don't you rule [be ruled]
Their rule is very unjust
The Apostle Paul says
When the enemy came in the garden
It's the woman who soonest paid heed to him

It's she who was the mother of us all
For she was a wife to Adam
Nevertheless it was she who lost the happiness
Of herself and for her children
It's she who lost the happiness
Whe she broke the command of God
When she took the advice of the dirty enemy
It's that which deceived her.

O, all you sons of men
That still remain in the world
Don't you covet the beauty
Of the the most beautiful woman who ever walked
But think you of David
And also of Solomon
How they were attracted by them
The wisest men that existed

This is an example to you, the youth
Take care in time
That you will not be tempted by them
In the way that the Scripture says
If you ever did but read of it
About the young man
That was walking in great ignorance
When he met a woman in the street

And with her sweet tongue
It's the stripling that she tempted with it
Just as the wolf
Walks with the kid goat
Or as the dumb creature
The butcher walks by the hand
Would go straight to destruction
If it had no knowledge what the purpose

O, many a wise man
Has suffered on account of women
If you ever read of Joseph?
Who threw him in prison?
It's the evilness of his mistress
That kept him under iron bolts
As just as he was to act
In the presence of God and Lord

If you were to remember Samson
And would think also of Job
What the evil was in their women
About to tempt them
Did you never hear of Naboth
How he died so cruelly?

It's on account of the wife of Ahab
It's she who was Jezebel

It's she who took the spoils of Naboth
And destroyed the Prophets of God
If you ever heard of her death
It's dogs that ate her
Also Athaliah
Her evilness was cruel
When she destroyed the people of Judah
And she herself took charge

O, who are you yourself, my friend
That would be attracted by women?
They're compared in the Scripture
Worse than the lion
They're compared to the lion
And to the dragon as well
Of their evilness further
I am ashamed to tell

Anyway it's in the Scripture
Before each individual
If you did ever but read of it
What the evilness women ever did
Their evilness is a sadness to me
To think of Saint John
That the blessed man was
Ever thrown in prison

O, think you, my friends
On the blessed man of God
How a young woman got for dances
Her desire before the King
John the Baptist was the man
If you heard of his death
His head she got for dances
Was she not completely without grace?

It's no wonder that Sirach's son
He was speaking against them so cruelly
That a bad woman is the worst
Of each creature in the world

Their evilness is again typified
[as being] Worse than anything
That's above the princes
Who punish wrongdoers [i.e. Satan's followers in Hell]

Is the situation not sad, my friends
Each Christian on the earth
That their actions are typified
[as being] Worse than the creature [i.e. Satan]
For it's he and the princes
Down shut in a cave of fire
And they that bring sin
Down with him they will reign

It's with him himself and Tubal
And Meshech and Elam
And with them also is Dives
In company with evil woman
And with them you will come, my friend
And the dirty tattler who walks
If you give way to sin
To these turn your back

And look closely in the Scripture
Every hour that you can give time
What the punishment is for sinners
Down in hell for ever
Down in hell in torment
In fire you will sharply call
Saying, "Sad is the day that came on me
When I chose the left-hand."

Saying that this was wholly my delight
When I took it as a choice
In fiddlers and cards
In wine and hitting people
In whoring and dances
I had pleasure night and day
And awaiting what the end came on me
When the Lord said to me:

"Is this the oath that you gave
When you were on both your knees

You were eating my flesh as bread
And drinking my blood as wine
You were promising as well to be thankful
And to increase in grace
But soonest you forgot me
And followed on the path of Judas?

"Anyway, in all your suffering
It's all your own fault
For I was always ordering you
Away from sin and evil women."
It's obvious in the Scripture
Before the children of mankind [literally, the seed of heaven]
That its the evil women who are the worst
Of each creeping thing

What the sort of women, my friends
O, ought you to be
That are listening to these words
About the evilness of women, what it is
Anyway what was their evilness
It's only some who were like that
For it's of a woman he was born,
The friend who took our part

It's she who was the blessed Mary
And also Mary Magdalene
And Deborah, in justice
Spent years ruling the realm
And many other women
Clearly the Scripture says
Led a life so righteous
As any that ever turned [to the bad]

For it's the same, my friends,
For a man or for a woman
If they will forsake sin
And follow Christ our Lord
And follow him with their will
Each gentle Christian will partake
Of the sweetness of the angels of paradise
Through the dear blood of Christ our Lord

It's through his blood, my friends
It's he who will come to meet us
And with a host of angels
In harmony and in music
Saying, "Glory to you in the Height
And on the earth peace
And good will to men,"
Constantly praying like that.

The final verse may suggest that the composer had seen St Luke 2:14 in Manx, which would put composition of this carval after 1763, when the Gospels and Acts of the Apostles in Manx were published. However, a number of the carvals, including some dated to the 1720s in 'Carvalyn Gailckagh', have a very similar form of words to describe this episode. The translation of St Luke may owe its format to the carvals rather than the other way round.

The first of the Gospels published by itself in 1748 was that of St Matthew, translated by Rev William Walker (1679-1729), Vicar-General to Bishop Wilson. His translation was thought to have been commenced about 1722, though waiting some twenty years for publication. Walker had also translated the other Gospels and Acts. Comparison between the 1748 edition of St Matthew and the version published under Bishop Hildesley from 1763 onwards shows Walker's orthography was akin to that of the Coyrle Sodjeh whilst the later text was revised to the comparatively standardised form of the Bible editors.

Translated by William Walker
Yn Sushtal Scruit Liorish Yn Noo Mian, *c.1722*

Cab. II
1. Nish tra va Yeesey er ny va Ruggitt ayns Bethlehem, dy Yudea, ayns laghyn Ree Herod, cur-my-ner haink deney creeney veih'n Shar gys Jerusalem,
2. Gra, Cre vel Ree ny Hewnyn te'r jeet er y teihl? Son honnick shin y Rollage echey ayns y Shar, as ta shin er jeet dy chur ooashley da.
3. Tra cheayl Ree Herod shoh, ve seaghnit as ovilley [ooilley] Jerusalem marish.
4. As tra ve er jaglym cooidjagh, ooilley ny ard-saggyrtyn as scruderyn y pobble, denee e jeu, cre'nraad va Creest dy heet er y teihl.
5. As doort adsyn rish, Ayns Bethlehem dy Yudea: Son shoh myr te scruit liorish y Phadeyr;
6. As uss Bethlehem ayns talloo Yuda, cha nee oo sloo ta, mastey Prinseyn Yudah: Son assyds hig Kiannoort nee reill my phobble Israel.
7. Eisht hug Herod fys gy follit er ny deney creeney, as, denee e jeu dy imneagh, cre'n tra va'n Rollage er ny akin.

8. As hug e ad gys Bethlehem, gra immee-jee as shir-jee magh dy kiarailagh son y lianoo aeg, as tra vees shin [shiu] er gheddyn e, tar-jee lesh fys hyms, dy voddyms myrgeddyn cheet as ooashley chur da.
9. Tra va'n Ree erreish loart, jimmee ad rumboo, as cur-my-ner, hie yn Rollage honnick ad ayns y Shar, roue, derrey haink ee as hass ee harrish yn raad, raad va'n lianoo.
10. Tra honnick ad y Rollage va'd lieent lesh boggey er skyn towse.
11. As tra vad er jeet stiagh ayns y thie, honnick ad y liannoo aeg marish Moirrey e Voir, as huitt ad sheese as hug ad ooashley da; as tra vad er vosley ny tashtaghyn oc, heb ad da giootyn, aer, as frankincese as myrrh.
12. As fakin dy row Jee er chur roue ayns ashlish, nagh row ad dy hyndaa gys Herod, jimmee ad gys nyn jeer hene raad elley.

Translation

The Gospel Written by Saint Matthew

Chap. II

1. Now when Jesus was born in Bethlehem of Judaea in the days of Herod the king, behold, there came wise men from the east to Jerusalem,
2. Saying, Where is he that is born King of the Jews? For we have seen his star in the east, and are come to worship him.
3. When Herod the king had heard these things, he was troubled, and all Jerusalem with him.
4. And when he had gathered all the chief priests and scribes of the people together, he demanded of them where Christ should be born.
5. And they said unto him, In Bethlehem of Judaea: for thus it is written by the prophet,
6. And thou Bethlehem, in the land of Juda, art not the least among the princes of Juda: for out of thee shall come a Governor, that shall rule my people Israel.
7. Then Herod, when he had privily called the wise men, inquired of them diligently what time the star appeared.
8. And he sent them to Bethlehem, and said, Go and search diligently for the young child; and when ye have found him, bring me word again, that I may come and worship him also.
9. When they had heard the king, they departed; and, lo, the star, which they saw in the east, went before them, till it came and stood over where the young child was.
10. When they saw the star, they rejoiced with exceeding great joy.
11. And when they were come into the house, they saw the young child with Mary his mother, and fell down, and worshipped him: and when they had opened their treasures, they presented unto him gifts; gold, and frankincesnse, and myrhh.

12. And being warned of God in a dream that they should not return to Herod, they departed into their own country another way.

William Walker was, according to George Waldron's 1726 publication, 'A Description of the Isle of Man', the only native of note of his day, and goes on to provide an interesting view of the people, their clergy and their language at that time:

> What eminent men this Island has formerly bred I know not, but at present I hear of none famous abroad; nor can boast of any more at home than one clergyman, who is indeed a man of letters, and who, I hope, will oblige the publick with his instructive and polite writings. He [William Walker], considering the profound ignorance of his countrymen, for their sakes undertook a translation of the New Testament into the Manks tongue; of which work he had (as I have been credibly informed) finished the four gospels, and had proceeded in it if the publication thereof had not been prohibited by a superior power. Books written in the Manks tongue they have none, except a catechism and instructions for youth, with some prayers not many years since compiled.
>
> Some, who are willing to entertain the most favourable opinion of this people, impute their general ignorance to their want of books; but I, who have lived and conversed some time among them, attribute their want of books to their innate ignorance. That this suggestion is not without grounds, appears from the little progress made in learning by those who have had the happy advantage of finishing their education in a Scotch or Irish college, which is commonly the case of such as are designed for Holy Orders; notwithstanding which, we find none of their writings made public, nor would most of their sermons pass on any but a Manks congregation. If to this they object that their language is obscure, and not well known in the world, let them write (as they frequently preach) in English, or in Latin, a language universally known to the learned world.
>
> To prevent controversies and support their imperious sway, the clergy (like those of the Church of Rome) hold the laity under a blind abject obedience; of which take this instance: When I once, in conversation with two young clergymen, lamented the above-mentioned prohibition, which debar'd the common people (who speak only their own language) from the delightful benefit and necessary duty of searching the Scriptures, they agreed in this answer, That it was happy for the people that the Scriptures were lock'd up from them, for it prevented divisions in the interpretation of them, which was given to themselves, and to themselves only, by their Great Dictator, who had substituted them his vicars and the interpreters of his law. It may, perhaps, not be unworthy the consideration of that power which presides over the diocese of Man, whether the greater inconvenience accrues from a publication, or a suppression of the translation I spoke of? In the first case, what was objected by the clergymen is not without some grounds, viz., that such a translation would lay the Scriptures open to the different interpretations of ignorant, prejudiced, or evil-designing men, and raise disputes even in matters of faith, carried on in a language strange to their metropolitan, nay even to their diocesan; by which means the unspotted discipline of the church might be polluted, her pure doctrine

corrupted, the laws of God perverted or broken, His holy name blasphemed, and yet the great offender escape unpunish'd, nay, untry'd. Yet for all this, such a translation is earnestly to be desired, when we consider the miserable condition of that unhappy people, who, surrounded by the most learned nations of Europe, remain in a state of utter ignorance, and rather imitate than conform to the purest church of God upon earth. They hear the Scriptures read, but not expounded, every Sabbath. Their prayer-books and Bibles are printed in English, and the minister mentally translates the service into the Manks tongue, as he delivers it to the people. From these two considerations I draw this question, as before mentioned, Whether the greater inconvenience or evil accrues from a publication or a suppression of a translation ? On the one hand there would be a fix'd, certain, known rule of faith which the people might in another generation be brought to comprehend, (that is, if those who ought to instruct them would do it) and by which they would be govern'd. As the case now stands, they are directed by the various interpretations of various preachers; nay, by the various interpretations of one preacher; for who can suppose that any man shall at all times (tho' on the same subject) use the same expressions, words, or terms. Does not this method open a door to that endless confusion, which some think they prudently exclude by prohibiting the publication? Besides, without being accounted malicious, would not any disinterested person ask the question, why these people are so ignorant, why there is not better care taken in forming their youth ?"

One of the early seventeenth-century clergymen who was also a carval writer was Rev Thomas Allen, Vicar of Kirk Maughold. Two of the carvals known to be written by him appear in 'Carvalyn Gailckagh'. One is ascribed to the year 1728, and is called, in 'Carvalyn Gailckagh', 'Tra Ta Mish Jeaghyn Er Yn Yrjid Heose, or, A Hymn On Man's Shameful Fall'. These are the opening twelve verses plus two 'floating' lines out of 47 verses as printed.

Thomas Allen

Tra Ta Mish Jeeaghyn Er Yn Yrjid Heose, *1728*

Tra ta mish jeeaghyn er yn yrjid heose
Kiongoyrt rhym's grian rollageyn as yn eayst
Lesh yindys ta mish rhympene sheer gimraa
Quoi hug daue soilshey, quoi ren oie as laa?

Shickyr dty keeayll's ren shoh, O Ree ny Gloyr
Dty obbraghyn ta feanish jeh dty phooar
Nagh nhee t'ayns niau as ooilley wass sy theihll
Liort hie er chroo lesh oardaghey dty veeal

Agh harrish ooilley dooinney v'ayns dt'imnea
My ren oo eh v'ou myr shoh jeh gimraa

Lhig da ve jeant lesh corp as annym glen
Ayns jalloo Yee erksyn dagh fer as Chiarn

Lheid shoh dy frioose va cowrey mooar dy ghrayse
As mieys Yee dy chroo eh wheesh ayns foays
Ny ainleyn hene agh feer veg er eh skyn
Ayns coondey Yee tra ve ayns cairys glen

O ghooinney aalin, maynrey v'ou sy traa
Cha row oyr olkys ayd noi oie as laa

Son Jee va lhiatt's as ooilley fo dty reill
Cha row ort laccal nhee erbee sy theihll
Stiagh Paradise hie oo er choyrt boayl veen
Ayns shen va gaase dy-chooilley vess jeh hene

As dooyrt eh rhyt tra v'ou sy gharey sthie
"T'ayd nish ayns shoh palchey dy veaghey mie
Cha vreayll yms voyd agh billey t'ayns y vean
Yn gharey gaase, ny jean uss gee jeh shen

"Shoh slane dty churrym, bee uss er dty hwoaie
Er pian dty vaaish ny jean, shen dooyrt mee roie
Faag void mee ammys ny t'ou tilgit ass
Ass fooayr dty Yee ny yiow 'sy tullagh baase"

Va'n sarey cairagh jir dagh fer eu ve
As vondeish Adam dy ver vreilley eh
She bioys as baase va echey nish ayns reih
Quoi eeagh jeh agh dooinney keoie gyn schlei?

Jeeagh nish er Adam as eh heshey Eve
Ayns Eden sthie va oc yn eiraght feeu
Yn Ardnieu vrinnagh te cheet huc as feysht
Cre smoo dooyrt Jee as myr shoh roosyn geaish

As dinsh ad da cre va nyn ghurrym slane
Agh dooyrt eh roo dyn imnea goaill jeh shen
Cha voghe ad baase ga goghe ad jeh as gee
Agh yrjid keeayll as toiggal myr va Jee

Er shoh yn ven ren jeeragh er eh raa
Dee ish jeh'n vess, O s'beg y feme v'ec da

Eisht ec da'n noid ny smoo ny sarey Yee
As choyrlee Adam dy ghoaill ayrn maree

Agh tra va heese ve dauesyn beaghey deyr
Son raa yn Jouyl prow dy ve coyrle molteyr
Dennee ad hene caghlaa veih mie gys sie
Woish stayd eh vea fo jymmoose Yee ny lhie

Translation

When I Am Looking on the Height Above, *1728*

When I am looking on the height above
Before me sun, stars and the moon
With wonder I am constantly saying to myself
Who gave them light, who made night and day?

It's certain that your intellect made these, O King of Glory
Your works are witness of your power
Each thing that is in heaven and all below in the world
By you they were created by command of your mouth

But above all man was in your concern
Before you made him you were thus saying of him
Let him be made with a clean body and soul
In the image of God above each one and Lord

Such attention as this was a great sign of grace
And the goodness of God to create him so much in benificence
The angels themselves but very little above him
In God's esteem when he was in perfect rectitude

O beautiful man, happy you were in the time
You had no reason for wickedness night and day

For God was with you and all were beneath your rule
You lacked for nothing at all in the world
Into Paradise you were given a dear place
In there every fruit was growing of its own accord

And he said to you when you were home in the garden
"You now have here plenty of good sustenance
I will not keep from you [any] but the tree that's in the centre
Of the garden growing, don't eat from that one

"This is the whole of your duty, be on your guard
On pain of your death, don't do it, what I said before
Refrain from disobedience, or you're thrown outside
Out of God's favour or you will in the instant die"

That the command was just, each one of you will say
And Adam's advantage had he kept it
It's life and death he had now in his choice
Who would eat of it but an artless, wild man?

Look now at Adam and his partner Eve
Home in Eden, the worthwhile heritage they had
The flattering Serpent he comes to them and asks
What more said God as thus listening to them

And they said to him what was their whole duty
But he said to them not to worry about that
They wouldn't die though they would take of it and eat
But get the height of knowledge and understanding like God

At this the woman did exactly as his word
She ate of the fruit, O little the need she had of it
Her attention [listening] to the enemy more than God's command
As she counseled Adam to partake with her

But when it was down it was to them expensive food
For the word of the Devil proved to be the advice of a deceiver
They felt themselves changing from good to bad
From the state of his life lying beneath the wrath of God

William Walker, who had translated the Gospels and the Acts of the Apostles, died in 1729, long before his work was published. His death and the death of his mother's son by a second marriage gave rise to 'A Sorrowful Ditty on the Death of her Two Sons, the Rev William Walker, LL.D., Vicar-General of the Diocese of Sodor and Mann, and Rector of Ballaugh; and Mr Robert Tear of Douglas. By Widow Tear of Ballaugh'. It was written about 1750.

Widow Tear of Ballaugh
A Sorrowful Ditty on the Death of Her Two Sons, *1750*

Roish my row mee rieau my voir
S'maynrey vaar mee eisht my hraa
My chree gyn loght, my chione gyn feiyr
My eddin lane dy vlaa

My aigney seyr veih laad chiarail
Sthill aashagh oie as laa
Agh nish my gherjagh t'er valleil
My chree ta brisht dy braa

As tra ren mee my stayd chaghlaa
Hug Jee dou bannaght cloan
Hrog mee ad seose dy voddym ghra
Nagh row nyn lheid agh goaun

Ayns aggle yee lesh ynsagh vie
Dy aalin as dy glen
As yerk mee roo dy chooney lhiam
Tra veign annoon as shenn

Dy insh jeh'n egin va mee ayn
Troggal myr shoh my chloan
Cha voddym scrieu's te doillee ginsh
Yn egin shen lesh goan

Arkys as feme ghow orrym greim
Haink faggys da my chree
Ny-yeih cha daink my raad yn chrem
Er-derrey daag ad mee

Er yn edjag-screeuee Robbin va
Ny vainshtyr ard ayns schlei

As v'eshyn gaase dy chooilley laa
Ny smoo ayns coontey sleih

Symbyl jeh'n ynsagh v'er e laue
Daag eh ayns bane as doo
Nee freayl e chooinaght fud sheelnaue
Er voalley ghiall Cheeill-Chroo

Illiam pessyn Cheeill Voirrey va
Bochilley chiaralagh Chreest
Laue yesh yn Aspick, sooill yesh y theay
Briw ny Hagglish neesht

Bannagh ny moght, scaa ny mraane hreoghe
Fendeillagh cloan gyn ayr
Da ny hannoonee dreeym nagh goghe
Veih treanee ghewill aggair

As ga dy row e churrym mooar
Va e chreenaght corrym rish
As er goo mie e hoiltyn hooar
Cooyrt reeoil Hostyn fys

Veih hooar eh ooashley's ennym noa
Ny mast'ain joarree roie
Lheid's nagh dooar Manninagh bio
As s'goan hooar lheid ny-yeih

E hoilshey ren soilshean dy gial
Trooid magh yn Ellan Slane
E hampleyr skeaylley dy chooilley voayl
E choyrle vie gys dagh ayrn

Gloyr Yee, as foays e helloo noo
Va kinjagh e chiarail
Biallagh gys e vochilley smoo
As veih shen jerkal faill

Myr va e hoilchyn ooilley mooar
Mannagh beagh eh dy bragh er ve ny smoo
Foast dreill eh yn leigh ayns pooar
Hug lesh meereiltys gys toyrt-mow

Oyr vooar ta ec ny Manninee
Lurg lheid yn charrey choe
Son stiark ny vud oc ta lheid y chree
Dy reayll drogh-yannoo fo

Jeh Saggyrt Walker cooinagh vees
Choud as ta Mannin ayn
As ayraghyn trooid mooarane eash
Vees ginsh jeh da nyn gloan

Kys hie eh seose gys cooyrt y ree
Noi ny kyndee brishey'n leigh
As ghow eh voue ooilley nyn mree
As hooar ad lhieggey veih

Quoi hyrmys eisht ny jeir ta roie
Veih groinyn yn chioltane
Keayney nyn mochill' graihagh mie
Nagh vel oc nish er-mayrn

Agh mish e voir tra smoo ayns feme
Hie eh er scarrey voym
Troggit dy leah shagh' harrish y cheim
'Sy Rullick hrimshagh hrome

Keayrt va mee mayrney ayns my chloan
Moir ghennal ren ad jeem
Dreill ad erskyn feme my chione
As v'ad sthill dou son dreeym

Nish ta mee coodit lesh slane oie
Gyn soilshey aym hiar ny heear
My chainle ta ass gyn saase erbee
Dy gherjagh moir ny ayr

Fo dorraghys doo, my aigney dooint
Gyn jerkal jeh soilshey reesht
Ayns diunid nagh vow acyr grunt
Mastey yn sterrym neesht

Translation
A Sorrowful Ditty on the Death of Her Two Sons, *1750*

Before I was ever a mother
So happy bore I then my time
My heart without blemish, my head without noise
My face in full bloom

My spirit free from a burden of care
Still easy night and day
But now my comfort has failed
My heart is broken for ever

And when I changed my state
God gave me the blessing of children
I raised them up so that I could say
That their like was not but scarce

In fear of God with good learning
Beautifully and cleanly
And I expected them to help me
When I would be feeble and old

To tell of the want of help I was in
Raising my children like this
I cannot write and it's difficult to tell
That want of help with words

Adversity and need took hold of me
Came near to my heart
For all that the soreness didn't come my way
Until they left me

With the quill pen Robbin was
The master high in skill
And he was growing every day
Greater in the estimation of people

A symbol of the learning that was in his hand
He left in white and black
That will keep his memory amongst mankind
On the bright wall of Keeill Chroo [Keeill Chragh in Kirk Patrick]

Illiam the parson of Keeill Woirrey [Ballaugh] was,
A caring shepherd of Christ
The right hand of the Bishop, the right eye of the people
A Judge of the Church [Vicar-General] as well

A blessing to the poor, shield of the widow women
The defender of fatherless children
To the feeble a bulwark [lit., a back or ridge] that would not yield
Before unrighteous cruel despots [lit., heroes!]

And though his duty was great
His wisdom was equal to it
And because of the good repute of his merit
The royal court of England got knowledge of it

From it he got honour and a new name
That were strangers amongst us before
Such as a living Manxman never got
And scarce received the like after him

His light shone bright
Throughout the whole Island
His example spreading everywhere
His good counsel to every part

The glory of God, and the benefit of his hallowed salve
Was always his concern
Obedient to his greatest shepherd
As from that hoping for his return

As were his deservings all great
If he would not for ever have been greater
Still he kept the law in force
He brought unruliness to destruction

There is great reason for the Manx people
To weep after such a friend
For scarce amongst them is such a heart
To keep wrong-doing down

Of Vicar Walker there will be memory
Whilst Mannin still exists
And fathers throughout many an age

Will tell of him to their children

How he went up to the king's court
Against those responsible for breaking the law
And he took from them all their energy
And they got a straightening from him

Who would then dry the tears that run
From the [im]pulses of the flock
Lamenting their loving, good shepherd
That does not now remain to them

But me, his mother, when most in need
He went to be parted from me
Lifted soon past over the stile
In the heavy, sad Graveyard

Once I was happy in my children
A contented mother they made of me
They kept my head above need
And they were still for me as a bulwark

Now I am coverered with a complete night
Without any light east or west
My candle is out without any way
To comfort mother or father

Beneath dense darkness, my spirit is closed
Without hope of a light again
In a depth that an anchor will not find ground
Amidst the storm as well

One of the Gaelic names in a Scandinavian context in the tenth century was Mail Brikti, becoming Mylvreeshey and then Bridson. In 1760, Joseph Bridson wrote a poetical description of the Island under the name Jeo Vreejey. In this work, he uses 'noain' on several occasions. It is possible that this is from 'shione' ('known'), but it is also possible that this is a late survival of the emphatic demonstrative, found in Phillips as 'shononi', but here as 'shoh noain'. This is the opening section which reveals it as a piece of doggerel. However, it shows a desire to bring Manx into print on a general topic.

Jeo Vreejey (Joseph Bridson)
Coontey-Ghiare Jeh Ellan Vannin, *1760*

Ayns Gailck

Jeh'n Ellan shoh, mychione eck ta fo'm loayrt
Nee'm y chooid share son coontey feer y choyrt.
T'ee Ellan veg ayns Keayn Noo Yeorge ny lhie.
'S ga d'el ee beg, t'ee costallagh dy mie.
Ta cheer ny Albey er y twoaie j'ee, soit
As Anglesey ta er y jiass j'ee lhie-t.
Ta Lancashire lhie vo'ee 'sy Chiar
As Nerin ayns y Sheear myr ta mee cur my ner.
Yn chummey eck ta, er yn aght shoh, noain
T'ee lane vie liauyr, cha vel ee agh feer choon.
Veih Kione-ny-harey 'syn ayrn sodjey twoaie
Er dys y Challoo, cha vel fys ayms quoi
Ren ee y howse, mish cha ren veg y lheid
Ta'd gra dy jean ee towse jeih veeilley as feed.
Er son y lheead eck slane, veih cheu dy heu
Myr ta mee lhaih, ta ny screeunyn streeu:
Paart sailliu nuy, ny jeih, ny red gyn veg
As paart ta shassoo er queig veeilley-yeig.
Agh lheid er-hastagh, ta mee cur dhyt my-reih
Dy ghoaill ee son nuy, queig-jeig ny jeih.

Translation
A Short Account of the Isle of Man, *1760*

Of this Island, about which I intend to talk
I'll do my best to give a true account.
It's a small Island which lies in St George's Sea.
And though it's small, it's precious to a goodly extent.
The country of Scotland on the north of her is set
And Anglesey is on the south of her, laid out.
Lancashire lies from her in the East
And Ireland in the West as I behold.
The shape of it is, in this way, understood
It's long to a goodly extent, but its only very narrow.
From the Point of Ayre in the part furthest north
To the Calf, I don't know who
Measured it, I myself never did the like
They say that it measures ten miles and twenty.

As for its full breadth, from side to side
As I read, the writings conflict:
Some, please you, nine, or ten, or some[thing] without anything
And some that maintain that it's five miles and ten.
But such for knowledge, I give to you as a choice
To take it for nine, fifteen or ten.

The poem goes on to deal with the towns and products of the Island, before concluding with something of the Island's folklore.

Ayns earish ter' ngholl shaghey, ny Manninee
Va ashoon niartal as sleih mooar chiaggee
Agh nish cha vel wheesh boirey cheet nyn raad
S'maynrey'n skeeal, feer vaynrey ta nyn stayd.
Yn cheer shoh noain, my ta shiu er chlashtyn jeh
Dyn dooyt nagh vel yn skeeal ta foddey shlea
Na'n cheer shoh hene, yn goo myr shoh ta goll,
D'el ferrishyn as beishtyn ayns dagh voayl
Jeh'n cheer veg shoh, as kinjagh te d'imraa
Dy vel ad er nyn vakin oie as laa;
Nish cre dy ghra 'sy chooish shoh, cha saym
Agh son lane pleat cha nakym monney feme
Part trooid faase chredjue, paart trooid gaasit vooar
Myr ennym jeu, myr shoh nee ad m'ansoor.
Ta lheid dy feer, cre oddyms roo y ghra?
My jirrym, dty hilley oo er dty volley ta.
Jir ad nagh vel, as cowraghyn ta'd ginsh
Ve myr shoh noain, v'eh cho baghtal shoh ny wheesh.
Cha jirrym roo, cha veer dhyt, as myr shen
Ta skeealyn gaase, t'ad credjit as ta'd beayn
Nish lhig dagh er, tra chlinnys eh lheid shoh
Edyr mychione corp varroo ny corp vio
Yn ymmyd saillish yannoo jeh yn skeeal
Cordail rish goo as sheeltys feer e veeal
Ta ginsh da lheid, agh share lhiam eh dy mooar
Eh ve dyn chredjal, as shickyr te dy liooar
Ta lheid ny niaghtyn toilliu lane dy chraid
Cooid ta'd dy gheddyn, dagh voayl t'ad goaill raad
Bunnys ny oddyms ghra mychione y cheer
Vel ooilley shoh ny taym's ve raa-it dy feer
Myr shen 'sy traa cha jeanyms lesh my veeal
Ny smoo y ghra, agh ta jerrey er my skeeal.

Translation

> In time that's gone past, the Manx
> Were a powerful nation and a great warrior people
> But now there's not so much bother coming their way
> So happy the story, very happy is their state.
> This very country, if you have heard of it
> Without doubt that's not the story that's far wider
> Than this country itself, the repute goes like this,
> That there are fairies and beasties in every place
> Of this little country, and always it's mentioned
> That they are being seen night and day
> Now what to say about this topic, I don't know
> But for complete prattle I will not see much need,
> Some through superstition, some through the great growth
> Of their name [i.e. the repute given to the stories], like this they will
>   answer me.
> The like is true, what can I say to them?
> If I say, your sight has deceived you.
> They will say that it hasn't, and they tell of signs
> It was this very way, it was as obvious as this or more so.
> I will not say to them, you aren't right, and thus
> The stories grow, they're believed and they're lasting
> Now let each one, when he hears the like of this
> Either about a dead body or a live body
> Make what use he wishes of the story
> According to the reputation and the true sobriety of the mouth
> Which tells him the like, but I much prefer
> That it is not credited, and it's certain enough
> That such newses are fully worthy of derision
> They gather goods [i.e. the stories are embroidered] each place they
>   go.
> Almost whatever I can say about the country
> It's all this that I've truly stated,
> So for the time being I will not with my mouth
> Say more, but there's an end to my story.

In 1760, the year of Jeo Vreejey's 'Coontey-Ghiare', a sea battle had been fought off the Island's west coast. On 28 February 1760 an action took place between a British squadron under Commander John Elliott and a French squadron under François Thurot. The flagship of Thurot was the 'Marshall Belleisle'. Thurot was known and liked in the Island, having been involved in trading in these waters for some years previously, but with a victorious Royal Navy squadron in Ramsey Bay, the Island celebrated with them. This event gave rise to a song. However, to sound a note of caution, William Harrison (1873) refers to 'the original MS. Copy, which, with the assistance of the Rev John Thomas Clarke, late chaplain of St. Mark's, is considerably enlarged, and the whole rendered into a more correct historical fact.'

Anonymous
Thurot as Elliot, *1760*

    Ec balley veg Frangagh er dorrin ny bleeaney
    Flodd veg dy hiyn-chaggee ren geddyn fo hiauill
    As choud's veagh Thurot kion-reiltagh e gheiney
    Cha bailloo ve orroo dy jinnagh ad coayl

    Sheer caggey noi'n ree ain, gyn aggle ny nearey
    As roostey as spooilley yn ymmodee siyn
    Yn gheay ren ee sheidey er ardjyn ny Haarey
    As gimman ad stiagh fo reeriaght yn ree ain

    Eisht hie ad dy ghoaill Carrick-Fergus ayns Nerin
    As myr v'ad cheet stiagh gys ny voallaghyn ayn
    Ard-chaptan y valley dooyrt rish e hidooryn
    Shane dooin ad y oltagh' lesh bulladyn ghunn

    Ny-yeih ayns traa gherrit v'an poodyr oc baarit
    Nagh voddagh ad shassoo as eddin chur daue
    Eisht captan y valley dooyrt reesht rish e gheiney
    Nish shane dooin roie orroo lesh cliwenyn ayns laue

    Va'n stayd oc danjeyragh dy cronnal ry-akin
    Eisht dooyrt eh roo, shane dooin cur seose huc ayns traa
    Son foddee mayd jerkal rish baase fegooish myghin
    Neayr's nagh vel shin abyl yn noid y hyndaa

    Myr shen haink ad stiagh ayns y valley laa-ny-vairagh
    Dy yannoo myr bailloo rish ooilley ny v'ayn
    Mysh lieh-cheead dy Rangee va currit er feayraght
    Daag Thurot cheu-chooylloo nyn lhie ayns y joan

    Tra va Carrick-veg-Fergus oc spooillit dy bollagh
    Nagh chiare ad dy roshtyn yn Ellan shoh noain
    Agh s'beg erree vocsyn er quoi veagh nyn rohaialtagh
    Yinnagh yn daanys oc ooilley dys kione

She Elliot veeit ad rish, ren orroo lhiggey
As lesh eddin ghebejagh doad orroo aile
Hug Thurot dy-chione lesh ooilley'n voyrn echey
As sheese beign da lhoobey er-boayrd yn Velleisle

Tra haink ad dy-cheilley as gunnaghyn lhiggey
As cronnagyn getlagh goll shiar as goll sheear
Fuill Frangagh myr ushtey dy palchey va deayrtey
As Belleisle vooar y Thurot va tholl't myr y chreear

Ny Frangee myr eeastyn va scarr't er ny deckyn
Tra hir ad son Thurot fud shilley cha grouw
Agh v'eshyn ny chadley ayns diunid ny marrey
Cha lhiass daue ve moyrnagh ass Thurot ny smoo

Slane shey-feed ayns coontey dy reih gunnaghyn Rangagh
Noi gunnaghyn Elliot queig-feed as kiare
Three lhongyn noi three ren ad caggey dy barbagh
Er derrey hooar Thurot e voynyn 'syn aer

Va oyr ec ny Frangee dy ghobberan dy sharroo
Son yn obbyr va jeant ayns three lieh-yn oor
Three-cheead reesht jeh'n cheshaght va lhottit ny marroo
As dussan dy cheeadyn goll stiagh 'sy thie-stoyr

Va queig jeh ny Sosthynee marroo myrgeddin
As 'nane-jeig-as-feed gortit 'sy chah
Agh shimmey v'er ennaghtyn guin yn laa cheddin
Er-bey dy ren Elliot cosney yn laa

Nagh dunnal yn dooinney va'n Offisher Forbes
Ghow cullyr lhong Thurot er-boayrd yn chied er
As Thomson myrgeddin hie sheese ayns yn aarkey
Dy yeigh ny thuill-vaaish eck lesh barragh as geirr

Fir-veaghee shenn Vannin v'er cheu heear yn Ellan
Eer Aspick Mark Hildesley as ooilley e hie
Ren jeeaghyn dy tastagh as fakin as clashtyn
Veih toshiaght dy yerrey yn caggey va cloie

Croan-spreie yn Velleisle tra ve currit er shiaulley
Ve eiyrit as immanit stiagh er y traie
Ve soit ec yn Aspick son cooinaght jeh'n chaggey

Er ynnyd ard-chronnal er-gerrey da e hie

Eisht mygeayrt Kione-ny-Haarey goll-rish deiney-seyrey
Hug ad lhieu nyn gappee seose baie Rhumsaa
Ec irree-ny-greiney ny Frangee va keayney
Tra honnick ad Thurot vooar currit dys fea

Tra hoig shin ayns Mannin cre'n ghaue v'er n'gholl shaghey
As c'raad va ny deiney v'er reayll jin yn ghaue
Ard phobble ny cheerey, eer mraane chammah's deiney
Haink roue dy veeiteil ad dy oltaghey daue

Va giensyn reih caarjyn ec theay as shiolteyryn
Va mooar jeant jeh'n Cheshaght ren cur lesh y laa
As rieau neayr's hiauill Ree Illiam dys Nerin
Cha ren lheid ny laaghyn soilshean er Rhumsaa

O sleih-cheerey as shiaulteyryn trog-jee seose arraneyn
Ny Frangee, ta'd castit er dy chooilley heu
Ta'n chaptan oc cadley ayns diunid ny marrey
Ny lhig daue ve moyrnagh ass Thurot ny smoo

Nish lhieen mayd yn veilley as iu mayd dy cheilley
Lesh Shee-dy-vea ghennal gys Georgee nyn Ree
Son she ny siyn-chaggee ta shin orroo shiaulley
Va'n saase dreill nyn noidyn veih ny Manninee

Translation
Thurot and Elliot, 1760

At a small French town at the stormy part of the year
A small fleet of warships got under sails
And as long as Thurot would be the chief of his men
They would not care to concede that they would lose

Fighting the utmost against our king, without fear or shame
And plundering and despoiling many vessels
The wind blew towards the area of the Ayres
And driving them in under the jurisdiction of our king

Then they went to take Carrickfergus in Ireland
And as they were coming in to the walls that were there
The chief captain of the town said to his soldiers

We must welcome them with gun bullets

Nevertheless, in a short time their powder was spent
So that they couldn't stand and face them
Then the captain of the town said again to his men
Now we must rush at them with swords in hand

The situation was dangerous, it was obvious to see
Then he said to them, We must surrender to them in time
For we can expect death without mercy
Since we are not able to turn the enemy

Thus they came into the town the following day
To do as they wished with everything that was there
About a half-hundred of Frenchmen who were put cold
Thurot left behind lying in the dust

When little Carrickfergus was despoiled by them completely
Did they not intend to reach this very Island
But little was their [inkling of] fate about who would be their
  quaaltagh [the first person to meet them]
That would bring their boldness to an end

It's Elliot they met with, who fired on them
And with a desperate face lit a fire on them
Thurot put an end to all his pride
And down he was forced to bend on board the Belleisle

When they came together with guns firing
And masts flying, going west and going east
French blood like water a-plenty was pouring
And Thurot's great Belleisle was holed like a sieve

The French like fishes were scattered on the decks
When they sought for Thurot amidst such a gloomy scene
But he was sleeping in the depth of the sea
They need not take pride in Thurot any more

A full six score in count of choice French guns
Against Elliot's five score and four guns
Three ships against three fought fiercely
Until Thurot found his heels in the air

There was reason for the French to lament bitterly
For the work that was done in three half-hours
Three hundred again of the company were wounded or dead
And a dozen of hundreds going into the hold [brig]

Five of the English were also dead
And eleven and twenty hurt in the battle
But many had felt pain the same day
Had not Elliot gained the day

Wasn't Officer Forbes a brave man
He, the first man, took the colour of Thurot's vessel on board
And also Thomson who went down in the ocean
To close her deadly holes with tow and tallow

The inhabitants of old Mannin who were on the west side of the
 Island
Even Bishop Mark Hildesley and all his house[hold]
Looked keenly and saw and heard
From beginning to end the fighting that was being played out

The bow-sprit of the Belleisle, when it was put afloat
Was washed and driven in on the shore
It was set by by Bishop for remembrance of the fighting
On a conspicuous place close to his house

Then around the Point of Ayre like gentlemen
They brought their captives up Ramsey Bay
At sunrise the French were lamenting
When they saw great Thurot put to rest

When we understood in Mannin what the danger that had gone past
And where the men were who had preserved us from danger
The chief people of the country, even women as well as men
Came to them to greet them and bid them welcome

O landsmen and sailors, raise you up songs
The French, they're defeated on every side
Their captain is sleeping in the depth of the sea
Don't let them take pride in Thurot any more

Now we'll fill the bowl and we'll drink together
With a pleasant toast to Georgie our King

> For it's the warships that we sail on
> That were the means of keeping our foes from the Manx people

---

Bishop Mark Hildesley, a witness to the sea battle between Thurot and Elliot, had been appointed as Bishop of Sodor and Man after the death of Bishop Wilson in 1755. Hildesley marshalled his clergy to provide a translation of the Bible into Manx, and they also translated the Book of Common Prayer. Attached to this were metrical versions of some of the psalms translated by Rev Matthias Curghey and Rev Robert Radcliff from the 1696 work of Nahum Tate and Nicholas Brady. The singing of metrical versions of psalms in church with the lines given out one by one is still practised in the Western Isles of Scotland, but was once widespread. Curghey's and Wilks's metrical psalms follow the metre of Tate and Brady's versions, but are quite free in dealing with the subject matter. After the Psalter, is a dedication:

> TO / THE RIGHT REVEREND FATHER IN GOD / MARK / (BY DIVINE PERMISSION) / LORD BISHOP OF SODOR & MAN. / MY LORD, / The annexed Translation, into our native Language, of the following Psalms, viz. I, IV, VIII, XV, XIX, XXII, XXIII, XXIV, XXV, XXXII, XXXCIX, XLV, LXVII, LXXXIV, XC, XCV, C, CIII, CXVI, CXVII, CXIX, CXXXV, CXLIII, CXLV, CXLVI, CXLVII, CXLVIII, with the Hymns and Doxologies subjoined, fitted to several of the Tunes, used in the Churches, are most humbly recommended to your Lordship, as proper to be made use of and sung in the several Churches of this Diocese, / By your Lordship's most dutiful / and obedient Servants, / ROBERT RADCLIFF. / MATTHIAS CURGHEY. / November 3, 1761.

The longest-surviving use of one of the metrical psalms in the Island seems to have been part of Psalm 90 which constituted the Kirk Christ Rushen Funeral Hymn. Funerals processions in Kirk Christ Rushen were accompanied by the slow singing of the metrical versions of verses 3 and 6. By the early twentieth century, this was still in use, albeit in the Tate and Brady English version rather than in Manx:

Robert Radcliff and Matthias Curghey
Psalm XC, *1761*

> 1. Hiarn, nyn saualtagh niartal rieau
> D'endeil dty reih hioltane;
> Veih eash dy eash t'ou er ny ve
> Yn sauchys shickyr ain.
>
> 2. Roish my ren sleityn cheet erash,
> Roish ren oo'n seihll y chroo:
> V'ou uss yn ooilley-niartal Jee,

Nish yn Jee cheddin oo.

3. T'ou caghlaa'n dooinney, Hiarn, gys joan,
Ass ren oo 'chummey eh;
Cha leah's ta'n sarey rait, Chyndaa,
Sheign baillys y ve.

4. Son ayns dty hilley thousane blein
Cha vel agh myr un laa;
Ny myr oor ceaut er dromm ny hoie,
Nagh vel mooar geill ain da.

5. Goit myr lesh thooilley, ta shin stroit,
As chea myr dreamal oie:
Gaase seose 'sy voghrey, goll-rish blaa,
Rere myr ta'n ghrian ceau bree.

6. Agh cre-erbee cha glass as te,
Cre-wooads yn aalid t'ayn:
Te giarit sheese, fiojit, as creen,
My jig y laa gys kione.

10. Seihll dooinney three feed blein as jeih,
Stiark ta goll seose er shen;
As my ta fer erbee cha trean
Dy heet gys kiare feed blein.

11. E hroshid eisht cha bee eh veg
Agh trimshey as angaish;
Snaih'n vea (ta faase) vees brish, as eisht,
Geyre farkiaght er ta'n baase.

Translation
Psalm XC, *1761*

1. Lord, ever our powerful saviour
To defend your chosen flock;
From age to age you have been
Our certain safety.

2. Before mountains came back,
Before you created the world:
You were the almighty God,

Now you are the same God.

3. You turn man, Lord, to dust,
From which you shaped him;
As soon as the command is spoken, Return,
There must be obedience.

4. For in your sight a thousand years
Is not but one day;
Or like an hour spent in the dead of night,
That we don't pay much heed to.

5. Taken as with a flood, we are destroyed,
And flee as a night's dream:
Getting up in the morning, like a flower,
According to whether the sun gives off energy.

6. But however green it is,
However great the beauty that exists,
It's cut down, faded, and withered,
Before the day will come to an end.

10. The world of man is three score and ten,
How few who go above that;
And if there's anyone so valiant
To come to four score years.

11. His strength then will be nothing
But sorrow and anguish;
The thread of life (which is weak) will break, and then,
Sharply waiting for him is death.

These are the corresponding verses in Tate and Brady's metrical psalm 90 for comparison:

1. O Lord the savior and defense
Of us thy chosen race,
From age to age thou still hast been
Our sure abiding place.

2. Before thou brought'st the mountains forth,
Or th' earth and world didst frame,
Thou always were the mighty God,

And ever art the same.

3. Thou turnest man, O Lord, to dust,
Of which he first was made;
And when thou speak'st the word, "Return,"
'Tis instantly obey'd.

4. For in thy sight a thousand years
Are like a day that's past,
Or like a watch in dead of night,
Whose hours unminded waste.

5. Thou sweep'st us off as with a flood,
We vanish hence like dreams;
At first we grow like grass that feels
The sun's reviving beams:

6. But howsoever fresh and fair
Its morning beauty shows;
'Tis all cut down and withered quite
Before the ev'ning close.

10. Our term of life is seventy years,
An age that few survive;
But if, with more than common strength,
To eighty we arrive;

11. Yet then our boasted strength decays,
To sorrow turned, and pain:
So soon the slender thread is cut,
And we no more remain.

For the translation of the Bible into Manx, Bishop Hildesley appointed Rev Philip Moore (1705–1783) as overall editor. Whilst at Bishopscourt on this work, Moore was discussing the Ossianic works of James MacPherson with Deemster Peter John Heywood. A gardener working outside the open window heard the names of Fin and Oshin, and said that his sister-in-law knew songs about them. From her Moore wrote down a song which had evidently survived from a much earlier period in the oral tradition, though not committed to writing until the 1760s. In 1829, Lord Teignmouth wrote that 'of literature there is no trace in the Manks language, excepting some songs composed in the style of Ossian, discovered by Bishop Hildesley'. This song would fit the chronology, but is the only Ossianic piece known to have been recorded in the Island. The refrain after each line (Fa la lo, fa la lay) is omitted.

Traditional
Fin as Oshin, *1763*

> Hie Fin as Oshin magh Laa dy helg
> Lesh sheshaght trean as moddee elg
> Cha row un dooinney sloo na keead
> Coshee cho bieau cha row nyn lheid
> Lesh feedyn Coo eisht hie ad magh
> Trooid Slieau as Coan dy yannoo Cragh
> Quoi daag ad ec y thie agh Orree beg
> Cadley dy kiune fo scadoo'n chreg
> Slane three feed Quallian aeg gyn unnane sloo
> Lesh three feed shenn Chaillagh dy yeeaghyn moo
> Dooyrt Inneen Fin ayns Craid as Corree
> "Kys yiow mayd nish cooilleen er Orree?"
> Dooyrt Inneen Oshin: "Kiangle mayd eh
> Lesh Folt e ching chionn gys y Clea
> As ver mayd Aile gys e chass cho bieau."
> Clysht tappee eisht hug Orree ass
> Tra dennee eh'n smuir roie ass e chass
> Loo Mollaght Mynney ad dy stroie
> Va er n'yannoo craid er Mac y Ree
> Dy farbagh breearrey ry Ghrian as Eayst
> Dy losht ad hene as thieyn neesht
> Hie Orree beg magh dys ny Sleityn
> As Speih mooar connee er e gheayltyn
> Hoght bart mooar trome hug eh lesh cart
> Hoght Kionnanyn currit ayns dagh Bart
> Hoght deiney lheid's sy theihll nish t'ayn
> Cha droggagh bart jeh shoh ny v'ayn
> Ayns dagh uinnag hug eh Bart, as ayns dagh dorrys
> Agh mean y Thie mooar hene yn Bart mooar sollys
> Va Fin as Oshin nish shelg dy chionn
> Lesh ooilley nyn treanee ayns ollish as joan
> Yaagh wooar ren sheeyney ass y neear
> Troggal ayns bodjallyn agglagh myr rere
> Roie Fin as roie Oshin derrey daase Oshin skee
> Agh she Fin mooar hene chum sodjey nish roie
> Eisht dyllee Fin huggey lesh Coraa trome
> "Cha vel faagit ain nish agh tholtanyn lhome."

Quoi ren yn assee shoh, nagh re Orree beg?
V'er chosney voue chelleerid gys ooig fo'n chreg
Raad plooght lesh Jaagh hayrn ad magh er y chass
Lesh cabbil keoi eisht raip ad eh gy baase

Translation
Fin and Oshin, *1763*

Fin and Oshin went out one day to hunt
With a valiant company and hunting dogs
There was not one man fewer than a hundred
There wasn't the like of such swift foot travellers
With scores of hounds then they went out
Through Mountain and Valley to wreak Havoc
Who did they leave at the house but little Orree
Sleeping quietly beneath the shadow of the rock
Full three score young pups without one fewer
With three score old women to look after them
Said Fin's daughter in Derision and Anger
"How will we now get revenge on Orree?"
Said Oshin's daughter: "We'll bind him
With the Hair of his head to the harrow bar
And we'll put Fire to his foot so swift."
Orree then gave a rapid leap out
When he felt the marrow running out of his foot
Swearing a curse of curses to destroy them
That had made a mockery of the Son of the King
Blazingly swearing by the Sun and the Moon
To burn those themselves and houses as well
Little Orree went out to the Mountains
With a large gorse-hook on his shoulders
Eight great heavy bundles he brought with a cart
Eight sheaves put in each Bundle
Eight men the like of which are in the world now
Would not lift a bundle of these that were in
In each window he put a Bundle, and in each door
But the middle of the great House itself the large bright Bundle
[i.e. on fire]
Fin and Oshin were now hunting closely
With all their heroes in sweat and dust
A great smoke stretched up from the west
Lifting in clouds to the utmost
Fin ran and Oshin ran, until Oshin grew tired

But it's great Fin himself who kept on further now running
Then Fin yelled to him with a heavy Voice
"There's only empty tholtans [roofless houses] left to us now.
Who did this harm, was it not little Orree?
Who had got away from them directly to a cave beneath a rock
Whom stifled with Smoke they hauled out by the foot
With wild horses then they ripped him to death

During Bishop Wilson's tenure of office, his Vicar-General, Rev William Walker, had translated not only St John's Gospel, which had been published during Wilson's time in 1748, but also the synoptic gospels and the Acts of the Apostles. However, before Bishop Hildesley caused them to be published in 1763, it appears that the texts were revised from the orthography of Bishop Wilson's publications to a further 'standardised' form under the editorial hand of Moore. Work on the Bible in Manx continued, with the first part of the Old Testament in 1771 and the second part in 1773. Bishop Hildesley had died the preceding December, but the final proofs of the pages which would complete the Manx translation of the entire Bible had been placed in his hand nine days before his death.

1763 was the year in which a Manx translation of 'The Christian Monitor' was published as 'Yn Fer-raauee Creestee'. The original had appeared in 1686. The Manx translation was by Rev Paul Crebbin of Santon. The translation given here is a literal one, not the original text.

Rev Paul Crebbin
Yn Fer-raauee Creestee – Cab.1, *1763*

Coyrle dy leeideil Bea Chrauee, marish Resoonyn breeoil dy ghreinnaghey Sleih huggey.

Te feer trimshagh dy smooinaghtyn, cha nee ynrycan cre'n earroo fardalagh dy Ashoonyn t'ayns y theihll ta goaill-rish y Chredjue Creestee, agh myrgeddyn jeh ny Ashoonyn shen ta goaill-rish, cre'n earroo fardalagh ayns cosolagh ta leeideil nyn mea cordail rish nyn Gredjue: Shen-y-fa te red feer jesh da ooilley sharvaantyn firrinagh Chreest, er skyn ooilley da Shirveishee e Hushtal, dy yannoo ooilley ny t'ayns nyn booar liorish nyn Ymmyrkey-bea as Ynsagh, liorish nyn Goyrle dy foshlit as er lheh, liorish nyn Breacheil as nyn Screeu, as liorish dy chooilley aght oddys ad, dy chur Craueeaght as Casherickys firrinagh er y hoshiaght mastey dy chooilley cheint dy leih, edyr ard ny injil, boght ny berchagh, fegooish y Chraueeaght as y Chasherickys cheddyn cha vod dooinney erbee ve maynrey, edyr ayns y theihll shoh ny ayns y theihll ta ry heet. As ga dy vel fyss feer vie aym dy vel, booise gys Jee, palchey dy lioaryn mie ny vud ain scruit son yn Oyr shoh; foast cha vel leid y

Choyrle ghiare as ta dy heet ny lurg shoh dy ve deyrit myr gyn ymmyd, fakin dy vod y lioar veg shoh, te laik, as y Choyrle t'ayn-jee ve ny smoo er ny skeailey, as shen fud yn ayrn s'boghtey dy leih, as foddee ad ve ny sassey er nyn lhaih as cooinaghtyn freailt jeu liorish nyn leid ocsyn as nagh vel Traa oc dy lhaih lioaryn mooarey, ny argid dy chionnaghey ad. Rish nyn leid shoh ta caa mennick aym dy veeiteil, as er y ghraih ocsyn er lheh ta mee scrieu yn lioar veg shoh; greinnit dy yannoo eh liorish paart dy phersoonyn crauee, chammah ayns cheer as balley, ta kiarrail dy ghiootal paart jeh ny lioaryn beggey shoh er sleih boghtey my-geayrt-y-moo, as va smooinaghtyn dy jinnagh feallagh elley myrgeddyn. As my scooidsaave lesh jee bannaght y choyrt da leid yn obbyr fardalagh as ta shoh, as eh y vishaghey son foays anmeenyn, sbeg geill verryms da ny foiljyn yow Fer-ynsee erbee mooar-alagh da'n lioar shoh.

Shen-y-fa fegooish arragh y ghra jeh'n lioar veg shoh, loarym riuish, er nyn nghraih ta mee scrieu ny lineyn shoh, myr Coyrle dy leeideil Bea Chrauee as Chreestee.

Translation

The Christian Monitor – Chap. 1, *1763*

Advice to lead a Holy Life, with vigorous Reasons to incite People to it.

It is very sad to think, not only what an insignificant number of Nations that are in the world which acknowledge the Christian Faith, but also of those Nations which acknowledge it, what an insignificant number in comparison are leading their life according to their Faith: That is the reason it is a very proper thing for all true servants of Christ, above all for Ministers of his Gospel, to do everything that is in their power through their Bearing in life and Learning/Teaching, through their Counsel openly and privately, through their Preaching and their Writing, and through every method they can, to promote true Piety and Sanctity amongst every sort of person, whether high or low, poor or rich, without which same Piety and Sanctity no man can be happy, either in this world or in the world that is to come. And though I know very well that there are, thank God, plenty of good books amongst us written for this Purpose; still the like of a short Instruction as is to come after this is not to be condemned as useless, seeing that this little book can, it is likely, and the Advice that is in it be more greatly dispersed, and that through the poorest portion of people, and they can be more easily read and remembrance kept of them by the like of those who have not Time to read large books, or money to buy them. With the like of these I often have an opportunity to meet, and for the love of them particularly I am writing this little book; encouraged to do it by some of the religious persons, both in country and town, who intend to make a present of some of these little books to poor people round about them, and were thinking that other people would do likewise. And if it is granted by God to give a blessing to such an insignificant work as this, and to increase it for the good of souls, little attention will I give to the faults that any haughty Man of learning will impute to this book.

That is the reason without speaking further of this little book, I will speak with you, for love of whom I am writing these lines, as Advice to lead a Religious and Christian Life.

The wreck of the Manx herring fleet in Douglas Bay on 21 September 1787 caused the death of 21 fishermen, and its economic consequences were a reduction of the Manx fishing fleet by about 18% as about 60 vessels were damaged beyond repair. A lament was written about the event by Quayle Vessie (i.e. Quayle, the son of Bessie).

Quayle Vessie
Coayl Jeh Ny Baatyn-Skeddan, 1787

Cooinee-jee, shenn as aeg
'Sy vlein shiaght cheead jeig
Kiare-feed as shiaght er keayn Ghoolish
Myr haink eh gy-kione
Va eeaystaght vie ayn
Lesh earish feer aalin as villish

Ny-yeih cha nee beayn
V'ayn earish cha kiune
My daink kione y chiaghtyn dys jerrey
Son va neeal yn aer
Soilshagh' magh danjeyr
Va sterrym feer agglagh er-gerrey

Oie'l Vian dy feer feayn
Choud's v'an flod ec y cheayn
Haink dewillys, as paart jeu ren scarrey
Veih dy chooilley nhee
Va deyr da nyn gree
Eer bioys, liorish dewillys ny marrey

Te doillee dooin gra
Cre whilleen as va
Oie'l Vian feer ching ec nyn greeaghyn
Cloan faagit gyn-ayr
Va keayney dy geyre
As mraane son ny sheshaghyn jeeaghyn

Trooid Skylley-Chreest
Va seaghyn as erreeish
Mraane jeeaghyn son nyn vendeilee
Skimmee Hom Kinlaie
V'ad keayney nyn-yei
As sheshaght Yuan Voore Croit-y-Caley

Thom Qualtrough myrgeddin
Va caill't 'syn oie cheddin
Marish y chooid elley jeh e gheiney
Cha row dooinney jeu bio
Jeh'n 'nane as feed shoh
Nyn ghaarjyn dy sharroo va keayney

Fastyr aalin feer ve
Tra hiaull adsyn jeh
Voish Doolish marish baatyn elley
As rosh ad yn voayl
V'an skeddan dy ghoaill
Dyn smooinaght er assee ny skielley

Agh gerrid v'an traa
Ren yn earish caghlaa
Yn gheay niar dy niartal ren sheidey
Dy leah datt yn cheayn
Lesh sterrym as sheean
Haink dorrin lesh dewillys as fliaghey

Eisht hrog ad dy leah
Nyn shiaull roish y gheay
Dy jeeragh lesh purt Ghoolish shiaulley
Tra rosh ad yn vaie
V'an cheayn magh er draie
As yn earish er-gholl foddey smessey

Ec aker 'sy vaie
Cha faggys da'n traie
Cre b'erree da ny ny baatyn va markiagh?
S'dorraghey myr ve
Fegooish soilshey er y key
Ayns aggle nyn maaish v'ad farkiagh

Dy fieau er y cheayn

Dy lhieeney dy lane
Ve chennid feer agglagh dy jarroo
Caabhil failleil
As baatyn sinkeil
As scoltey ayns peeshyn, cheet thalloo

Ve cha dorraghey dhoo
Nagh b'leayr daue yn chlieau
Ny tonnyn va freayney stiagh harroo
Nagh atchimagh ve
Lesh dorrin as kay
Dy roie roish yn gheay dys thalloo

Er-creau voish yn cheayn
Lesh sterrym as sheean
Ny tonnyn myr sleityn v'ad girree
As ooilley'n traa shen
Va'n cheayn brishey bane
Nagh b'leayr daue'n phurt v'ad dy yeearree

Mysh oor roish y laa
Ve smooinit va'n traa
Hie Qualtrough dy roie son y thalloo
V'eh hen as Juan Voore
Caill't 'syn un oor
As ooilley yn skimmee va maroo

Myrgeddin Kinlaie
Ec faagail yn vaie
Cha b'leayr da yn raad dy roie jeeragh
Traa s'dorraghey ve
V'eh bwoailt noi'n key
As va'n vaatey sinkit chelleeragh

Cha row saase 'sy theihll
Nyn gour dy scapail
Yn vaase va kiongoyrt rish nyn sooillyn
Yn eam oc va treih
Lesh cree er ny lheie
Ec toshiaght sinkeil boayl va whilleen

Dy hrial nyn schlei
Cha voddagh ad reih

Nyn lheid as v'ad shoh ooilley cooidjagh
Ny deiney mie cheayn
Ayns y vinnid shen
Ny tonnyn y vaaish ren ad choodagh

Son nyn gaarjyn deyr
Va oyr oc shilley yeir
Chammah mraane as mraane-hreoghe as cloan veggey
Lesh osnaghyn hreih
V'ad currit lhieu thie
As oanluckit marish nyn cleinney.

Translation
The Loss of the Herring Boats, *1787*

Remember you, old and young
In the year seventeen hundred
Four score and seven on [the] sea [at] Douglas
As it came about
There was good fishing
With weather that was very beautiful and sweet

Nevertheless it's not everlasting
Was such calm weather
Before the weekend came to an end
For the aspect of the air
Showed danger
There was a very dreadful storm near

St Matthew's Eve very expansively
Whilst the fleet was at sea
There came inclemency, and parted some of them
From everything
That was dear to their heart
Even life, because of the severity of the sea

It's difficult for us to say
How many there were
On St Matthew's Eve, very sick at their hearts
Children left without a father
There was bitter lamenting
And women searching for their partners

Through Kirk Christ [Rushen]
There was sadness and sympathy
Women searching for their defenders
The crew of Tom Kinley
They were lamenting after them
And the company of Juan Moore, Croit e Caley

Tom Qualtrough as well
Was lost in that same night
With the remainder of his men
There was not a man of them alive
Of these twenty-one
The friends were bitterly keening

Truly it was a beautiful afternoon
When these ones sailed off
From Douglas with other boats
And they reached the place
That the herring were occupying
Without thinking of hurt or harm

But soon was the time
The weather changed
The east wind strongly did blow
Soon swelled the sea
With storm and clamour
A tempest came with severity and rain

Then they soon raised
Their sail before the wind
Sailing directly for Douglas port
When they reached the bay
The sea was out on the ebb
And the weather had gone far worse

At anchor in the bay
So close to the shore
What would be the fate of the boats that were riding?
So dark was it
Without a light on the quay
In fear of their death they were waiting

To wait for the sea

To come to high tide [literally, to fill completely]
It was very dreadful distress indeed
Cables failing
And boats sinking
And splitting in pieces, coming ashore

It was so dark black
That the mountain wasn't clear to them
The waves were overflowing in across them
Was it not awful
With tempest and fog
To run before the wind to land

A-quiver from the sea
With storm and clamour
The waves like mountains they were rising
And all that time
The sea was breaking white
So that the port they were yearning for wasn't clear to them

About an hour before the day
It was thought was the time
Qualtrough went to run for the land
He himself and Juan Moore were
Lost in the same hour
And all the crew that were with them

Likewise Kinley
On leaving the bay
The way to run directly wasn't clear to him
When it was so dark
He was struck against the quay
And the boat was sunk immediately

There was no way in the world
For them to escape
The death that was before their eyes
Their cry it was sad
With heart [courage] melting away
At first sinking where there were so many

To test their skill
They couldn't choose

Such as were here all together
The good seamen
In that minute
The waves of death covered them

For our dear friends
There was reason for us to shed tears
Wives as well as widows and little children
With sad sighs
They were taken home
And buried with their kinfolk

Another song of the sea concerns the voyage of a Manx privateer called the Tiger (or Tyger) which dates to events in 1778 and 1779. The author of the song was John Moore of Camlork in Braddan, who was a Lieutenant on the Tiger under Captain Richard Qualtrough. Moore later bought an inn in Bride. He sang his song so often that he was known as 'Moore the Tiger'.

John Moore
Marrinys Yn Tiger, *1779*

Ren deiney-seyrey Vannin
Ayns yrjid, stayd as moyrn,
Nyn bingyn ceau dy-cheilley
As chionnee ad shenn lhong.

Va ynnyd oc ayns Doolish,
As boaylyn er y cheer,
Raad cheau ad pingyn cooidjagh
Dy chionnagh privateer.

Ny pingyn hie dys Sostyn,
Va ymmyd daue ayns shen,
Dy chionnaghey'n chenn "Tiger,"
'S dy choyrt ee dys y cheayn.

Hie eam magh trooid yn Ellan
Son guillin jeh ynsagh-cheayn,
Ny guillin roie dy Ghoolish,
Tra cheayll ad lheid y sheean.

Ayns sheshaghtyn v'ad chymsagh,
Cheet voish dagh ayrn jeh'n cheer,
Dys thie Nick Voore ayns Doolish,
Cho liauyr as grenadier.

She Qualtrough vees nyn gaptan,
As marish nee mayd goll.
As feiyr vooar hie fud Doolish,
Lesh lheimmyraght as kiaull.

Caggee mayd noi ny Frangee,
As noi America.
Ta guillin-vie ayns Mannin,
Nagh jean voish noid chyndaa.

Liorish nyn jebbyn aalin,
Ny guillyn hayrn ad lhieu,
Ny eirinee va gyllagh,
"Kys yiow mayd jeant yn traaue?"

Va shoh daue ard oyr aggle,
Quoi eiyragh er y cheeaght
Dy goan veagh guillin Vannin,
Son coltar chur fo chreagh.

Va Illiam mooar y Condray
As dooinney vooar yn chronk
V'ad gyllagh son ny guillin
Va wheesh d'inneenyn oc.

O shiuish inneenyn Vannin,
Ta dobberan ayns doo,
Gra, "nagh vel guillyn faagit
Agh paitchyn nagh vel feeu.

"Dy vel ad ooilley failt
Er boayrd yn phrivateer,
As s'goan my ta wheesh faagit
As roshys fer er kiare.

"As tra nagh vel wheesh faagit
As roshys fer y pheesh,
Te foddey share ve follym,

Cha nee fer eddyr jees."

Giu as cloie er ny caartyn
Chum roinyn oie as laa
Gra, "blebeeyn ny guillin
Nagh jed noi America."

Myr eignit hie mee maroo,
As hass mee seose dys gunn,
As kinjagh va mee dobberan,
Dy row my ghraih rey rhym.

Ny cheayrtyn va mee smooinaghtyn
Nagh vaikin ee dy braa,
As ceau my laghyn seaghnagh,
Ny lhie ayns baie Rumsaa

Tree laa va shin er hiaulley
Lesh dooin faagail Rhumsaa.
Tra veeit shin rish y sterrym
Hug er yn eill ain craa

Va deiney tooillit teaymey
As guillin coayl nyn mree
As Harry Voore va gyllagh
"My ghuillin cum nyn cree."

Yn cheayn va gatt as freaney
Ve rastagh erskyn towse,
Yn chronnag ain va caillit,
Cha dod shin freayl nyn goorse.

Lurg da ve tammylt sheidey,
Yn sterrym reesht ghow fea;
As rosh shin shenn oie Ollick
Gys aker ayns Mount Bay.

Ec kione three laa reesht aarloo.
Eisht hie shin son y cheayn;
As veeit shin lhong voish Holland,
As ghow shin ee dooin hene.

Eisht haink shin thie dy Ghoolish,

Lesh gunneraght as kiaull,
As deiney-seyrey Vannin
Dy moyrnagh haink nyn guaill.

Ga blaik lhieu fakin spooilley,
Va'd moyrnagh gyn resoon,
Loayrt baggyrtagh nyn oi ain
Dy choyrt shin ayns pryssoon.

Leah hoig shin dys nyn drimshey,
Lurg dooin v'er roshtyn thie,
Yn lhong va shin er hayrtyn,
Dy row ee goit noi'n leigh.

Dooyrt ad dy row'n chooish ain
Trieit feanish yn chiannooyrt
As "cha vel briw ayns Mannin
Ne briwnys diu y choyrt.

"Nish gow shin [shiu] reue dys Sostyn,
As meeit mayd shiu ayns shen,
As shooyl mayd rieau er thalloo,
Ny shiaull mayd rieau er keayn."

Agh ta mish nish ayns Mannin,
As vouesyn ta mee seyr;
Cha vod ad mee y lhiettal
Veih sheshaght my ghraih gheyr.

Shoh'n erree ghow'n chenn "Tiger,"
Va'n oyr jeh wheesh dy chiaull;
V'ee creckit jeh son toghyr,
Da'n lhong va shin er ghoaill.

Ga va shin sheshaght ghennal,
As trean ayns corp as cree,
Drogh choyrle as drogh leeideillee
Ver naardey cooish erbee.

Ta'n foill ta geiyrt da'n Vanninagh,
Oyr treihys fer-ny-ghah,
Te'h creeney lurg laa'n vargee
Agh s'beg vondeish te da.

O shiuish my gheiney cheerey
Ta geaishtagh rish m'arrane,
My choyrle te diu ve creeney,
Choud's ta'n traa er-mayrn.

She'n chooish ta ooilley lhie er,
Dy ghoaill kiarail ayns traa,
Roish bee laa'n vargee harrish,
Nyn drimshey son dy braa.

Translation

The Voyage of the Tiger, 1779

The gentlemen of Mannin
In grandeur, state and pride
Threw their pennies together
And they bought an old vessel

They had a place in Douglas
And places in the country
Where they threw pennies together
To buy a privateer

The pennies went to England
There was use for them there
To buy the old Tiger
And to put her to sea

A call went out through the Island
For lads with knowledge of the sea
The lads ran to Douglas
When they heard such a clamour

In companies they were gathering
Coming from each part of the country
To Nick Moore's house in Douglas
As tall as a grenadier

It's Qualtrough who'll be our captain
And with him we'll go
As a great noise went through Douglas
With capering and din

We'll fight against the French
And against America
There are good lads in Mannin
Who won't turn from an enemy

Through their beautiful offers
They drew the lads with them
The farmers were shouting
'How will we get the ploughing done?'

This to them was a great cause of fear
Who would follow the plough
Manx lads would be scarce
For to put the coulter to the clod

There was Big William Condra
And a great man from the hill
They were shouting for the lads
They had so many daughters

O you daughters of Mannin
Who are lamenting in black
Saying that there aren't lads left
But children who aren't worthwhile

That they're all hired
On board the privateer
And scarce if there's as many left
As will reach [do for] one in four

And when there are not as many left
As may do for one a piece
It's far better being without
Not one between two

Drinking and playing at cards
Kept us night and day
Saying, 'Fools are the lads
Who won't go against America'

So compelled I went with them
And I stood up to a gun
And always I was lamenting

That my love was done with me

Sometimes I was thinking
That I'd nevermore see her
As spending my sorrowful days
Lying in Ramsey bay

Three days we had sailed
After we left Ramsey
When we met with a storm
That made our flesh quiver

Men were exhausted bailing out
It was stormy above measure
Our crosstree was lost
We couldn't keep our course

After it had been blowing a while
The storm again took a respite
And on old Christmas day we reached
To anchor in Mount Bay

At the end of three days ready
Then we went for the sea
And we met a ship from Holland
As we took her for ourselves

Then we came home to Douglas
With gunfire and din
And the gentlemen of Mannin
Proudly they came to meet us

Though they liked seeing plunder
They were proud without reason
Speaking threateningly against us
To put us in prison

Soon we understood to our sorrow
After we had arrived home
The ship we'd caught
Was taken against the law

They said that our case was

Tried before the governor
And 'There's not a judge in Mannin
Will give a judgement for you

'Now get you hence to England
And we'll meet you there
And we'll walk with you on land
Or we'll sail with you on sea'

But I'm now in Mannin
And from them I'm free
They couldn't hold me back
From the company of my dear love

This is the fate of the old Tiger
That was the reason for so much din
She was sold for a dowry [i.e. as compensation]
For the ship we had taken

Though we were a happy band
And valiant in body and heart
Bad counsel and bad leaders
Will bring to nothing any cause

The fault that follows the Manxman
A cause of grief for one or two
He's wise after the market day
But little advantage it is to him

O you my countrymen
Who are listening to my song
My advice to you is to be wise
Whilst there's time remaining

It's the thing that everything depends on
To watch out in time
Before the market day will be over
Our sorrow for ever

Moore the Tiger was also a carval writer, noted in 'Carvalyn Gailckagh' as the composer of 'Carval yn Noo Paul, or, Carol on St Paul'. His name has also been associated with 'Carval ny Drogh Vraane'. In a paper on the carvals, Cyril Paton describes the pieces in an original carval book and notes:

> As to the authorship [of 'Carval ny Drogh Vraane'], George Borrow thought that it was by ... Moore the Tiger; Philip Caine informs me that he has seen it attributed to William Kinrade, of Ballachrink, Maughold, who was the author of nine or ten carvals, 'Carval Noah' amongst others. It is here stated to be 'Metreit Liorish John Moore jeh Balla Cammaish Skeeyl Andreas' i.e. metred by John Moore of Balla Cammaish, Parish of Andreas'. I know not if this is the same as the 'Tiger'.

As 'Carval ny Drogh Vraane' was dated to 1720, and Andreas and Bride are different, albeit adjoining, parishes, it probably is not. Paton mentions William Kinrade, to whom P W Caine attributes the Question and Answer carval above. That also was shown in 'Carvalyn Gailckagh' to date to 1720. However, William Kinrade was born in 1769 and died in 1854. If by Kinrade, the Question and Answer carval may properly belong to the period between 1790 and 1850 rather than to 1720. Another carval attributed to William Kinrade is 'Lhig Da'n Slane Seihll Cur Clashtyn, or, Let The World Give Hearing', of which these nine verses are the second half of the carval as printed in 'Carvalyn Gailckagh'.

Attributed to William Kinrade
Lhig Da'n Slane Seihll Cur Clashtyn, *c.1790*

Shiuish king lheeah, chyndaa-Jee [chyndaa-jee]
Bee'n traa eu leah ec kione
Ny kirp eu ta gaase appee
Dy hyndaa reesht gys joan
Nagh bee shiu lhiggey shaghey
Ta'n tra dy siragh roie
Yn noid ta still er arrey
As kiarit shiu y stroie

Bee boggey mooar ayns flaunys
Ec cheet ny aryssee
Nyn greeghyn er ny chowragh
Lesh seal jeh graih Mac Yee
Dy gerrit nee ad joinal
Marish yn agglish heose
Ny cooyrtyn beayn nee feiyral
Cur moylley braa da Creest

Trimshey erbee ny osney
Cha vel ry ennaght ayn

Sidooryn Chreest ter chosney
Yn caggey slane ec kione
Ny smoo cha bee ad tossit
Fud faarkaghyn dy ghaue
Nyn noidyn as nyn roshtyn
Dy yannoo skielley daue

Nyn anmeeyn maynrey garditt
Trooid Jordan feayr jeh baase
Satan cha vow nyn raad oc
Dy violagh ad dy bragh
Te nish buirrogh myr lion
Erchee sheelnaue y stroie
Mec as inneenyn Sion
Te tossal ad dy creoi

O, giall dy vod thousaneyn
Dy si'yragh cosney thie
Dy iu ass ny farraneyn
Dy vaynrys nagh vel traih
Te geam diu dy cheet huggey
Dy chooilley stayd dy sleih
As slane sheelnaue dy chroymmey
Gys reiltys Mac e Ghraih

O, shiuish y hirveishee
Smooar ter nyn gurrym lhie
Shir shiu son voayl ny kirree
Bee ad ayns phastyr vie
Vel ushtey ec ny shioltaneyn
Ayns bree as chiass yn laa
Leeideil ad dys farraneyn
Dy ooraghey nyn baa?

Erbee nyn lhiggey shaghey
Heeagh shiu laaghyn mie
Sheelnaue myr roayrt ny marrey
Dy siyrragh cosney thie
Ayns soylagh gys calmaneyn
Veagh getlagh dys nyn duill
Chymsaghey ayns shioltaneyn
Lesh kesmad gastey shooyl

Shiuish vraaraghyn as chaarjyn
Cre'n fa ta shiu cumrail?
O, tar shiu gys ny cuirraghyn
Ta Yeesey er nordrail
Yn lheiy beiyht ter ny varroo
Te gialdyn dagh nhee mie
Te booiagh skealley harrin
Yn cullee eckey graih

My chaarrjyn, cur shiu tastey
Da ny ta mee er loayrt
Son ta'n traa tayrn ergerrey
Traa shegin dooin coontey choyrt
Traa vees mayd symnit cooidjagh
Liorish feiyr yn ard cayrn
As nooghyn yn er syrjey
Vees goit dys gloyr. – Amen.

Translation

Let the Whole World Give Hearing, *c.1790*

You grey-headed ones, turn
Your time will soon be at an end
Your bodies are growing ripe
To turn again to dust
Don't be procrastinating [allowing past]
Time is running hurriedly
The enemy is still on watch
And intent on destroying you

There will be great joy in paradise
At the coming of the repentent
Ther hearts being marked
With the seal of the love of the Son of God
Soon they will join
With the church above
The eternal courts will be sounding
Giving everlasting praise to Christ

Any sadness or sighing
Are not to be felt in it
The soldiers of Christ have won
The whole war at an end

No longer will they be tossed
Amidst oceans of danger
Their enemies out of reach of them
To do harm to them

Their happy souls guarded
Through cold Jordan of death
Satan will not find their road
To tempt them ever
He now bellows like a lion
About to destroy mankind [the seed of heaven]
Sons and daughters of Sion
He tosses them roughly

O, promise that thousands can
Hurriedly make it home
To drink out of the fountains
Of happiness that do not abate
He calls to them to come to him
Every condition of person
And for the whole of mankind to bow
To the government of the Son of his Love

O, you who are his ministers
On whom great is the duty that lies
Seek for the place of the sheep
They will be in the good pasture
Do the flocks have water
In the vigour and heat of the day
Leading them to fountains
To refresh their thirst?

But for your procrastinating
You would see good days
Mankind like the spring tide
Hurriedly making it home
In comparison with doves
That would be flying to their roosts [holes]
Gathering in flocks
Walking with a lively step

You brothers and friends
Why are you delaying?

O, come you to the feasts
That Jesus has ordained
The fatted calf has been killed
He promises every good thing
He is content to spread over us
His banner of love

My friends, take notice
To what I have said
For the time is drawing nigh
When we must give account
When we may be summoned together
By the noise of the great trumpet
And saints of the highest being
May be taken to glory. – Amen.

An extremely well-written carval believed to date from about 1790 is 'Roish My Row Flaunys Er Ny Chroo, or, Before The Heavens Were Created'. It is thought to have been composed by Rev Thomas Christian (1754-1828). Christian also composed 'Pargys Caillit', published in 1796, and which is a paraphrased and abridged version of Milton's 'Paradise Lost'. Similar turns of phrase have been identified in the carval and poem, and it is thought that the carval is the earlier work.

Attributed to Thomas Christian

Roish My Row Flaunys Er Ny Chroo, *c.1790*

Roish my row flaunys er ny chroo
Ny ainleyn sollys kiaddit ayn
Roish my row soit er-lheh yn stoo
Glen hug eh'n mirril shoh gys kione
Cre eisht v'ayn? Cre eisht v'ayn?
Na mooar feeu ronsagh er y hon?

Roish my row soilshey, eayst ny ghrian
Ny rollage hollys heose chyndaa
Ny whilleen pooar ayns niau soilshean
As ren towse kiart gys oie as laa
Cre eisht va? Cre eisht va?
Cre v'ayn my row imbagh ny traa?

Roish my hrog sleityn seose nyn gione

My daink y thalloo injil rish
Roish my row awinyn roie cha shliawin
Sheese trooid dagh glion, myr hee shin nish
Cre v'ayn eisht? Cre v'ayn eisht
My row'n mooir mooar as traieyn mysh?

Dowin fegooish grunt, as ard gyn barr
Lhean neesht gyn oirr as liauyr gyn kione
Ve follym feayn, gyn ooir, gyn aer
As cha row aile ny ushtey ayn
Cha moo va – stoo ny staa –
Agh y Jee niartal ynrican

She er dy rieau, va eshyn Jee
As veih hene toshiaght ren eh goaill
Cur toshiaght da dy chooilley nhee
As undin shickyr da dagh boayl
Roish va Ayrn – lhieent veih'n slane
Lesh Jee as lesh e phooayr gloyroil

Veh ooilley niartal ayns E phooar
As ooilley creeney ayns E schlei
E vaynrys slane va ayns E gloyr
As cha row nhee dy ghoaill shen veih
Cha row seihll – cha row foill
Ny oyr dy yannoo veg y leigh

Ga nagh row rieau ny niaughyn ayn
Ny cretoor bio gennit ayndoo
Ga nagh row thalloo, aer ny keayn
Ny veg ny bioee er ny groo
Cha row pooar – cha row gloyr
Yn ooilley niartal, veg ny sloo

Shoh yn Jee creeney chiaddey niau
Marish ny ainleyn bannee t'ayn
As hug eh'n gioot spyrrydoil shoh daue
Dy beagh oc bea liauyr fegooish kione
Gloyr as phooar – as manrys vooar
Va oc gyn lheamys ve er unnane

Myr sy ghlen oie ver shiu my-ner
Ny aileyn baney t'er nyn skyn

Lossey dy gennal ayns yn aer
As lieh my lieh cur soilshey hooin
Dagh rollage – mooar as beg
Ta lane jeh'n soilshey hee mayd ayn

Earroo erskyn earroo va ayn jeu
As va nyn eiragh cha roomoil
Nyn aigney hene va kiarit daue
My baillen ve dy bragh gloyroil
Sy stayd shoh – kinjagh bio
Ayns fenish Jee nyn Ree graysoil

Nyn gurrym aashagh ynsit va
As va ad oarderit dy chur geill
Lesh kiaull, lesh bingys, oie as laa
Cur moylley booise da nyn fer reill
Biallagh – ammyssagh
Veih nyn slane gree gys goan y veeal

Yn ooilley niartal ren coraa
As dooyrt Eh roo, 'She un Vac t'aym
My ynrican Vac, my eirey braa
My pooar, my niart, Eh shinney lhiam
She y fa – cur jee da
Yn ooashley cair da Eirey yn Rheim

Croym ad nyn ging lesh biallys
Myr booiagh jeh ny ve dy ghra
Ayns maynrys slane as gennalys
Cur bannaght, booise as moylley da
Goaill arrane – gys nyn Jiarn
Kiaulleeaght – Alleluia

Shoh ooilley yn churrym as yn cheesh
Va oardit da ny flaunyssee
She shoh va'n mayle as y shirveish
Ooilley ny va dy eek da'n Ree
Ammyssagh – son dy bragh
Nyn stayd gloyroil ayns fenish Jee

Foast yn ard-ainle va roie goit stiagh
Ayns foayr rish Jee harrish mooarane
Trooid troo as moyrn ren girree magh

Ayns caggey foshlit n'oi nyn Jiarn
Veih yn laue yesh – hayrn eh lesh
Jeh theay nyn maynrys, yn trass ayrn

Sharroo as dewil va'n caggey v'ayn
Cheen [Heeyn] ooilley niartal plooghey neose
Veih stoyl-yreill, chaill cloan ny moyrn
Yn Chiarn leeideilagh hoie Eh seose
Ayns E phooar– as E gloyr
Ta ayns yn yrjey erskyn towse

Shoh raad va Miall as ainleyn mie
Er cheu ny cairys fo cullee Yee
Shoh raad van dragon as y greie
Streeu mysh y reiltys shirrey stroie
Foast cha row saase – yinnagh baase
Da spyrridyn aileagh va lossey cooie

Cha vel ny ainelyn myr sheelnaue
Fo pooar e vaase stroie as toyrt mow
Cha vod greie caggee baase chur daue
Ny'n dooghys ocsyn y chur mow
Foast van caggey – v'ocsyn chea
Lesh gahyn ailagh er dagh cheu

Agh yn Messias, Mac deyr Yee
Coamrit lesh ooashley, niart as pooar
Haink magh ayns room ny flaunysee
As da harvaantyn chur Ee foayr
Yn traitoor – as eh phooar
Hie mow dy leah lesh brishey mooar

Hie ad er eebyrt magh as niau
Veih maynrys vooar ny flaunyssee
Gys niurin vroghe rieau kiarit daue
Raad nagh vel scaa dy vioys erbee
Gyn treishteil – dy scapail
Agh dy bragh kianlt fo corree Yee

Shoh ny va ynsit jeh ny v'ayn
Roish my row'n seihll shoh er ny chroo
Cre'n erree hie er cloan ny moyrn
Tra hoill ad Jee ve corree roo

Ga va'd mooar – rish ayns foayr
Trooid cairys yiar eh yn eiraght jew

Nish va'n trass ayrn jeh reeriaght niau
Folmit jeh cummaltee gloyroil
Shen-y-fa chiaddee Jee sheelnaue
Giootit lesh anmeeyn spyrrydoil
Lheid as veeagh – bio dy bragh
Ayns ynnyd ainleyn hie er coayl

Yn noidys vooar, shoh dinsh mee diu
Goaill toshiaght ec ny ainleyn glen
Ta tannaghtyn sy laa tayn jiu
Yn drogh-spyrryd troo mysh doomney [dooiney] as ben
Dy voghe ad – lheid y stayd
As va roie caillit echey hene

Cre'n saaseyn croutagh te goll mysh
Dy hayrn nyn miallys voish Jee
Dy choontey ny dy loayrt jeh nish
Dy beeagh aym traa as schlei, ve'n skee
Gerjagh tain – foast er mayrn
Dy vel e violaghyn fegooish bree

Son y Messias niartal Chreest
Hooar barriaght roie er y traitoor
Trooid foayr te cheet neose hooinyn nish
Dy obbragh ny saualtys mooar
Chebbal grayse – dooin son saase
Dy chosney eiraght veayn ayns gloyr

Booisal eisht lhisagh shin y ve
Ammys as ooashley feeu chur da
Dy ren E shin nyn flaunyssee
As dy ve bio ayns niau dy braa
Lhig dooin guee – dy jean Jee
Earroo ny nooghyn lhieeney traa – Amen.

Translation

Before the Heavens Were Created, *c.1790*

Before heaven was created
Or bright angels were formed in it

Before the substance was specially placed
Clean he brought this miracle to an end
What then existed? What then existed?
Would it not be greatly worth researching for it?

Before there was light, moon or sun
Or bright star above turning
Or so much power shining in heaven
And gave the correct measure to night and day
What then was? What then was?
What existed before season or time?

Before mountains raised up their head
Before the low land appeared
Before rivers were running so slippy
Down through each glen as we see now
What existed then? What existed then?
Before the great sea and shores about it

Deep without bottom and high without top
Wide too without edge and long without end
It was empty and expansive, without earth, without air
And there was not fire or water in existence
Neither was there substance at all
But the mighty God alone

It's from eternity that he was God
And from himself did he make a beginning
Giving a beginning to everything
And a sure foundation to each place
Before there was a Part filled from the whole
With God and with his glorious power

He was almighty in his power
And all-wise in his skill
His whole happiness was in his glory
And there was nothing to take that from him
There was not a world, there was not a fault
Or reason to make the least law

This was the wise God who made heaven
With the blessed angels in it
And he gave this spiritual gift to them

That they would have a long life without end
Glory and power and great happiness
They had without a single one having a blemish

As in the clear night you will behold
The white fires that are above us
Burning pleasantly in the air
And turn and turn about giving light to us
Each star, little and big
Is full of the light we will see in him

Number above number there existed of them
And their heritage was so spacious
Their own will was intended for them
If they wished to be for ever glorious
In this state ever alive
In the presence of God their gracious King

Their easy duty was taught
And they were ordered to give heed
With music, with harmony, night and day
Giving thankful praise to their ruler
Obedient, respectful
From their whole heart to the utterance of the mouth

The almighty made a voice
And he said to them, 'It's one Son I have
My only Son, my heir for ever
My power, my strength, he is beloved of me
For that reason, render to him
The honour rightful to the Heir of the Realm

The bent their heads in obedience
As contented about what he was saying
In complete happiness and pleasure
Giving a grateful blessing and praise to him
Taking song to their Lord
Singing Alleluia

This was all the duty and the tribute
That was ordered to the heavenly host
It's this was the rent and the service
All that was to pay to the King

Respectful for ever
Their state glorious in God's presence

Yet the archangel that previously was brought inside
In favour with God above many
Through envy and pride rebelled
In open war against our Lord
From the right hand he drew with him
Of the people of happiness, the third part

Bitter and cruel was the battle that went on
The almighty stretched down a stifling
From the throne, the children of pride lost
The leading Lord he set up
In his power and his glory
That is in the height above measure

This is where Michael was and the good angels
On the side of right under God's banner
This is where the dragon was and the equipment
Striving over the government, seeking to destroy
Yet there was no way that death would [be dealt]
To fiery spirits that were a natural [appropriate] flame

The angels are not like mankind
Under the power of death that destroys and consumes
A weapon of war cannot bring death to them
Or destroy their nature
Yet there was the fighting they had to flee
With fiery stings on each side

But the Messiah, the dear Son of God
Clothed in honour, strength and power
Came out in the presence of the heavenly host
And to his servants he gave favour
The traitor and his power
Soon went to destruction, with a mighty breaking

They were driven out of heaven
From the great happiness of the heavenly host
To filthy hell ever intended for them
Where there is no shadow of life at all
Without hope of escaping

But for ever bound under God's anger

This is what was taught of what existed
Before this world was created
What fate it was that befell the children of pride
When they deserved God's being angry with them
Though they were great with him in favour
Through justice he cut off the heritage from them

Now was the third part of the kingdom of heaven
Emptied of glorious inhabitants
That's the reason that God formed mankind
Gifted with spiritual souls
Such as would be alive for ever
In the place of angels who were lost

The great enemy, this I told you
Starting with the pure angels
Is continuing in this very day
The evil spirit envious of man and woman
That they would get such a state
As was formerly lost by him himself

What crafty methods he goes about
To pull their obedience from God
To give account or to talk about it now
If I had time and skill, it was tiresome
We have comfort still remaining
That his temptations are without force

For the strong Messiah Christ
Gained a victory before over the traitor
Through favour he comes down to us now
To work a great salvation
Offering grace to us as a method
To gain an everlasting heritage in glory

Thankful then we ought to be
To give respect and worthy honour to him
That he make us the heavenly host
And to be alive in heaven for ever
Let us pray that God will
Fill the number of saints [in] time – Amen.

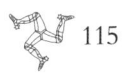

Rev Thomas Christian's paraphrase and abridgement of 'Paradise Lost', his 'Pargys Caillit', consists of over 4,000 lines. The following 74 lines include some phrases close to those in the above carval.

Thomas Christian
Pargys Caillit (lines 150–224), *1796*

Cha row ny seihill fo niau foast er nyn yannoo,
as seose 'syn aer meiht cha row'n ooir ny shassoo,
agh raad ta'n ooir nish, chemmit lesh y cheayn,
raad ta roltageyn, eayst chaghlaa, as grian,
va eaynagh ghowin gyn grunt, gyn oirr, gyn kione,
gyn doaie, gyn cummey, dorraghey as feayn.
Cha row ayn hiar ny heear ny twoaie ny jiass,
chamoo v'ayn heese ny heose ny hoal ny wass,
imbagh ny traa, daahghyn doo ny bane –
foast lesh ny rassyn oc shoh ooilley lane –
aer, ooir, aile, ushtey, nyn giare kione-y-cheilley,
as un oie eajee, ghoo, reill harrish ooilley.

Agh niau nish jeant marish ny cummaltee
rere pooar ooill'-niartal as ard chreenaght Yee,
er laa dy row – son laghyn ta ayns niau
dy howse yn braa beayn nagh vod traa y cheau,
's ga t'eh gyn oie foast ta ayn lheid y traa
as ta shirveish dy scarrey laa veih laa –
er lheid y laa shen sheshaght-chaggee niau,
freggyrt gys symney reeoil chie'r chur daue
ooilley dy heet kiongoyrt rish stoyl y gloyr
dy chlashtyn aigney 's leigh y Chroodagh mooar,
haink fodd' as gerrid veih dagh boayn jeh'n reill,
seraphim gial as pooaryn ard leeideil
ny troopyn sollys; kiaull ving flaunyssagh
lhieen yn aer vannee myr v'ad getlagh stiagh
'sy valley wooar shen trooid ny dor'syn ard,
maynrys as boggey lhieeney ayns dagh straid.

Yn Ooilley-niartal soie er stoyl-reeoil
ard 'skyn dagh yrjid 's erskyn-towse gloyroil,
ainelyn, ard-ainleyn, as slane ooashley niau
myr whilleen grian nyn shassoo er dagh laue
jeh'n phooar gloyroil; crownyn as slattyn-reill

hilg ad er laare ayns cowrey jeh nyn gheill
as biallys, goaill rish dy nee veih Jee
va oc nyn mea, nyn maynrys, as dagh nhee.
As va Mac Yee ayns oghrish 'Ayr ny hoie,
gys nish freilt follit veih ny flaunyssee –
cherubyn sollys er dagh lhiattee va,
gial myr y ghrian ain, ard ec y vunlaa –
gloyr, pooar as reill va grainnit er e ghruaie,
as veih e hooillyn graih myr stroo ren roie,
lesh va flaunys villish er ny lhieeney;
dagh ainle streeu quoi smoo yinnagh cooilleeney
ayns graih sp'rydoil as aigney mie dy-cheilley.
Shoh'n aght va flaunys myr un cheayn dy ghraih
as jeh dagh eunys nagh vel, nagh jean traih.

Eisht hug y Croodagh niartal magh coraa
lesh ren niau veih yn undin ooilley craa:
"Un vac ennoil," dooyrt eshyn roo, "ta aym
jiu er ny gheddyn, as eh shynney lhiam,
my yalloo hene, my chreenaght as my phooar,
my Ghoo smoo niartal 's corrym rhym ayns gloyr.
Mish Jee, as mee ta cur y leigh shoh diu
mychione my vac ta shiu dy akin jiu;
echey ta pooar, voym's, harrish ooilley niau,
as dagh nhee ta livreit stiagh ayns e laue;
niau as ny t'ayn ta echey fo e reill,
da ta mee goardagh shiuish neesht dy chur geill.
Ayns niau, na mish, cha vel unnane ny smoo,
As liorym pene kiongoyrt riuish ta mee loo,
dy chooilley ghlioon nagh groym ayns ammys da
vees tilgit magh as m'eanish son dy braa,
as veih my vaynrys, veih my ghrayse as foayr,
veih ooilley'n cairys t'echey ayns my ghloyr."
shoh loayr y Jee, as ooilley cheayll e ghoo,
lesh skell e ghloyr va 'eddin follit voue;
ny ainleyn, myr dy beagh ad booiagh lesh,
chroym sheese nyn gione as ghlioon ayns biallys.
'Myr dy beagh ad booiagh' ta mee gra,
son ayrn cha row, myr hee shiu ayns y traa.
Eisht hrog yn eanish wooar ayns un choraa,
"Gloyr, booise as moylley gys Mac Yee dy braa;
eh ayns [e] ghloyr ta shin er akin jiu,
t'eh Jee dy braa as v'eh Jee er-dy rieau."

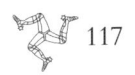

Literal translation
Paradise Lost (lines 150–224)

The worlds beneath heaven had not yet been created,
And up in the air measured out the earth was not standing,
But where the earth is now, hemmed round with the sea,
Where there are small stars, changing moon, and sun,
Was a deep waste without bottom, withour edge, without end,
Without order, without form, dark and expansive,
There didn't exist east or west or north or south,
Neither did there exist down or up or over or here,
Season or time, colours black or white –
Yet with the seeds of these things completely full –
Air, earth, fire, water, their four [elements] mixed –
And one odious, black night, ruling over all.

But heaven now made with the inhabitants
According to the almighty power and high wisdom of God,
On [in] one particular day – for days in heaven are
Of the measure of eternity that time cannot expend,
And though it's not yet night, such a time exists
As serves to separate day from day –
On such a day as that the battle-host of heaven
Answering a royal summons that was given to them
All to come before the seat of glory
To hear the will and the law of the great Creator,
Came far and near from each far reach of the realm,
Bright seraphim and high powers leading
The bright troops; harmonious heavenly music
Filling the blessed air as they were flying in
To that great town through the main doors,
Happiness and joy welling in each street.

The Almighty sitting on a throne
High above each height and glorious above measure,
Angels, archangels, and the full nobility of heaven
Like so many suns standing on each hand
Of the glorious power; crowns and sceptres
They threw on the ground in a sign of their attention
And obedience, admitting that it's from God
They had their life, their happiness, and everything.
And the Son of God was seated in the bosom of the Father,
Till now kept hidden from the heavenly host –

Bright cherubim on each side there were,
Bright as our sun, high at the midday –
Glory, power as authority were carved on his countenance,
And from his eyes love like a current did run,
With which sweet heaven was filled;
Each angel striving who most would fulfil
In spiritual love and good will together.
This is the way that heaven was as one sea of love
And of each delight that doesn't, that will not abate.
Then put the strong Creator forth a voice
With which heaven from its foundation was all a-quiver:
"One beloved son," he said to them, "I have
Today begotten, and he is beloved of me,
My own image, my wisdom and my power,
My most powerful Word and equal with me in glory.
I am God, and I'm giving this law to you
About my son that you are seeing today;
He has power, from me, over all heaven,
And everything is delivered into his hand;
Heaven and what is in it is his under his rule,
To which I am ordering you as well to give heed.
In heaven, [other] than me, there is not one greater,
And by myself before you I swear,
Every knee that does not bow in respect to him
Will be thrown out of my presence for ever,
And from my happiness, from my grace and favour,
From all the rights he has in my glory."
This spoke the God, and all heard his word,
With the ray of his glory was his face hidden from them;
The angels, as if they were content with it,
Bent down their heads and knees in obedience.
'As if they were content,' I say,
For a part were not, as you will see in time.
Then raised the great audience up in one voice,
"Glory, thanks and praise to the Son of God for ever;
He in his glory we have seen today,
He is God for ever and he was God since eternity."

Thomas Christian was at one time the Vicar of Marown. It is thought that his work in writing 'Pargys Caillit' may have been a form of penance for having been dismissed for fornication and drunken and aggressive behaviour. However, he was, or had been, a member of the clergy. John Feltham was a visitor to the Island in 1797 and 1798. He notes that:

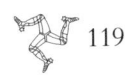

> The enlightened Manksman, if he is fond of his native language, must lament the barrenness of its literary field, and the almost daily disuse of his mother tongue. The English language is preferred in general. In the Church and in the Courts of Law, it is indispensably necessary: in general the lower class understand English, and few are wholly ignorant of it; yet they are more ready at, and attached to, their Manks.
>
> ...They have neither grammar nor dictionary, and few except the clergy know Manks well enough to compose in it.

The Nineteenth Century

The amanuensis to Rev Philip Moore in editing the Manx Bible was John Kelly (1750–1809). Kelly also went on to take holy orders. In 1803 he wrote 'A Practical Grammar of the antient Gaelic or language of the Isle of Mann, usually called Manks'. In 1805 he intended to print 'A Triglot Dictionary of the Celtic tongue, as spoken in the Highlands of Scotland, in Ireland, and in the Isle of Man'. Unfortunately, a fire at the printing works destroyed the stock. Kelly's work did not become more generally known until the Manx Society published his grammar in 1859 and, in 1866, a Manx-English dictionary with appended English-Manx dictionary based on his work. However, he had prepared an introduction to his Triglot Dictionary, dated 1805:

> To cultivate a language and to improve a people are similar offices. Under a conviction of this truth I have, with much labour, compiled a Dictionary of the Gaelic Language as it is spoken in Scotland, Ireland and Man. The writers who have preceded me on this subject have endeavoured to obtain the attention of the public by dwelling on the great antiquity of the Gaelic, by commending the vast energy of its phraseology, and by displaying the etymological purity of its words. On all these accounts it is highly worthy the attention of the scholar and the antiquary. But these are confined objects, embracing words and neglecting men. The enlarged minds of the primitive bishops, Wilson and Hildesley ... studied it with a higher view, – to render it by publication instrumental in removing ignorance, communicating truth, and obtaining a knowledge of English. Their motives were religious and moral; but the present state of the empire holds out to government and individuals another motive at this time not less imperious, that unity of language is the surest cement of civil as well as of religious establishments.
>
> ... It is true that in process of time this cultivation of the Gaelic language will destroy the language itself, as a living language; but it will have produced the knowledge of a better and will descend to posterity by means of the press in a more perfect state, than if it should be found only in the conversation of unlet-

tered individuals. There would be no more cause for regret, then, that it was not a living language, than there is at present, that the Hebrew, Greek, and Latin are no longer such ... the knowledge of the English language in consequent of the publication of the Gaelic Scriptures and Gaelic books, is everywhere gaining ground. And when there shall be one national language, then only will the union of the empire be completely established."

Kelly's avowed aim was to use Manx as a means of acquiring English, which would replace it. In 1820 a book of 13 songs was published under the title 'The Mona Melodies'. The words accompanying the tunes were poor lyrics in English specially written for the book, but eleven of the titles were given in Manx. These included 'Illiam Dhone' and 'Ny Kirree fo Niaghtey' which we have already met. Sets of Manx lyrics are known for another eight of these songs, including 'Mylecharaine'. 'Mylecharaine' is a Manx surname. The song appears to be an amalgamation of disparate strands, each apparently old in itself. There may be a play on words in the emphasis placed on 'carranes'. A *carrane* is a calf-hide shoe, with the hair left on and on the outside of the shoe. Despite the rather strange lyrics, the tune was held in great esteem, and was described as the 'Manx national melody' long before W H Gill used it in 1907 as the basis for what became the National Anthem, 'O Land of our Birth'. In the song 'Mylecharaine' there is a refrain after each line. In some versions this is a vocable, but in others is 'My lomarcan daag oo mee', 'Alone you left me'. This is omitted here.

Anonymous
Mylecharaine, *c.1800*

O Vylecharaine, c'raad hooar oo dty stoyr?
Nagh dooar mee 'sy Churragh eh dowin, dowin dy liooar?

O Vylecharaine, c'raad hooar oo dty sthock?
Nagh dooar mee 'sy Churragh eh eddyr daa vlock?

O Vylecharaine, c'raad hooar oo ny t'ayd?
Nagh dooar mee 'sy Churragh eh eddyr daa foaid?

Hug mee my eggey-varree as my eggey-lieen
As hug mee dow-ollee son toghyr da'n 'neen

O yishig, O yishig, ta mee nish goaill nearey
T'ou goll gys y cheeill ayns dty charraneyn baney

O yishig, O yishig, jeeagh er my vraagyn stoamey
As uss goll mygeayrt ayns dty charraneyn baney

She, un charrane ghoo as fer elley vane
Cheau uss, Vylecharaine, goll dy Ghoolish Jesarn

She, daa phiyr oashyr as un phiyr vraag
Cheau uss, Vylecharaine, ayns kiare bleeantyn jeig

O vuddee, O vuddee, cha lhiass dhyts goaill nearey
Son t'ayms ayns my chishtey ver orts dy ghearey

My hiaght mynney mollaght ort, Vylecharaine
Son uss v'an chied ghooinney hug toghyr da mraane

She mollaght dagh dooinney ta ruggyr inneen
Kyndagh rish Juan Drommey as Mylecharaine

Son hooar Juan Drommey y chooid er y chronk
Hooar Mylecharaine y chooid er y faaie

Translation

Mylecharaine, c.1800

O Mylecharaine, where did you get your store?
Did I not get it in the Curragh, deep, deep enough?

O Mylecharaine, where did you get your stock?
Did I not get it in the Curragh between two blocks?

O Mylecharaine, where did you get what you have?
Did I not get it in the Curragh between two sods?

I gave my web of tow and my web of flax
And I gave an ox for a dowry to the daughter

O father, O father, I am now ashamed
You are going to the church in your white carranes

O father, O father, look at my fine shoes
And you going about in your white carranes

Yes, one black carrane and the other white
You wore, Mylecharaine, going to Douglas on Saturday

Yes, two pair of stockings and one pair of shoes

You wore, Mylecharaine, in fourteen years

O lassie, O lassie, there's no need for you to be ashamed
For I have in my chest [something] that will make you laugh

My sevenfold deadly curse on you, Mylecharaine
For you were the first man who gave a dowry to women

A curse on each man that a daughter is born to
Because of Juan Drommey [Juan of the Ridge] and Mylecharaine

For Juan Drommey got the wealth on the ridge
Mylecharaine got the wealth on the flat [the field nearest the house]

Another translation of religious material to Manx was made, it is thought, by Rev John Thomas Clarke (1799–1888) in about 1820. These were some homilies of the Church of England, of which this is part of the first.

Attributed to John Thomas Clarke

Yn Chied Homily Jeh Agglish Hostyn: Ny Coyrl Vondeishagh Mychione Lhaih As Toiggal Ny Scripytryn Casherick, *c.1820*

Cha vod nhee erbee ve ny s'ymmyrchee ny ny s'vondeishee da Creesteenyn, na tushtey jeh ny Scriptyryn Casherick: er-yn-oyr dy nee ayns shen ta Goo firrinagh Yee soiaghey magh yn ghloyr echeysyn, as myrgeddin currym dooinney. As cha vel firrinys ny ynsagh erbee ymmyrchagh gys nyn seyrey as saualtys dy bragh farraghtyn, nagh vod ve er ny hayrn veih'n farrane shen dy irriney. Shen-y-fa whilleen as ta aggindagh dy ghoaill toshiaght er y raad cairagh, as jeeragh gys Jee, shegin daue tastey y choyrt dy hoiggal ny Scriptyryn Casherick; n'egooish cha vod eddyr enney ve oc er Jee as e aigney, ny er nyn oik as nyn gurrym hene.

As myr ta jough millish dauesyn ta paagh, as bee dauesyn ta accryssagh, myr shen ta lhaih, clashtyn, as ronsaghey ny Scriptyryn Casherick dauesyn ta aggindagh dy gheddyn tushtey jeh Jee ny jeu hene, as dy yannoo yn aigney echey: as ta tushtey flaunyssagh as ooraghey jeh Goo Yee skeeagh as feohdoil dauesyn ny-lomarcan ta wheesh sluggit seose lesh fardaillyssyn seihltagh, nagh vel blass oc eddyr jeh Jee ny craueeaght: son shen yn oyr dy vel ad graihagh er lheid ny fardaillyssyn, as cha nee er tushtey firrinagh Yee. Myr t'adsyn ta ching jeh ny crayne, cre-erbee t'ad giu, ga dy beagh eh ass-towse millish ayn hene, ny-yeih te dauesyn cha shiarroo as ullymar; cha nee veih sherriuid yn beaghey, agh veih'n vroid as sherriuid t'ayns nyn meeal hene; myr shoh ta miljid Goo Yee sharroo, cha nee ayn hene, agh ynrican dauesyn ta ny aignaghyn oc millit lesh cliaghtaghyn peccoil as graih yn theihll shoh.

Translation

The First Homily of the Church of England: Or Advantageous Advice About Reading and Understanding the Holy Scriptures, *c.1820*

Nothing at all could be more useful nor more advantageous to Christians, than knowledge of the Holy Scriptures: because in that is the true Word of God setting out his glory, and also the duty of man. And no truth or learning is necessary for our release and everlasting salvation, that cannot be drawn from that fount of truth. For that reason as many as are desirous of making a start on the road which is righteous and direct to God, they must pay attention to understanding the Holy Scriptures; without it they can recognise neither God and his will, nor their office and their own duty.

And as drink is sweet to those who are thirsty, and food to those who are hungry, like that is reading, hearing, and researching the Holy Scriptures to those who are desirous of obtaining knowledge of God or of themselves, and to do his will: and heavenly and refreshing knowledge of the Word of God is tiresome and abhorrent only to those who are so much swallowed up with wordly vanities, that they don't have the taste either for God or religion: for that's the reason that they love the vanities, and not the true knowledge of God. As are they that are sick of the ague, whatever they drink, though it were sweet beyond measure in itself, nevertheless it is to them as bitter as wormwood; not from bitterness of life, but from the filth and bitterness that is in their own mouth; like this is the sweetness of the Word of God bitter, not in itself, but only to those whose wills are marred by sinful habits and the love of this world.

Amongst other religious tracts published by the Society at Bristol of the Church of England was one on the life, work and martyrdom of William Tyndall.

Anonymous

Coontey Jeh Saggyrt William Tyndall, *1829*

Va William Tyndall, Shirveishagh firrinagh Chreest, as fer hur baase son y credjue, as tooilloo dy v'er ny reayll ayns cooinaghtyn er-yn-oyr dy nee eshyn ren ny Scriptyryn hoshiaght y hyndaa as y phrintal ayns Baarle, er ny ruggey er cagliaghyn thalloo Vretnagh, tammylt roish y vlein 1500. Neayr's ve ny lhiannoo v'eh ynsit ec yn Ard Schooil ec Oxford, raad myr daase eh ayns eash, daase eh ayns tushtey jeh ny chied ghlaraghyn. Hug eh tastey er-lheh da ny Scriptyryn Casheric, as ren eh lhiah ad lesh spyrryd meen as imlee, as lesh padjer son creenaght flaunyssagh. Chamoo va aigney echey dy choyrt fo saagh yn soilshey hooar eh veih e ynsagh, son choud's ve beaghey ayns Magdalen Hall lhaih eh Lecturyn er y chredjue gys sheshaght ny scoillaryn va cummal ayns shen, as dynsee eh ad ayns tushtey as firrinys

Goo Yee. Myr v'eh ny ghooinney jeh ymmyrkey bea crauee v'eh mooar soit jeh liorish e ainjyssee. Tra veh er choyrt jerrey er e ynsagh ec Oxford, hie eh gys Cambridge, raad duirree eh tammylt, as ren eh bishaghey ayns tushtey jeh ny Scriptyryn. Veih shoh hie eh dy chummal marish dooinney ooasle ayns Gloucestershire enmyssit Welsh myr fer-ynsee da e chloan. Va'n dooinney seyr shoh foylt as arryltagh dy choyrt oltaghey bea da troailtee, as va dy mennic Saggyrtyn ayns e naboonys ec e voayrd, maroo ren Tyndall taggloo mychione ny deiney ynsit v'ayns ny laaghyn shen, lheid as Luther, as Erasmus, as mychione ny streeuaghyn mysh y chredjue, as ynsagh ny Scriptyryn Casheric. Ayns ny cooishyn shoh va Tyndall cliaghtey dy osley e aigney lesh lane reamys, as tra v'adsyn smooinaghtyn er aght elley na v'eshyn yinnagh eh soilshaghey daue ny ayrnyn jeh Scriptyr va prowal ny v'eh hene dy ghra, as coyrt oghsan da'n marranys ocsyn. Ec y jerrey va Priestyn y cheerey jymmoosagh rish, er-yn-oyr dy row eh taggloo wheesh mychione ny Scriptyryn, as denmys ad eh fer eh shaghyryn ayns y chredjue, as hug ad playnt noi gys Chancellor quaill yn Aspick, ren symney eh dy heet kionfenish, as dy ansoor gys ny reddyn n'er nyn goyrt gys e lhieh. Tra haink eh kionfenish, ren y Chancellor baggart er dy trome as goltooan eh dy scammyltagh, as hug eh ymmodee reddyn gys e lhieh, nagh row fer erbee ayn dy phrowal. Lurg da Tyndall ve feyshtit dy mennic lhig ad yn raad da, as hyndaa eh gys e chummal.

Translation
An Account of the Priest William Tyndall, *1829*

William Tyndall, a true Minister of Christ, and one who suffered death for his belief, and deserving to have been kept in remembrance because it is he who first translated the Scriptures into and printed them in English, was born on the borders of Wales, a while before the year 1500. From being a child he was taught at the High School in Oxford, where as he grew in age, he grew in knowledge of the first languages. He gave particular attention to the Holy Scriptures, and he read them with a meek and humble spirit, and with a prayer for heavenly wisdom. Neither was his will to put beneath a vessel [hide under a bushel] the light he got from his learning, for whilst he was living in Magdalen Hall he read Lectures on the faith to the company of scholars who were living there, and he taught them in the knowledge and truth of the Word of God. As he was a man of religious bearing he was highly esteemed by his acquaintances. When he had put an end to his learning at Oxford, he went to Cambridge, where he stayed a while, and he increased in knowledge of the Scriptures. From this he went to live with an honourable man in Gloucestershire called Welsh as a teacher to his children. This gentleman was generous and willing to give a reception to travellers, and there were often Priests in his neighbourhood at his table, with whom Tyndall spoke about the learned men who lived in those days, such as Luther, and Erasmus, and about the strivings about the faith, and learning of the Holy Scriptures. In these debates Tyndall was accustomed to opening his mind expansively [with full room], and when they were thinking in a different way than he was he would explain to them the parts of Scripture that proved what he himself said, and giving a reproof to their mistake. In the end the country Priests were angry with him, because he was talking so much about the Scriptures, and they named him as a heretic [one astray in the faith], and they put a complaint against him to the Chancellor of the Bishop's court, who summoned him to come before him, and to answer to the things that had been put to his account. When he came before him, the Chancellor threatened him heavily and reproached him scandalously, and he put many things to his account, that there was no one at all there to prove. After Tyndall had been questioned frequently they let him go, and he returned to where he was living.

In 1795, a collection of hymns in Manx had appeared, though already a second edition. There were five versions of the collection printed between 1795 and 1846. These were mainly translations of hymns and spiritual songs by Wesley, Watts and others. In the 1830, fourth, edition (and repeated in the fifth, 1846, edition), Hymn 150 is shown as '[Originally composed in Manks.]'.

Anonymous

Hymn 150, *1830*

    1. Er jeet dy cheilley ass-y-noa,
    Dy hebbal booise da'n Chiarn;
    Cre'n yindys eh dy vel shin bio,
    Fud whilleen gaue er-mayrn?

    2. Da'n Jee ta choud er nyn sparail
    Lhig dooin cur gloyr as booise:
    Ta coadey, as goaill j'in kiarail,
    Ayns mean dangeyrn [sic] wheesh.

    3. Dangeyryn ta ass shilley sooill,
    'S shen ver mayd tastey da,
    Yn chramp 'sy dorraghys ta shooyl,
    As stroider y vun-laa.

    4. O trog-jee nyn goraaghyn seose,
    As lhig dooin voylley eh:
    T'er neam shin veih yn dorraghys,
    Dy hooyl ayns raad y vea.

    5. Lhig dooin coyrt moylley son e ghrayse,
    Erskyn dy chooilley nhee;

Dy daink nyn Jiarn's dy hur eh'n baase,
Dy choardail shin rish Jee.

6. O lhig dooin lesh un aigney prayll,
Er son e Spyrryd mie;
Dy jean eh shin 'sy raad leeideil,
Gys nee mayd roshtyn thie.

7. Ayns shen cha bee paartail dy bragh;
Agh marish flaunyssee,
Goaill jeh ny messyn flaunyssagh
Dy bragh, as moylley Jee.

Translation
Hymn 150, *1830*

1. Having come together anew,
To offer thanks to the Lord;
What wonder is it that we are still alive,
Amidst so many dangers remaining?

2. To the God that thus far has spared us
Let us give glory and thanks:
Who protects, and takes care of us,
In the middle of danger so great.

3. Dangers that are out of sight of eye,
And that we must give heed to,
The plague that walks in the darkness,
And the destroyer of the midday.

4. O raise you your voices up,
And let us praise him:
Who has called us from the darkness,
To walk in the way of life.

5. Let us give praise for his grace,
Above everything;
That our Lord came and that he suffered death,
To bring us to accord with God.

6. O let us with one will pray,
For his good Spirit;

That he will lead us in the way,
Until we will reach home.

7. In that there will never be parting;
But with heaven's inhabitants,
Partaking of the heavenly fruits
For ever, and praising God.

John Lewin was the Sumner (a church warden or official) of the Parish of Jurby in the 1830s. One of the carvals in 'Carvalyn Gailckagh' is attributed to Lewin by P W Caine. Caine names it 'Carval er Feeyn as Jough' ('Carval on Wine and [strong] Drink') and dates it to 1836. 'Carvalyn Gailckagh', does not attribute or date it, and it appears as 'My Chaarjyn Gow Shiu Tastey, or, My Friends Take Notice'. In 1895, William Gill collected a tune called 'Lewin's Total Hymn' from John Kissack, which suggests that Lewin was teetotal, an abstainer. The carval and tune would fit together. However, ten of this carval's verses show that Lewin was by no means against the use of alcohol, only against its abuse.

Attributed to John Lewin

My Chaarjyn, Gow Shiu Tastey, *c.1836*

Messyn y theihll va palchey
Dy arroo, ooil as feeyn
Kiarit er son cloan deiney
Dy yannoo magh nyn veme
Cha nee son scooyr ny meshtallys
Cha moo son peccah erbee
Agh baarail ad dy cairagh
Myr te soit ayns goo Yee

Yn shenn seihll daase meechrauee
As Jee ren ad y stroie
Cheu moie jeh lught thie Noah
Va sauit ayns arg dy fuygh
Tra ren yn thalloo chirmagh
Yn lhong hoie er y clieau
Eisht hoie eh garey feeyney
Ar [As] ren eh feeyn y iu

Hug yn feeyn eh er meshtey
As cha row peccah ny leih
Agh cursit va yn dooinney

Nagh ren eh choodaghey
Te raait, smerg dhyts ter meshtey
Cha nee lesh feeyn ny jough
Leeideil lurg saynt ny foaley
As tannaght foe dy loght

Hug Jacob lesh gys Isaac
Tra hooar eh vannaght hene
Veih y laue ghow eh beaghey
As myrgeddin ghow eh feeyn
Ren Joseph gee dy gennall
Marish e vraaraghyn
Hug eh daue naightyn maynrey
Goll thie gys cheer Canaan

She shoh ta scruit 'sy Psalmyn
Ec phadeyr reeoil Yee
Feeyn cur gennallys syn eddin
As niartaghey yn cree
Myrgeddin ta mac Sirach
Er choontey eh gyn loght
Cre'n cree oddys ve'c dooinney
Ta fegoish feeyn ny jough?

Ta Paul er scriu gys Timothy
Jeeaghyn er dy ve ching
Nagh iu ny sodjey ushtey
Agh iu red beg dy feeyn
Va Yeesey hene ec bannish
Un cheayrt ec Galilee
As ren Eh feeyn jeh ushtey
She shoh va merril Yee

Yn oie va Chreest er ny vrah
Nagh vannee Eh yn feeyn
As ren Eh shoh y yiootal
Neesht er ny ostylyn
Gra, "Shoh jeana jee cha mennick
She ayns cooinaghtyn jeem"
Kys sloys dhyts gra, O ghooinney
D'el peccah ayns jough ny feeyn

Nish my t'ad er my yiootal

Naght myr t'an goo dy ghra
Shickyr ta towse jeh ymmyrchagh
Myr ver mayd tastey da
Leeideil nyn mea kiaralagh
As gyn dy ghoaill yn scooyr
Son shimmey ta stroit liorish
Er faarkey as er yn ooir

Nagh abbyr shiu ny sodjey
Ta peccah ayns yn stoo
Agh ayns ny creeghyn ocsyn
Ta jannoo drogh-ymmyd jeu
Agh giu ad hene er meshtey
As gweeaghyn as loo
Foast ta paart elley sober
T'ad cur rish saynt as troo

Ta maarlee as molteyryn
Breagyryn as dunveryn
Laccal ad hene reayll sober
Nyn sayntyn dy chooilleen
As shickyr ny meeghiastylee
Ga nagh vel oc yn scooyr
Chyndaa ersooyl ny boghtyn
Lesh jeirkyn treih dy liooar

Translation

My Friends, Take You Notice, *c.1836*

The fruits of the world were a-plenty
Of corn, oil and wine
Intended for the issue of men
To make out their needs
It's not for intoxication or drunkenness
Nor yet for any sin
But expending them carefully
As is set down in the word of God

The old world grew ungodly
And God did them destroy
Apart from Noah's family
That was saved in an ark of wood
When the land dried out

The ship sat on the mountain
Then he set a vineyard
And he drank wine

The wine made him inebriated
And there was not sin on his behalf
But cursed was the man
Who didn't cover him
It's said, woe to you who is drunk
It's not the wine or [strong] drink's fault
Leading to the lust of the flesh
And remaining beneath your sin

Jacob brought it to Isaac
When he obtained his own blessing
From the hand he took sustenance
And likewise he took wine
Joseph ate pleasantly
With his brothers
He gave them good news
As they went home to the land of Canaan

It's this that's written in the Psalms
By the royal prophet of God
Wine gives pleasantness in the face
And strengthens the heart
Likewise the son of Sirach
Has reckoned it without sin
What heart could a man have
That's without wine or [strong] drink?

Paul has written to Timothy
Seeing that he was ill
Don't drink water any more
But drink a small amount of wine
Jesus himself was at a wedding
One occasion in Galilee
And He made wine from water
It's this that was a miracle of God.

The night that Christ was betrayed
Did He not bless the wine
And He offered this

As well to the apostles
Saying, "This do you so often
It's in memory of me"
How dare you say, O man
That there is sin in [strong] drink and wine

Now if they're offered to me
In the [same] way as the word says
It's certain that an amount of it is necessary
As we will take note of
Leading our life carefully
And without resorting to inebriation
For many a person that's destroyed by it
On sea and on the soil

Don't say any more
That there is sin present in the stuff
But in the hearts of those
Who abuse it
But they drink themselves into drunkenness
And swear and curse
Still there is another section who are sober
Who practise lust and envy

There are robbers and deceivers
Liars and murderers
Wanting to keep themselves sober
And certainly the uncharitable
Though they are not inebriate
Turning away the poor
With expectations that are miserable enough

John Lewin also explored this theme in a poem called 'Pingyn yn Ommidan', 'The Fool's Pence', composed in association with Evan Christian. These are nine out of the 24 verses. There was also a prose version of the story. Both were published by M A Quiggin of Douglas.

John Lewin and Evan Christian
Pingyn Yn Ommidan, *c.1845*

Cur tastey mie, my chaarjyn
Da shoh neem's soilshagh diu

Te mygeayrt-y-mysh fer cheirdey
Ghow taitnys mooar ayns giu
Dooiney jeh yn valley-vargee
Va geddyn yn aill vooar
Agh baarail lane jeh 'hoilliu v'eh
Er jough ta coyrt yn scooyr

Cha row eh er ve ass obbyr
Rish bleeantyn liauyr dy hraa
My baillish hene agh gobbraghey
Myr ver mayd tastey da
Agh veagh eh cur roi ny cheayrtyn
Myr dooyrt eh, son y *spree*
Dy chummal seose niart yn challin
Lurg garrey d'obbyr chreoi

Ayns y voghrey tra v'eh goll magh
V'eh goll roish dy'n thie-oast
Aynshen ren eh giu veih'n cappan breinn
Hug lesh eh dy ve boght
Agh foast lane yindys v'eh dy ghoaill
Jeh'n argid v'eh baarail
Er aght erbee, cha chronnee eh
Cre'n red va stroie e aill

E chloan, v'ad feer frytlagh
Eh-hene ny rytlag vooar
Cha row eh wheesh as cur tastey
Cre'n assee v'ayns y scooyr
Yn bine v'eh dy ghoaill 'sy voghrey
Cha row cur da yn scooyr
Shen ny v'eh giu ec y vunlaa
V'eh gra nagh row eh mooar

Chamoo dod eh geeck yn Mainshter
Son gynsagh daue nyn schoill
As dy feer olk shen v'eh goaill rish
Yn ven ve geddyn foill
Yn choardail vie va eddyr oc
Hyndaa gys troiddey dewil
Gys baggyrt, bwoalley as oltooan
As jannoo aigney'n jouyl

Er-lesh nagh b'lhiass j'ee ve feiyral
Son y bine v'eshyn goaill
As ayns jannoo wheesh dy woirey
V'eh fakin red feer voal
V'eh goaill-rish shoh, dy onneragh
Kiongoyrt rish dagh unnane
Dy bynney mie lesh yn thie-oast
Dy cheau ayn Laa yn Chiarn

Fy-yerrey haink yn arreyder
Stiagh huc, gyn-yss, cooyl-thie
Yn Doonaght shen va'n iuder boght
Ayns y thie-oast ny hoie
Eisht deie y ven-oast ayns tullogh
'*Thom* veen! tar seose er 'lout
Ta tammylt mie er y Doonaght
Dy chreck cha vel mish lowit'

'Bee mayd sumnit er-gys y whaiyll,'
Ny sodjey ren ee gra
'Eishtagh caill-yms kied yn oastys
As creeuit veem son dy bra'
She heose er y lout v'eh follit
Raad va ny reddyn s'boie
Va *Thom* boght caillit ayns yindys
Cha vaik eh rieau lheid roie

Hug eh my-ner yn coodagh bwaagh
Va skeaylt dy lhean er 'laare
As siyn argid va londyrnee
Myr sollysid yn aer
Eisht yeeagh eh 'sy ghless-thuarystal
Raad va e chaslys hene
Coamrit ayns fritlaggyn dy liooar
E gharmad moal as breinn

Translation

The Fool's Pence, *c.1845*

Give good attention, my friends
To this that I'll explain to you
It's about a tradesman
Who took great delight in drinking

A man of the market-town
Who was getting the big wage
But spending the whole of his earnings he was
On drink that causes inebriation

He hadn't been out of work
For long years of time
If he himself wished but to work
As we will take note of
But he would be making provision sometimes
As he said, for the spree
To keep up bodily strength
After a bout of hard work

In the morning when he was going out
He was heading to the pub
There he drank from the stinking cup
That brought him to be poor
But still wholly amazing it was to note
The money that he was spending
In some way, he didn't discern
What it was that was destroying his wages

His children, they were very ragged
He himself the great ragged one
He didn't so much as take heed
What the harm was in the drunkenness
The drop he was taking in the morning
Didn't make him inebriated
That's what he was drinking at the midday
He was saying that it wasn't great

Neither could he pay the Master
For teaching them in school
And very badly he acknowledged that situation
The wife was getting the blame
The good accord that was between them
Turned to severe quarreling
To threatening, beating and reproach
And doing the devil's will

He thought that she needn't be making a noise
About the drop that he was taking

And in making so much fuss
He was seeing something very despicable
He admitted this, honestly
Before each and everyone
That he well loved the pub
To spend the Lord's Day in it

Finally came the watchman
Into it, unknown, the back way
That Sabbath the poor drinker was
Sitting in the pub
Then shouted the landlady in an instant
'Dear Tom, come up to the loft
There's a good while on the Sabbath
[When] to sell I'm not allowed'

'We'll be summonsed to the court,'
Further she said
'Then I'll lose the hostelry licence
And I'll be cowed for ever'
It's up in the loft he was hidden
Where the most beautiful objects were
Poor Tom was lost in wonder
He never before saw the like

He beheld the beautiful carpet
That was spread wide on the floor
And silver vessels that were dazzling
Like the brightness of the sky
Then he looked in the mirror
Where was his own reflection
Clothed in rags enough
His garment poor and stinking

The title page of 'A Dictionary of the Manks Language with the Corresponding Words or Explanation in English' shows it to have been published in 1835. However, the date of publication is thought to have been 1838. The compiler was Archibald Cregeen (1774-1841), a stone mason and Coronor (an administrative official of government). In the Preface he writes:

That a language so venerable for its antiquity and so estimable on many accounts should be so generally neglected, is much to be lamented. The consequence of this neglect has been, that numerous corruptions have crept into the dialect in general use, and so many anglicisms been adopted, that the Manks is now seldom spoken or written in its original purity. Despised and neglected, however, as the language appears to be at present it is susceptible of high improvement, and justly entitled to the attention of the scholar. The sublime strains of OSSIAN mark the capabilities of the language, and commend it to the regard of the philologist as a subject of curious enquiry, and deserving accurate investigation ... let it not be said that the natives of Mona regard "Chengey ny mayrey Vannin veg veen" with disgraceful apathy and heartless indifference. As long as the Manks Bible and the Manks Liturgy remain they will testify that our ancestors thought and felt more correctly.

After the Preface is an 'Introduction to the Manx Language'. Towards the end of his Introduction, Cregeen writes that:

I cannot but admire the construction, texture, and beauty of the Manks Language, and how the words initially change their cases, moods, tenses, degrees, etc. It appears like a piece of exquisite network, interwoven together in a masterly maner, and framed by the hand of a most skilful workman, equal to the composition of the most learned, and not the production of chance.-The depth of meaning that abounds in many of the words must be conspicuous to every person versed in the language.

Earlier, Cregeen has observed that:

I am well aware that the utility of the following work will be variously appreciated by my brother Manksmen. Some will be disposed to deride the endeavour to restore vigour to a decaying language. Those who reckon the extirpation of the Manks a necessary step towards that general extension of the English, which they deem essential to the interest of the Isle of Man, will condemn every effort which seems likely to retard its extinction.

A writer who would not have derided or condemned Cregeen's efforts was William Kennish (1799–1863). About 1840 he wrote a piece lamenting the dismissive attitude towards the language.

William Kennish

Dobberan Chengey Ny Mayrey Ellan Vannin, *c.1840*

Myr va mee my-lomarcan troaylt harrish Sniaul
Tra va yn coleayrtys y hayrn
E coamrey harrish cheu Vannin jeh'n theihll
As dooghys cur biallys d'an Chiarn

Dy choodaghey'n seihll lesh cloagey yn oie
As aash y chur-lesh gys sheelnaue
Veih boiraghyn seihltagh as laboraght creoi
Son ooilley cretooryn e laue

Myr shoh va mee faagit dou hene er y clieau
Fegooish nhee dy heshiaght erbee
Dy ghobberan harrish dagh boirey as streeu
Ta seaghney Mannin-my-chree

Tra honnick mee ben voght ayns coamrey glass
Cheet my-whail ny mastey yn freoagh
Lesh ooilley mygeayrt-y-mooie frytlagh as rasst
Roie myr dy beagh ee er-keoiagh

Va my chree er ny ghleayshaghey ayns my cheu-sthie
Tra honnick mee stayd yn cretoor
Son ec y chied hylley jee honnick mee mie
Dy row ee er dhuittym veih pooar

Tra haink ee ny sniessey dou, cheayll mee ee gra
"Ogh! Ogh! Ta mee heaghyn dy trome
Myr shoh dy ve scart veih sheelnaue son dy braa
Gys diunid shenn Traa dy gholl roym!"

Va yn ushag veg ruy goll ro-ee gys yn crouw
Va ny gheayin gys nyn moiraghyn roie
Va yn oie er yn 'aarkey lesh cochaslys grou
Dy gastey cheet veih yn niar-hwoaie

Va fainagh ny ghrianey er n'eiyrt harrish oirr
Ny farkiaghyn dowin yn sheear-ass
Va yn eayst ayns yn shiar er n'irree ayns gloyr
Va ya [yn] sheear ayns y coamrey glass

Tra hoie shin sheese cooidjagh er lhuss glass ny faaie
As dooyrt ee rhym, "Vanninagh, eaisht
As nee'm dhyt ass ny scriunyn shoh lhaih
My hrimshey fo soilshey yn eayst"

Eisht ren ee goaill toshiaght as lhaih ee myr shoh
"Ayns laghyn ta er ny gholl shaghey
Cha row mee rieau laccal my coamrey noa

Dy reayll mee veih feiraght as fliaghey

Son mish, bee fys ayd er, ta scaan y chenn ghlare
Ec cloan Vannin er my hregieil
Agh s'beg fys ta ocsyn dy beeagh eh ny share
Daue mish dy ve harroo dy reill

Son mish ta er reayll yn fer joarree ersooyl
Son keeadyn dy vleintyn dy hraa
As va mee er reill veih yn traie gys Barool
Da Manninee dooie son dy braa

Agh nish ta yn voyrn oc er chur lesh yn Vaarle
Eer seose yn glione mooar Tolt-y-Will
As mastey ny reeastyn er lhiattee Wooar Cardle
As creggyn yn Creg-Willy-Syl

Myr ta'n croaghan 'sy tourey yn maase cur er-ouyl
Ta'n voyrn er ny chur orroo roie
Lesh y ghah, veih kione heear yn Niarbyl gys Groudle
As veih Colloo as ny Ein gys y twoaie

Dy-lhiattee veih raaidyn nyn ayraghyn dooie
Nagh ren rieau myr shoh m'y hregeil
Son va'n aigney oc gyn y Ellan dy stroie
Ny chur ayns y joarree treishteil

O! dy jinnagh adsyn ta sthill er y cheu
My Ellan veg nish chaglym cooidjagh
Dy chloh veih my hraieyn lesh siyr yn toyrtmow
Ta mygeayrt-y-moom nish er 'noaill toshiaght

As chyndaa nyn gleayshyn veih ooilley yn chiaull
Ta jeant mygeayrt Mannin Veg Veen
Lesh deiney ta gys dy chooilley nhee doal
Er-lhimmey son berchys daue hene

Agh quoi ta ad hene ta geamagh myr shoh
Agh adsyn ta laccal pooar dy reill
Harrish Manninee dooie, lesh lorg-reill noa
My yiow ad sleih doue dy chur-geill?

O! gow shiu my choyrle, shiuish sthill ta er-mayrn

Jeh cummaltee dooie Vannin voght
As ny chur shiu geill da nyn raaidyn shenn vraane
Mygeayrt-y-mysh lhiggar as jough

O! dy jinnagh cummaltee Vannin cordail
Ny shenn leighyn oc keillit dy reayll
As gyn sodjey nyn draa dy stroie ayns fardail
Dy eaishtagh rish deiney gyn keeayl

Agh son aym pene, neem chelleeragh goll roym
Dy ollagh mee hene ayns y joan"
Dooyrt yn red trimshagh, lesh osney dy trome
"Son jeeagh cre cha lheeah ta my chione"

Translation

Lamenting the Mother Tongue of the Isle of Man, *c.1840*

As I was alone travelling over Snaefell
When the gloaming was drawing
Its clothing over the Manx side of the world
And nature was offering obedience to the Lord

To cover the world with the cloak of the night
And to bring ease to mankind
From worldly troubles and hard labour
For all the creatures of his hand

Like this I was left to myself on the mountain
Without anything at all of a companion
To lament over each trouble and strife
That saddens Mannin of my heart

When I saw a poor woman in grey clothing
Coming to meet me amongst the heather
With all about her ragged and ripped
Running as if she were maddened

My heart was moved in my inside
When I saw the state of the creature
For at the first look of her I saw well
That she had fallen from power

When she came nearer to me, I heard her say

"Oh! Oh! I am afflicted heavily
Like this to be separated from mankind for ever
To the depth of old Time to make my way"

The little red bird was making its way to the sprig
The lambs were running to their mothers
The night was on the ocean with a gloomy form
Nimbly coming from the north-east

The chariot of the sea had followed over the edge
Of the deep seas of the south-west
The moon in the east had risen in glory
The west was in grey clothing

When we sat down together on the green herb of the field
And she said to me, "O Manxman, listen
And to you out of these writings I'll read
My grief beneath the light of the moon"

Then she made a start and she read like this:
"In days that have gone past
I was never lacking my new clothing
To keep me from cold and rain

For I, you will know it, am the ghost of the old language
By the children of Mannin forsaken
But little do they know that it would be better
For them for me to be over them to rule

For it's me that has kept the stranger away
For hundreds of years of time
And I had ruled from the shore to Barrule
Over true Manxmen for ever

But now their pride has brought the English language
Even up the great glen of Tholt-y-Will
And amongst the uncultivated lands on the side of Great Cardle
And the rocks of Creg Willy Syl

As the horsefly in the summer maddens the cattle
The pride has made them run
With the sting, from the western point of Niarbyl to Groudle
And from Calf and Chickens to the north

Aside from the ways of their true fathers
That never like this forsook me
For they were minded not to destroy the Island
Or put trust in the stranger

O! that those who are still on the side
Of my little Island would now gather together
To chase from my shores with haste the destruction
That about me now has begun

And turning their ears from all of the din
That is made about Mannin Veg Veen
With men who are to everything blind
Except for wealth for themselves

But who are they themselves who shout like this
But those who want power to rule
Over true Manxmen, with a new sceptre
If they get people to give heed to them

O! that the inhabitants of Mannin would agree
To keep their old hidden laws
And no longer their time to destroy in vain
To listen to men without wit

But for myself, I will immediately head off
To hide myself in the dust"
Said the sad thing with a sigh heavily
"For look how grey is my head"

William Kennish set his poem in the mountains. Mountain areas had long been considered as commons with open grazing. Attempts to privatise parts of the mountains were resisted by force. A famous incident came in 1857 with The Battle of Pairk-ny-hEarkan when the Sulby Cossacks (the inhabitants in and around a northern village) tore down newly-built walls which were to demarcate privatised land and fought with the authorities. Similar incidents occurred on the southern hills. In 1860 the government brought in legislation to make mountain land available for purchase. Protests continued. In 1863 the government issued a proclamation about an incident arising from one such incident. The proclamation was issued in two versions, one of them in Manx. The Manx is here rendered as printed.

The Nineteenth Century

Proclamation
Eam Er Y Theay, *1863*

Liorish yn Kiannoort
Ellan Vannin, Ta shen de ghra.
Son wheesh as, er y queigoo lhaa jeh mee veanagh y Gheurey s'jerree, va Eam er ny chur magh trooid yn Ellan shoh liorish yn Kiannoort s'jerree, chebbal Leagh jeh Keead Punt da Persoon erbee yinnagh hoshiaght cur stiagh lheid y phlaiynt as feanish as lheeidagh gys feddyn magh as gheddyn foiljagh yn Persoon ny ny Persoonyn ren, er oie jedoonee yn sheyoo lhaa yeig jeh mee Sauiney s'jerree, lhieggal sheese as stroie liurid voar dy voalley cloaie bentyn da Illiam Fine Moore, Doiney-seyr, ec Faaie Llewellyn, ayns Skeerey Chreest-ny-Heyrey as Skeerey Maughold; Goaill carail nagh row yn Persoon yinnagh cur stiagh lheid y phlaiynt, er ve goaill ayrn eh hene ayns stroie yn voalley cheddin; As son wheesh as te briwnyssit cooie dy chaghlaa yn ayrn s'jerree imraait jeh'n Eam cheddin; Ta mish liorish shoh ny sodjey chebbal yn Leagh cheddin jeh Keead Punt da Persoon erbee, quoi erbee vees eh, nee hoshiaght cur stiagh yn plaiynt as feanish roie raait; As ny sodjey ta mee liorish shoh fockley magh dy jean yn Ard Ordralagh son Cooishyn Thie y Ream cur coyrle da'n Ven-Reinn de ghialdyn Leih Nastee da un Persoon erbee ta er n'ghoaill ayrn ayns stroie yn voalley cheddin, as nee hoshiaght cur stiagh lheid y phlaiynt as feanish as nee leeideil gys feddyn foiljagh ooilley ny ayrn erbee jeh ny Persoonyn ghow ayrn ayns lhieggal sheese as stroie yn voalley cheddin. Jeant er ye kiarroo lhaa as feed jeh yn Vart, 1863. Henry B. Loch, Kiannoort. Dy Bannee Jee Yn Ven-Reinn!

Translation
A Call to the Populace, *1863*

By the Governor

Isle of Man, That is to say.
For as much as, on the fifth day of the middle month of Winter [December] last, there was a Call being put out through this Island by the last Governor, offering a Reward of a Hundred Pounds to any Person who would first lodge such a complaint and evidence as would lead to finding out and finding guilty the Person or the Persons who, on Sunday night the sixteenth day of November last, knocked down and destroyed a large length of stone wall pertaining to William Fine Moore, Gentleman, at Faaie Llewellyn [normally Pairk Llewellyn], in Kirk Christ Lezayre and Kirk Maughold; Taking care that the Person lodging such a complaint had not been taking part himself in destroying the same wall; And for as much as it is judged appropriate to change the last part mentioned of the same Call; I am by this further offering the same Reward of a Hundred Pounds to any Person, whoever it may be, who will first lodge the complaint and evidence before stated; And further I am by this proclaiming that the Minister for Home Affairs will advise the Queen

to promise a Free Pardon to any Individual who has taken part in destroying the same wall, as will first lodge such a complaint and evidence as will lead to finding guilty all the other part of the Persons who took part in knocking down and destroying the same wall. Done on the fourth day and twenty of the [month of] March, 1863. Henry. B. Loch, Governor. God Save The Queen!

Another example of 'official' Manx arises from the annual open-air Tynwald ceremony. The short title of Acts which have received the Royal Assent are still required to be read out in Manx and English in order to promulgate them, a necessary step in the Island's legislative process. In former days, the entire legislation was read out. The following example was reprinted in 'Coraa Ghailckagh' No 11 (May 1955). It was there said to be from a manuscript of about 1835 held by the Cannell family of Ballacarnane. However, the Act was made in 1855 and promulgated in 1856. It is given here without comment as to spelling or grammar.

Offical Document

Acts Which Have Received Royal Assent, *1856*

Slattys son cur naardey yn eajeeys girree veih jaagh veih coirraghyn as Thieyn-obbyr-lauee ayns as er-gerry da Baljyn yn Ellan shoh.

Son wheesh as dy vel eh ymmyrchagh dy chur naardey yn eajeeys ta girree veih jaagh coirraghyn cheusthie jeh Baljyn yn Ellan shoh, as er-gerrey da dagh valley. Te er y fa shen jeant ny leigh, veih as lurg yn chied lhaa jeh January lurg fockley magh yn Slattys shoh, dy bee dy choilley choirrey ta ymmyd jeant eh ayns mwyllin, thie obbyr-laue, thie-prental, thie-daah, thie son lheie yiarn, thie-imbyl, thie-fuinney, obbraghyn-gas, obbraghyn-ushtey, ny thieyn erbee ta ymmyd jeant jeu son cur rish keird ny obbyr-laue, cheusthie jeh veg jeh ny Bailjyn jeh Doolish, Ballachashtal, Purt ny hinjey ny Rumsaa, ny cheusthie jeh dhaa veeiley veih unnane erbee jeh ny bailjyn cheddin, as eddyr jeshaght-steam ve gobbraghey ayns shen ny dyn, dy bee dagh lheid y choirrey er ny yannoo, ny er ny caaghlaa, er lheid yn aght as dy lhostey ny dy stroie yn jaagh ta girree veih'n choirrey cheddin: as my nee person erbee lurg yn chied lhaa jeh January lurg fockley magh yn Slattys shoh, jannoo ymmyd jeh coirrey erbee nagh bee er ny yannoo er lheid yn aght as dy lostey ny dy stroie yn jaagh echey hene, cheusthie jeh veg jeh ny bailjyn roie-rait, ny cheusthie jeh dhaa veeilley veih unnane erbee jeh ny vailjyn cheddin, ny my nee eh jannoo ymmyd jeh unnane erbee jeh lheid ny choirraghyn er lhied yn aght lhagcharailagh nagh bee yn jaagh ta cheet voish dy foandagh losht ny stroit, ny my nee eh cur rish keird ny obbyr erbee nee jannoo soar brein ny asslayntagh, ny eajeeys erbee da cummaltee yn Naboonys fegooish goaill ny saaseyn share son lhiettal, ny son cur naardey lheid yn eajeeys, nee dagh lheid y phersoon myr shen foiljagh, eddyr yn thie ve lesh hene, ny ayns y cummal echey, tra t'eh feddynit oollee kiongoyrt rish Briw, ny dhaa Briw-chee, farvish as geek sym argid nagh bee erskyn queig puint, ny ny sloo na dhaa eed skillyn as my teh feddynit oollee yn nah cheayrt, yn sym jeh jeih puint, as son dagh cheayrt elley t'eh feddynit oollee lurg shen, sym dhaa cheayrt wheesh as yn sym stierree farvishit: goaill carail dy kinjagh nagh bee ny focklyn "lostey ny stroie yn jaagh" er ny hoiggal, ayns dy chooilley chooish dy veanal "lostey ny stroie ooilley yn jaagh" as cha jean yn Briw ny ny Briwnyn-chee feddyn oollee jeh'n foill roie-rait, my nee ad smooinaghtyn dy vel yn persoon cheddyn er n'yannoo ny er chaghlaa yn choirrey echey myr shen as dy lhostey ny dy stroie choud as oddys y ve ooilley yn jaagh cheet voish lheid y choirrey, as er chur tastey dy charailagh da'n chooid cheddin, as er stroie ny er lhostey wheesh as oddys y ve yn jaagh cheet voish lheid y choirrey.

My nee persoon erbee ta thie echey lesh hene ny ayns yn cummal echey, gobbal dy hurranse yn thie echey dy ver ny ronsaghey liorish persoon t'er gheddyn pooar veih'n Baillee dy yannoo myr shen, foddee Constable erbee t'er gheddyn pooar fo laue unnane jeh ny Briwnyn, marish ny fegooish persoon erbee dy chooney lesh, entreil stiagh ayns lheid y thie, as ronsagh thie erbee raad ta coirrey, as dy ghoail baght jeh'n cummey echey, as yn aght t'eh gobbraghey, as my nee persoon erbee lhiettal constable ta myr shen cooilleeney yn currym echey, as feddynit oollee jeh'n loght cheddin, nee eh farvish as geek sym argid erbee nagh bee erskyn jeih puint.

Goaill carail dy kinjagh nagh bee playnt erbee jeant noi persoon erbee cour geddyn fine erbee fo'n Slattys shoh, er lhimmey jeh fo pooar Turnere y Ven-reinn ny jeh'n Baillee.

Translation

Acts Which Have Received Royal Assent, *1856*

An Act for abolishing the nuisance arising from smoke from furnaces and Workshops in and near to the Towns of this Island.

For as much as it is useful to abolish the nuisance that arises from the smoke of furnaces within the Towns of this Island, and near to each town. It is for that reason made for law, from and after the first day of January after the promulgation of this Act, that every furnace of which use is made in a mill, workshop, printworks, dyehouse, iron smelting works, brewhouse, bakehouse, gasworks, waterworks, or any other premises where use is made of them for practising a trade or handicraft, within any of the Towns of Douglas, Castletown, Peel or Ramsey, or within two miles of any one of those same towns, and whether a steam engine be working there or not, that each such furnace be made, or be altered, in such a way as to burn or destroy the smoke that arises from that same furnace: and if any person after the first day of January after the promulgation of this Act, shall make use of any furnace that is not made in such a way as to burn or to destroy its own smoke, within any of the aforesaid towns, or within two miles of any one of the same towns, or if he shall make use of any one of such furnaces in such a neglectful way that the smoke which comes from it shall not be effectively burnt or destroyed, or if he practices a trade or any work that shall cause a foul or unhealthy smell, or any nuisance to the inhabitants of the Neighbourhood without applying the best methods for abatement, or for abolishing such a nuisance, each such person like that shall be culpable, whether the premises are his, or in his tenancy, when he is found guilty before a Deemster, or two Justices of the Peace, forfeiting and paying a sum of money that shall be not more that five pounds, nor less that forty shillings and if he is found guilty for a second time, the sum of ten pounds, and for each other time he is found guilty after that, a sum two times as much as the last sum forfeited: always provided that the words "burning or destroying the smoke" shall not be understood, in every case to mean "burning or destroying all of the smoke" and the Deemster or the Justices of the Peace shall not find guilty of the aforesaid fault, if they shall think that the same person has made or has altered his furnace so as to burn or to destroy as far as can be all the smoke coming from such furnace, and has carefully given attention to the same issue, and has destroyed or has burnt as greatly as possible the smoke coming from such furnace.

If any person who is the owner of the premises or in whose tenancy they are shall refuse to permit his premises to be searched by a person who has obtained authority from the Bailiff to so do, any Constable who has obtained authority under the hand of one of the Deemsters, with or without any person to assist him, enter into such premises, and search any premises where there is a furnace, and to give evidence of its appearance, and the way it works, and if any person shall obstruct a constable who is thus executing his duty, and is found guilty of the same offence, he shall forfeit and pay a sum of money that shall be not more than ten pounds.

Always provided that any complaint shall not be made against any person for obtaining any fine under this Act, except under the authority of the Attorney General (the Queen's Attorney) or of the Bailiff.

The appearance of an official proclamation regarding the law and the full text of an Act in Manx at this date is perhaps surprising in view of comments by Rev William Gill in editing John Kelly's manuscript grammar of about 1770 for publication as 'The Manx Grammar', Manx Society Vol II, in 1859:

> The object of this reprint is not to uphold the Manx as a spoken language,-that were a hopeless attempt, were the end ever so desirable; ... The decline of the spoken Manx, within the memory of the present generation, has been marked. The language is no longer heard in our courts of law, either from the bench or the bar, and seldom from the witness-box ... It is rarely now heard in conversation, except among the peasantry. It is a doomed language,-an iceberg floating into southern latitudes.
>
> Let it not, however, be thought that its end is immediate. Among the peasantry it still retains a strong hold. It is the language of their affections and their

choice,-the language to which they habitually resort in their communications with each other. And no wonder; for it is the language which they find most congenial to their habits of thought and feeling.

Against a growing tide of Anglicisation, there were those who sought to promote Manx. In 1872, a meeting called Yn Lhaih Gailckagh, The Manx Reading, was held of people supportive of Manx in 1872. The chairman was Rev T Caine of Lonan. This is part of his speech to the meeting:

Rev T Caine
Loayrtys Yn Arr T Caine, Caarliagh, *1872*

My chaarjyn as gheiney cheerey, cha row mee rieau er-yerkal dy akin lheid yn chaglym mooar as t'syns [t'ayns] shoh nyoie[yn oie] noght, or [er] jeet dy cheilley dy chlashtyn arraneyn as co-loayrtys Ghailckagh as myrgeddyn Goo Yee er ny lhaih ayns chengey ny mayrey Ellan Vannin. Te boggoil dy akin lheid y shilley. Ta prowal dy vel ny Manninee bwooiagh clashtyn glare nyn chenn-ayraghyn. Va'n traa, as cha vel eh foddey er-dy-henney, te shen cheu-sthie jeh three feed blein, tra va feer veg dy Vaarle loayrit ayns yn Ellan shoh cheu-mooie jeh ny baljyn-mergee, as va'n Goo er ny phreacheil ayns Gailck ayns ny kialteenyn skeerey ghaa ny three dy ghooneeyn 'syn vee ... tra haink yn ayrn s'jerree [jeh'n Vible] va pryntit gys Aspick Hildesley, yiow eh lheid y boggey jeh, ga nagh row eh hene toiggal eh, dy dooyrt eh " Hiarn nish t'ou cur kied da dty harvaant paartail ayns shee cordail rish dty ghoo, son ta my hooillyn er vakin dty haualtys" (Luke ii. 29). Va shoh Jesarn; daa laa lurg shen v'eh bwoailt leh palsy myr shen nagh loayr eh arragh, as shiaghtin lurg shen phaart eh. ... Ve cliaghtey ve grait ayns Mannin tra va fer erbee goll gys Balla-ny-hinjey dy chummal, "t'eh cur seose yn seihll as gell [goll] gys Purt-ny-hinjey," agh cha vel eh myr shen nish, son ta deiney Purt-ny-hinjey soiaghey sampleyr rein [roin] veagh eh mie dooin geiyrt er, ta shen dy reayll seose yn ghlare ain hene, glare nyn chenn-ayraghyn.

Translation
Speech of the Rev T Caine, Chairman, *1872*

My friends and countrymen, I never expected to see such a large gathering as there is here to-night, come together to hear Manx songs and conversation, and also the Word of God read in the mother tongue of the Isle of Man. It is joyous to see such a sight. It is a proof that the Manxmen are pleased to hear the language of their forefathers. There was a time, and it is not long since, that is within three score years, when there was very little English spoken in this Island outside of the market towns, and the Word was preached in Manx in the parish churches two or three Sundays in the month ... when the last part [of the Bible] which was printed came to Bishop Hildesley, he rejoiced so much at it, though he did not himself understand it, that he said: "Lord, now lettest Thou Thy servant depart in peace, according to Thy word, for mine eyes have seen Thy salvation" (Luke ii. 29). This was on Saturday; two days afterwards he was struck with palsy, so that he never spoke again, and a week afterwards he died ... It was the custom to say in Man, when anyone was going to Peel to live, "He is giving up the world and going to Peel"; but it is not like that now, for the men of Peel are setting an example to us which it would be well for us to follow, that is to keep up our own language, the language of our forefathers.

Another contribution delivered at the meeting was by Rev John Thomas Clarke (1799–1888). We have already seen a translation into Manx of Church of England Homilies, thought to have been made by him about 1820. His interest in Manx continued, even though his religious calling took him to Wales. From Wales he wrote a letter to Rev Caine to be read out at Yn Lhaih Gailckagh in 1872.

Rev John Thomas Clarke

Screeuyn Yn Arr J T Clarke, *1872*

My ghooinney cheerey, te jannoo lane taitnys da my chree (ga bunnys three keead veeilley jeh) dy chlashtyn dy vel Manninee feiy-yerrey, ga yn laa lurg y vargey, doostey seose ass nyn merriud-haveenagh [merriuid-] dy hauail chengey ny mayrey veih ve ooilley-cooidjagh oanluckit 'syn oaie. Ga dy vel eh roie dy tappee gour-y-vullee goll-rish ny banglaneyn elley jeh'n chenn ghlare-ghooie, va keayrt dy row gurneil un tress [trass] ayrn jeh'n Rank, ny-yei cha vel eh yindys erbee, dy vel ad ooilley goll sheese ny lhargey, agh er-lheh yn Ghailck Vanninagh son te cha beg dy chummaltee 'syn Ellan. Ta Jee er choyrt wheesh dy cheeayl da dooinney nish, dy vel eh gimman ny greinyn-aileagh t'eh jannoo eer er famman ny geayee, as ta wheesh dy schlei currit da dy vel eh er n' yannoo mollagyn-aeragh dy chur lhieu seose eh dys ny bodjallyn. Ta siyn-hiaullee echey myrgeddyn dy gholl veih cheer dy heer, eer noi sooill-ny-geayee, tidaghyn ny marrey as gaalyn yn aer. Eer er grunt y cheayn-vooar hene ta saase ec dooinney dy chur chyrrys veih un ayrn jeh'n seihll dys ayrn elley lesh vieauid yn tendreil. Shen-y-fa ta sleih ny cruinney mestit fud-y-cheilley wheesh shen smoo na v'ad rieau roie dy re yn ghlare s'cadjin te 'sy theihll vees y ghlare smoo ymmyd vees jeant j'ee. She shoh yn oyr son y chooid smoo dy vel yn Ghailck Vanninagh ain er gholl kione-ny-lhie cha tappee. Ta Mannin nish jeant myr dy beagh ee ayrn jeh Sostyn raad ta'n Vaarle glare chadjin y theay. Ayns Sostyn er-y-fa shen cha vel yn Ghailck dys ymmyd erbee. Myr shoh ta'n Vaarle goaill yn reiltys as yn reiltys vees ec. Ta'n oyr feer vaghtal. Ta dellal Vannin currit lesh cheu-sthie jeh queig ny shey dy ooryn dys margaghyn Hostyn, as dy ghellal ayndoo shen she Baarle as Baarle ynrickyn sheign ve oc. Ta sleih-aegey Vannin myrgeddyn chammah as yn chenn-diaght troilt veih boayl dy voayl er-feiy-ny-cruinney, paart dys yn aill, paart dys keird, as paart elley goll er-shiaulley foddey jeh dy hagglym cooid as cowreyn gour y laa-fliaghee. Son y cooid smoo she Baarle t'ad loayrt as ayns Baarle t'ad dellal . Fakin shoh ro-laue eisht ta sleih coontey begjeh'n ghlare ghooie oc-hene, ec y traa cheddin oddagh Gailck ve oc chammah as y Vaarle, fegooish yn derrey yeh cheet ayns raad y jeh elley. Ta yn fardailys smoo 'sy theihll dy chredjal dy jinnagh tushtey jeh taggloo as lhaih yn Ghailck dy bragh cheet 'sy raad oc ayns gynsagh y Vaarle. Cha daink shoh my raad's ayns gynsagh yn Vaarle. Ec jeih bleeaney dy eash va mee abyl dy loayrt dy floail ayns Gailck rish cotlaryn my yishag nagh row Baarle erbee oc, as roish va mee feed blein dy eash va ymmoddee lioaryn veggey Vaarlagh chyndaait aym gys Gailck as er nyn gloughey son ymmyd y theay. Nish lesh ooilley'n obbyr shoh ayns Gailck cha row eh rieau ayns my raad eddyr ayns loayrt ny lhaih y Vaarle. Agh ta ard-reiltee Ellan Vannin noi yn Ghailck; ta shirveishee yn Goo jeh dy chooilley chredjue noi ec; ta briwnyn as leighderyn noi ec; as ta'n aegid troggit seose nish ny s'mee-hushtey jeh chengey-ny-mayrey na maase dy vagheragh cliaghtey ve. Ayns traa Aspick Wilson as Aspick Mark Hildesley; cha voddagh dooinney aeg erbee gheddyn stiagh ayns oik y taggyrtys fegooish Gailck vie echey. Tra va kiare-as-feed ny gharrane reill roish nish, she Gailck ooilley v'oc. As ayns [traa] yn Vriw Lace as yn Vriw Crellin cha b'loys da turneyr erbee cheet kiongoyrt roo nagh voddagh argane eh ayns Gailck. Ta cooinaghtyn aym-pene ayns laghyn my aegid dy re ayns Gailck va shin ooilley loayrt rish nyn gabbil as nyn ollagh. Eer moddee hene mannagh loayragh shin roo ayns Gailck, cha jinnagh ad cloh dooin, agh jeeaghyn mygeayrt-y-moo goaill yn yindys smoo 'sy theihll c'red va shin laccal ad dy yannoo dooin. Cha row ny moddee voghtey hene toiggal Baarle, son she Gailck ooilley v'oc, as cha row ad goaill nearey j'ee noadyr!

Translation
Letter of the Rev J T Clarke, *1872*

My fellow countryman, it delights my heart (though nearly three hundred miles away) to hear that at last Manxmen, although the day after the fair, are waking up out of their lethargy to save the mother tongue from being altogether buried in the grave. Though it is rapidly hastening to its end, like the other branches of the old native tongue, it once held sway over the third part of France. Nevertheless it is no wonder that they are all going down-hill, but especially the Manx Gaelic, for there are so few inhabitants of the Island. God has given so much wisdom to man nowadays that he drives the steam engines (fiery engines) he makes even on the tail of the wind, and has given him so much skill that he has made balloons to take him up to the clouds. He has vessels also to go from country to country, even against the eye of the wind, the tides of the sea and the gales of heaven. Even on the bottom of the ocean itself man has means to send a message from one part of the world to another with the speed of lightning. Therefore the people of the world are mixed together much more than they ever were before, so that the most common language in the world will be that of which the most use will be made. This is the reason, for the most part, why our Manx Gaelic has declined so rapidly. The Isle of Man is now become as it were a part of England, where English is the common language of the people. In England, therefore, Manx is of no use at all. Thus the English takes the rule, and the rule she will have. The reason is very plain. The trade of the Island is brought within five or six hours to the markets of England, and to trade there English, and English only, they must have. Young people of the Isle of Man also, as well as the old, travel from place to place throughout the world, some to service, some to business, and others go sailing far off to amass goods and wealth against a rainy day. For the most part it is English they speak, and in English they trade. Foreseeing this then, people despise their native tongue, yet they could have both Manx as well as English, without the one coming in the way of the other. It is the greatest mistake in the world to believe that the knowledge of talking and reading Manx would ever come in their way in learning English. This never came in my way in learning English. At ten years of age I was able to speak fluently in Manx to my father's tenants, who had no English at all, and before I was twenty years of age I had translated many little English books into Manx and printed them for the use of the people. Now with all this work in Manx, it was never in my way either in speaking or reading English. But the rulers of the Isle of Man are opposed to the Manx; the ministers of the Word of every faith are against it; judges and lawyers are against it; and the youth are now brought up more ignorant of the mother-tongue than the beasts of the field used to be. In the time of Bishop Wilson and Bishop Mark Hildesley, no one could enter the office of the priesthood unless he had good Manx. When the twenty-four keys of the carrane ruled the land formerly they all had Manx. And in the time of Deemster Lace and Deemster Crellin no advocate dared come before them unless he could plead in Manx. I myself remember in the days of my youth that it was in Manx that we all spoke to our horses and cattle. Even the dogs themselves, unless we spoke to them in Manx, would not herd for us, but would look around them wondering what in the world we were wanting them to do. The poor dogs themselves were not understanding English, for they all had Manx, and they were not ashamed of it either!

Professor John Rhys was a visitor to the Island in the late nineteenth century, and he spent time pursuing the language as well as folklore. In his Preface, written in 1894, to 'The Outlines of the Phonology of Manx Gaelic', Rhys describes what he found in the Island:

> It is to me a cause of grief and profound sadness to see how rapidly the men and women who can talk and read Manx are disappearing ... I might describe all those who rendered me assistance in Manx, as persons who had reached the prime of life or else had already passed it ... With regards to the prospects of Manx as a living language, one has frankly to confess that it has none. So far as my acquaintance with the Island goes, there are very few people in it now who habitually talk more Manx than English. Among those few one may perhaps

mention the fishermen living in the little village of Bradda, in Rushen, some of whom I have surprised conversing together in Manx. Such is their wont, I learn, when they are out of doors, but when they enter their houses they talk English to their wives and children, and in this conflict of tongues it is safe to say, the the wives and children have it ...

One cannot help contemplating with sadness the extinction of a language, even though confined to such a small area as the Isle of Man; but ... it is not rash to prophesy that in ten or fifteen years the speakers of Manx Gaelic may come to be counted on the fingers of one hand.

The appearance of two books in 1896 demonstrates the increased trend towards English and away from Manx. The first was 'Manx National Songs' Melodies collected in the Island were arranged for the Victorian drawing room, and frequently altered and amended. The book has remained in print, and Manx music has frequently been thought to be these stylized with piano accompaniment, though the arranger, William Henry Gill, said that it was only one approach to the music. The second was A W Moore's 'Manx Ballads & Music', mainly a collection of words to songs in Manx, collected from broadsides and other printed sources, and some from oral tradition. It had a few associated melodies as an annex. Whilst 'Manx National Songs' has remained popular and is still in print, in more recent times the search for original Manx material has led to at least two reprints of 'Manx Ballads & Music', but at the time created little interest other than as a reference book for antiquarians.

More material from the nineteenth century might have been available if the Manx people themselves had shown greater appreciation of those in the community who wrote songs and poems. Edward Faragher (sometimes Farquar) of Cregneash was familiarly known as Neddy Beg Hom Ruy. He spent some time in Liverpool working in a safe-making factory, but returned to the Island to go to the fishing and crofting. In 1899, he wrote of his earlier years (here rendered in standard orthography).

Neddy Beg Hom Ruy (Edward Faragher/Farquar)
Early Years, *1899*

Cha vel Manninee gollrish ashoonyn elley. Cha vel ad goaill monney taitnys [ayns] arraneyn gollrish Sostynee as Bretnee. Cha vel cummaltee Vannin goaill taitnys erbee ayns yn screeu ayms as my horch. Agh ta joarreeyn coontey feer vie jeu. Tra va mish my ghooinney aeg, va mee mie dy screeu arraneyn graihagh gys ny mraane aegey. Agh cha row mraane aegey Vannin goaill taitnys erbee ayndoo. Agh tra va mee cummal ayns Sostyn, va mee coyrt ny mraane aegey er fennue lesh my arraneyn. Va mee dy mennick eignit dy furriaght ec y thie fastyr Jedoonee er yn oyr dy row rour jeu cheet er my eiyrt. As va mee shirveish ad ooilley er yn un chlaare. Tra veagh mish screeu arrane da unnane, veagh ee lhaih eh da e cumraagyn as veagh ad ooilley streeu dy gheddyn ainjys orrym, as dy gheddyn mee dy yannoo arrane orroo hene gys v'ad boirey my chione. Agh ayns my ellan hene cha row ad coontey veg jeu. Shen-y-fa ren mee cur seose screeu arraneyn graihagh as goaill toshiaght dy screeu arraneyn spyrrydoil. As shen ta mee er screeu rish ymmodee bleeantyn as ta mee er stroie ymmodee jeh ny arraneyn ommidagh ren mee screeu ayns laghyn my aegid. Ta ny joareeyn Albinagh jannoo magh dou dy re Albinagh mee as dy re Farquhar yn sliennoo aym. Ny-yeih cha [vel] e monney maadyr dou cre ta'n sleih coontey mee. Ta my vea er ve seaghynagh dy mie ayns traaghyn, myr laa arree dy frassyn as ghrian.

Translation
Early Years, *1899*

The Manx people aren't like other nations. They don't take much pleasure in songs like the English people and the Welsh people. The inhabitants of Mannin don't take any pleasure in the writing of me and of my sort. But the strangers make very good account of it. When I was a young man, I was good to write love songs to the young women. But the young woman of Mannin weren't taking any pleasure in them. But when I was living in England, I was putting the young women in a frenzy with my songs. I was often forced to stay at the house on Sunday afternoon because there were so many of them coming following after me. And I was serving them all on the same plate. When I would be writing a song to one, she would be reading it to her comrades and they would be all striving to get acquaintance with me, and to get me to do a song for themselves until they were bothering my head. But in my own island they think nothing of them. That's the reason that I gave up writing love songs and started to write spiritual songs. And that have I written for many years and I've destroyed many of the foolish songs that I wrote in the days of my youth. The Scottish strangers (visitors) make out to me that I am a Scot and that Farquhar is my surname. For all that it doesn't much matter to me what the people think of me. My lifetime has been well sorrowful at times, as a spring day of showers and of sun.

This was, of course, a private letter rather than something written for publication. Carl Roeder was a German businessman living in Manchester. His great interest was in folklore, and he became a well-known figure in the south of the Island, where his main source was Neddy Beg. Through Roeder came the publication in 1901 of Neddy Beg's 'Skeealyn Aesop: A Selection of Aesop's Fables: Translated into Manx-Gaelic. Together with a Few Poems'. This is one of the fables.

Neddy Beg Hom Ruy (Edward Faragher/Farquar)
Yn Moddey-Oaldey As Yn Eayn, *1901*

Veeit moddey-oaldey eayn er-shaghryn veih yn woaillee, as ghow eh ayns laue gyn dy ghoaill eh ayns fuill feayr, agh dy gheddyn oyr ennagh liorish oddagh eh jannoo magh da'n eayn hene dy row cairys echey dy ee eh. Myr shen dooyrt eh rish, "Wooidjeen, nurree ren oo jannoo faghid j'eem." "Dy jarroo," dooyrt yn eayn lesh coraa feer trimshagh: "Cha row mee ruggit ec y traa shen." "Eisht," dooyrt yn moddey-oaldey, "t'ou gyndyr er yn aber ayms." "Cha vel, vainster mie," dooyrt yn eayn, "cha vel mee rieau er vlastyn faiyr." "Eisht," dooyrt yn moddey-oaldey, "ta shiu giu ass my hibber." "Cha vel," dooyrt yn eayn, "Cha ren mee rieau giu ushtey, son ta bainney my vayrey jannoo beaghey as jough d'ou." Er-shen ren yn moddey-oaldey tayrtyn er as gee eh seose gra: "Cha bee'ms fegooish my hibber, ga dy vel oo er heyrey oo hene jeh ooilley ta mee er ghra."

Yiow yn tranlaasagh dy mennick leshtal son e hranlaase.

Translation
The Wolf and the Lamb, *1901*

A wolf met a lamb astray from the fold, and he undertook not to take him in cold blood, but to find some reason by which he could justify to the lamb itself that it was his right to eat it. So he said to it, "Miscreant, last year you mocked me." "Indeed," said the lamb with a very sad voice: "I wasn't born at that time." "Then," said the wolf, "you graze on my meadow." "I don't, good sir," said the lamb, "I've never tasted grass." "Then," said the wolf, "you drink from my well." "I don't," said the lamb, "I never drank water, for my mother's milk provides sustenance and drink to me." At that the wolf caught it and ate it up saying: "I'll not be without my supper, even thou you've absolved yourself of everything I've said."

The tyrant will often find an excuse for his tyranny.

In 1907, Edward Faragher was obliged to leave the Island to live with his son in Derbyshire, where he died in 1908. This is one of his poems about being separated from the Island

Neddy Beg Hom Ruy (Edward Faragher/Farquar)
Vannin Veg Veen, *c.1907*

Vannin Veg Veen ayns yn aarkey ny lomarcan
Ta soar millish chonnee goll nish lesh ny geayee
Ta'n Arragh ayn reesht lesh frassyn as sumarkyn

Ny croink ooilley coamrit lesh aittin as freoaie

O Vannin Veg Aalin, yn boayl va mee ruggit
Raad cheau mee ny laghyn d'aegid ayns shee
Rish lhiattee Cronk Veayl yn boayl va mee troggit
As blaaghyn yn chonney va gerjaghey mee

Ny yeih, va mee eignit dy gholl ayns traa gerrid
Dy hiaulley yn cheayn as m'Ellan d'aagail
Yn sourey dy liauyr as yn geurey 'sy gyrrid
Ayns cheeraghyn elley dy mennick rouail

Ny yeih, ayns ashlish 'syn oie er yn aarkey
My smooinaght gys Mannin veagh 'mennick chyndaa
Va nish faagit my chooyl ayns tid[e]y ny carrickey
As ayns m'arrane mennick urree gimraa

Boayl va my chumraagyn ayns laghyn m'aegid
Ny cheayrtyn goll marym dy eeastagh 'sy Vaie
Tra veagh ny croink veggey soilshean ayns nyn aalid
As foillanyn soie er ny creggyn 'sy traie

Agh ga dy vel ooilley yn traa er gholl shaghey
As mish er rouail choud ersooyl voish my voayl
Ayns smooinaght ta mee foast fud creggyn yn Stackey
Marish my chaarjyn rouail er nyn oayl

O Vannin Veg Veen, raad va my hennayraghyn
Traaue ayns ny magheryn as shooyl er y clieau
Yn Cheer Veg 'sy Cheayn, yn boayl va my vraaraghyn
Eeastagh yn skaddan glass yn cliaghtey v'oc rieau

Ny yeih ta mish seaghnit son chengey ny mayrey
Te doillee meeiteil nish rish Manninagh dooie
Yn Vaarle ta er choodagh myr tonnyn ny marrey
Yn Ellan veg ain veih'n jiass gys y twoaie

Translation

Dear Little Mannin, *c.1907*

Dear Little Mannin in the sea all alone
There's a sweet smell of gorse going now on the winds
It's Spring again with showers and primroses

The hills all clothed in gorse and heather

O Beautiful Little Mannin, the place I was born
Where I spent the days of youth in peace
On the slopes of Meayll Hill the place I was raised
And the flowers of the gorse were comforting me

Nevertheless, I was forced to go in a short time
To sail the sea and my Island to leave
The summer of length and the winter in shortness
In other countries often roaming

Nevertheless, in a dream in the night on the ocean
My thought to Mannin would be often turning
That was now left behind me in the tide of the carrick
And in my song often referring to it

Where my comrades in the days of my youth
Sometimes going with me to fish in the Bay
When the little hills would be shining in their beauty
And seagulls settling on the rocks on the shore

But though all the time has gone past
And me having strayed so far away from my place
In thought I am yet amongst the rocks of the Stackey
With my friends rambling as was our habit

O Dear Little Mannin, where my forefathers were
Ploughing in the fields and walking on the mountains
The Little Land in the Sea, where my forefathers
Fishing the grey herring was ever their custom

Nevertheless I am saddened for the mother tongue
It's difficult meeting now with a true Manxman
The English has covered like the waves of the sea
Our little Island from the south to the north

The Twentieth Century

The work of Neddy Beg Hom Ruy is from the late nineteenth and just into the twentieth century. The work of John Joseph Kneen (1873-1938) is from just at the end of the nineteenth century into the first third of the twentieth century. As an obituary by William Cubbon published in 'The Journal Manx Museum' Vol IV No 58 in 1939 tells us,

> He first attracted attention by his writings in Manx, with interlinear literal translations in English, which appeared in the Isle of Man Examiner as early as 1895, when he was only 22 years of age. In 1897 these contributions came to the notice of the Speaker of the Keys, Mr. A. W. Moore, who had several interviews with the present writer and with the young man, which resulted in the formation two years later of the Manx Society [The Manx Gaelic Society].
>
> Thus encouraged, his enthusiasm for the preservation of the language and the study of the folk-lore and history of his country, continued to the end of his days. He wrote many booklets and compiled lessons for the use of students. Having a fine poetic sense, he translated many ballads and hymns, all of which were useful in the cause of Manx language and literature.

An example of Kneen's facility at versifying can be found in the National Anthem. The anthem was written by W H Gill in 1906 and published in 1907. J J Kneen's version is a very close paraphrase of Gill's English words, without distorting the Manx (other than a slight straining of grammar in odd places).

Translated by John Joseph Kneen
Yn Arrane Ashoonagh, *1907*

O Halloo nyn ghooie
O Chliegeen ny 's bwaaie

Ry gheddyn er ooir aalin Yee
Ta dt' Ardstoyl Reill-Thie
Myr Barool er ny hoie
Dy reayll shin ayns seyrsnys as shee

Tra Gorree yn Dane
Haink er traie ec y Lhane
Son Ree Vannin v'eh er ny reih
'S va creenaght veih Heose
Er ny chur huggey neose
Dy reill harrin lesh cairys as graih

Ren nyn ayr'yn gimraa
Va Nooghyn shenn hraa
Yn Sushtal dy Hee fockley magh
Shegin yeearree peccoil
Myr far aileyn Vaal
Ve er ny chur mow son dy bragh

Vec ooasle yn Theill
Ayns creioghys tooilleil
Ta traaue ooir as faarkey, Gow cree
Ny jarrood yn Fer mie
Ta coadey'n lught thie
Ren tooilleil liorish Loch Galilee

Deiyr yn sterrym noon as noal
Yn baatey beg moal
Fo harey hug Eh geay as keayn
Trooid ooilley nyn ghaue
Ta'n Saualtagh ec laue
Dy choadey nyn Vannin veg veen

Lhig dorrinyn bra
Troggal seose nyn goraa
As brishey magh ayns ard arrane
Ta nyn groink aalin glass
Yn vooir cummal ass
As coadey lught thie as shioltane

Ny Ellan fo hee
Cha boir noidyn ee
Dy bishee nyn eeastyn as grain

Nee'n Chiarn shin y reayll
Voish streeughyn yn theihll
As crooinagh lesh shee 'n ashoon ain

Lhig dooin boggoil bee
Lesh annym as cree
As croghey er gialdyn yn Chiarn
Dy vodmayd dagh oor
Treishteil er E phooar
Dagh olk ass nyn amneenyn 'hayrn

Translation

The National Anthem

(Literal translation of Kneen's version)

O Land of our nature (or kind)
O jewel most beautiful
To be found on the beautiful earth of God
Your Throne of Home Rule
Like Barrule [a mountain] being set
To keep us in freedom and peace

When Gorree the Dane
Came onshore at the Lhen
For the King of Man he was chosen
And there was wisdom from Above
Sent down to him
To rule over us with justice and love

Our fathers mentioned
The Saints in old time
The Gospel of Peace were pronouncing
Sinful desires must
Like the false fires of Baal
Be destroyed for ever

You worthy Sons of the World
In hardship toiling
Who plough earth and ocean, Take heart.
Don't forget the good Man
Who protects the household
Who toiled by Lake Galilee.

The storm followed hither and yon
The poor little boat
Under command He put the wind and sea
Through all our danger
The Saviour is at hand
To protect our Mannin veg veen

Let tempests ever
Raise up their voices
And break out in a high song
Our beautiful green hills
Keep the sea out
And protect our household and flock

Our Island at peace
No foes will bother it
May our fish and grain increase
The Lord will keep us
From the strivings of the world
And crown with peace our nation

Let us joyful be
With soul and heart
And depend on the Lord's promise
That we can each hour
Trust in His power
To extract each sin from our souls

Translation

The National Anthem

(original version by W H Gill)

O land of our birth
O gem of God's earth
O Island so strong and so fair
Built firm as Barrool
Thy Throne of Home Rule
Makes us free as thy sweet mountain air

When Orry, the Dane
In Mannin did reign
'Twas said he had come from above

For wisdom from Heav'n
To him had been giv'n
To rule us with justice and love

Our fathers have told
How Saints came of old
Proclaiming the Gospel of Peace
That sinful desires
Like false Baal fires
Must die ere our troubles can cease

Ye sons of the soil
In hardship and toil
That plough both the land and the sea
Take heart while you can
And think of the Man
Who toiled by the Lake Galilee

When fierce tempests smote
That frail little boat
They ceased at His gentle command
Despite all our fear
The Saviour is near
To safeguard our dear Fatherland

Let storm-winds rejoice
And lift up their voice
No danger our homes can befall
Our green hills and rocks
Encircle our flocks
And keep out the sea like a wall

Our Island, thus blest
No foe can molest
Our grain and our fish shall increase
From battle and sword
Protecteth the Lord
And crowneth our nation with peace

Then let us rejoice
With heart, soul and voice
And in the Lord's promise confide
That each single hour

We trust in His power
No evil our souls shall betide

Whilst Kneen might celebrate the Isle of Man in Manx, Manx has not been universally blessed by Gaelic scholars. Writing in 1929, Professor Carl Marstrander observed that 'The material I have collected will without doubt have significant value when Celtic speech has completely disappeared from the island in 5-10 yrs. Time ...' In 1932, T F O'Rahilley published his Irish dialects past and present. In the Preface he says that 'It is, perhaps, too much to expect that Manx, that Cinderella of Gaelic tongues, should ever attract many students ...' In his book he writes the following in respect (or rather disrespect) of Manx:

> From the beginning of its career as a written language English influence played havoc with its syntax, and it could be said without much exaggeration that some of the Manx that has been printed is merely English disguised in a Manx vocabulary. Manx hardly deserved to live. When a language surrenders itself to foreign idiom, and when all its speakers become bilingual, the penalty is death.

Rahilly would no doubt have disapproved of the request by the Manx Museum Trustees in 1934 to J J Kneen to provide a translation of the Rubaiyat of Omar Khayyam from Fitzgerald's well-known English version. The request had come to the Museum from an Indian scholar, Mr J E Saklatwalla. Kneen's translation of the 75 quatrains was published in the Journal of the Manx Museum No 38-41 (March-June-September-December 1934). These are the closing nine quatrains:

John Joseph Kneen
Rubaiyat of Omar Khayyam *(extract)*, 1934

>LXVII.
>Tra fioghys Bio's jean mee lesh Feeyn 'chiarail,
>As niee my Chorp tra ta mee er phaartail;
>Eisht soaill mee ayns Brelleein jeh Duillag Feeyn,
>'S ayns Coyr Fuygh feeyney oanluck mee ayns Keyll.
>
>LXVIII.
>Tra ta mee fo yn Thalloo nee my Leoie
>Y skeayley magh 'syn Aer lheid y Soar mie
>Dy bee yn Meshtallagh ayns Ribbey goit
>Gynys, tra hig eh faggys da my Oaie.

LXIX.
Ny Jallooyn dy bynney lhiam dy-deyr,
T'er n'yannoo ayns Sooill Ghooinney dou Aggair;
T'er vaih yn Onnor aym ayns Cappan beg,
As er loayrt noi'n Ardghoo aym lesh Drogh-ghlare.

LXX.
Dy-jarroo, jarroo, loo mee Arrys rieau,
Agh row mee rieau sheelt tra ren mee loo?
Eisht haink yn Arragh as lesh Rose my laue,
Ersooyl hie m'Arrys lhome-cheaut roish dy-bieau.

LXXI.
Ga varr yn Feeyn my Onnor as my Ghaill,
Gys yiowym Baase cha jeanym rish 'phaartail;
As ga dy voddagh eh my Chorp y stroie,
Erskyn dy-chooilley red nee'm Feeyn 'phriseil.

LXXII.
Ah treih! dy ragh yn Arragh lesh e Ghraih!
Dy beagh Lioar Aegid villish er ny jeigh!
Yn Ushag reagh chiaull er y Vangan glass,
Quoi ec ta Fys c'raad d'ettyl ee? Ah treih!

LXXIII.
Ah ghraih! dy goardagh uss as mish rish Jee
Dy chur Saase Reddyn seaghnagh shoh ass Bree,
Nagh brishagh shin ayns meeryn eh – as eisht
Ny s'niessey 'chummey eh gys Yeearree'n Chree!

LXXIV.
Ah! Eayst my Haitnys nagh b'ione Baarney jee,
Ta Eayst Niau g'irree keayrt reesht ayns e Shee;
Quoid keayrt ny yei shoh nee ee ayns fardail
Shirrey my lurg 'sy Gharey? Ughanee!

LXXV.
Tra hed uss shaghey, Saki, chiart goll ree'sh,
Fud Goaldee skeaylit er yn Aiyr ghlass neesht;
As er dty Haght'raght ghennal hig d'yn Voayl
Raad ren mee nane – chyndaa Gless follym sheese!

Literal translation from Kneen
Rubaiyat of Omar Khayyam *(extract)*

LXVII.
When Life itself may wither tend me with Wine,
And wash my Body when I have departed;
Then wrap me in a Sheet of Vine Leaf,
And in a Wooden Wine Cask bury me in a Wood.

LXVIII.
When I am under the Ground my Ash will
Broadcast in the Air such a good Smell
That the Drunkard will be caught in a Trap
Without realising, when he will come close to my Grave.

LXIX.
The Images that I loved dearly,
That have done in the Eye of Man to me a Wrong;
That have drowned my Honour in a little Cup,
And have spoken against my Repute with Rough speaking.

LXX.
Indeed, indeed, I always swore Repentance,
But was I ever sober when I swore that?
Then came the Spring and with the Rose to hand,
Away went my worn-out Repentance quickly.

LXXI.
Though Wine killed my Honour and my Stomach,
Until I Die I will not part with it;
And though it could destroy my Body,
Above everything I prize Wine.

LXXII.
Alas! that Spring should go with its Love!
That the sweet Book of Youth should be closed!
The Bird that arranged its music on the green Branch,
Who Knows where it flies? Alas!

LXXIII.
Ah love! that you and I would agree with God
To put this sad Way of Things out of Commission,
Would we not break it in pieces – and then

Closer shape it to the Desire of the Heart!

LXXIV.
Ah! Moon of my Delight that no Gap is known to it,
The Moon of Heaven rises once again in its Peace;
How many times after this will it in vain
Seek for me in the Garden? Woe is me!

LXXV.
When you go past, Saki, just as it does,
Amongst Guests scattered on the green Grass again,
And on your cheerful Message will go to the Place
Where I made one – turn an empty Glass down!

The role of Yn Cheshaght Ghailckagh (The Manx Gaelic Society) since 1899 has been influential in making available dictionaries, grammars, primers and reading material in Manx and of Manx interest. 'First Lessons in Manx' by Edmund Goodwin (1843-1924) was published in 1901. A revised edition has been in continuous print since 1965. It is regarded by many as the 'Bible' of Manx grammar. In 1935 Yn Cheshaght Ghailckagh published 'Beginning Manx Gaelic/A Manx Primer', based on 'First Lessons in Manx'. Publishing a second edition in 1940, the Foreword notes:

> When this book was first printed, in 1935, it was regarded merely as a necessary tool for the language classes that were then being formed in various parts of the Island, and it was believed that a small edition of 500 would meet the needs of those classes for some time to come.
>
> Such has been the popularity of the primer, however, with individual students abroad as well as with classes at home, that the 1935 edition was sold out rapidly, and copies have now been virtually unobtainable for over two years. Yn Cheshaght Ghailckagh, therefore, issues this new edition in response to many requests in the hope and faith that it may prove as good a missionary for the Manx language revival as its predecessor.

The continuation of the lessons came in 'Lessons In Manx' published in 1936. The book acknowledges 'much additional matter which enhances the value of this little volume' by J J Kneen, who made a translation of an Irish legend 'especially for students'. The story is in sections throughout the book. This is the first section.

John Joseph Kneen
Cheer Nyn Aeg, *1936*

Va Oshin fer s'jerree ny Fenee faagit syn Erin. V'eh yn fer smoo jeh ny Fenee va firchaggee myrgeddin. V'eh mac da Fynn, agh v'eh foast bio ayns lhing Pharick. Hoiagh eh taggloo rish y noo as eer g'eaishtagh rish.

Va'n noo er spreih ushtey casherick er yn Eniagh. Ny yeih cha row eh shickyr son tammylt beg by chair da taggloo rish lheid y fer er-lhimmey jeh taggloo mysh Creestiaght. Va Oshin ro henn tushtey dy ve echey mychione y chredjue shoh. Agh d'ansoor daa ainle ny ourysyn echey. Dooyrt ad rish dy lhisagh eh screeu sheese goan Oshin, er-lheh ny skeealyn echey jeh'n chennaghys Er-yn-oyr [sic], as yn ainle, verragh ad boggey da deiney ayns ny laghyn va ry-heet.

Va Oshin nish cha meein as Creestee erbee. Cha yarg eh markiagh, cha yarg eh roie, cha yarg eh kiaulleeagh monney. Agh yn chooid smoo jeh'n traa echey hoiagh eh lieh-lhie er e hoshiaght er e leiy. V'eh goll rish billey-ooyl ennagh v'er choayl ooilley agh unnane jeh ny banglaneyn echey as rish foddey nagh row er n'ymmyrk mess erbee er-lhimmey jeh cliegeenyn dy gheul. Ve'h bentyn da sluight va'n jannoo as yrjid as aght beaghee echey jeeaghyn dy ve ny s'cooie da'n thalloo na shen v'ec Creesteeyn, ny smoo ayns cordail rish sleityn, keylljyn, faarkaghyn dorrinagh, as niaughyn. Eaishtagh eh rish skeealyn craueeaght, agh cha d'od cagh eh y hyndaa gys Creestiaght. V'eh ro henn as foawragh ooilley cooidjagh, as va'n cooinaghtyn echey ro lane. Tra ghow Parick ny saggyrt ny s'moal-hushtee ennagh elley orroo dy ghriennaghey [sic] eh liorish gra nagh row Fynn as e vraaraghyn ayns Flaunys, d'reggyr eh: Mannagh bee adsyn ayns shid, cre yinnins ayns shid? Cre'n-oyr dy je'ms gys shid?

Translation
The Land of the Young, *1936*

Oshin was the last one of the Fenians left in Ireland. He was the greatest of the Fenians who were warriors as well. He was the son of Fynn, but he was still alive in the era of Patrick. He would sit talking with the saint and even listening to him.

The saint had sprayed holy water on the Fenian. Nevertheless he wasn't certain for a short while that it was proper for him to talk to such a one except for talking about Christianity. Oshin was too old for him to have knowledge about this belief. But two angels answered his doubts. They told him that he ought to write down Oshin's utterance, particularly the stories he had about history Because [sic], said the angel, they would give pleasure to men in days that were coming.

Oshin was now as tame as any Christian. He couldn't ride, he couldn't run, he couldn't make music much. But the most part of his time he would sit leaning forward on his spear. He was like some apple-tree that had lost all but one of its branches and for a long time it had not born any fruit except for loops of mistletoe. He was connected with a line of which the action and height and way of life seemed to be more appropriate to the land than that of the Christians, more in accord with mountains, woods, tempestuous oceans, and heavens. He would listen to religious stories, but not a single one could convert him to Christianity. He was too old and giant-like all together, and his memory was too full. When Patrick or a priest or some of the most dimwitted took it upon themselves to say that Fynn and his brothers were not in Paradise, he replied: If they'll not be over yonder, what would I do yonder? What reason would I be going over yonder?

From Spring 1951 to New Year 1957, Yn Cheshaght Ghailckagh published 14 issues of 'Coraa Ghailckagh' ('Gaelic Voice'), edited by John Gell. The publication included a range of material including original and translated work by a variety of authors, and provides a rich seam. The second edition (summer and autumn 1951) included a long poem written in 1939 by Juan Comish, originally from Castletown but since settled in Kirkland Lake, Ontario. His poem of 246 lines divided into 18 non-standard sections is about the gift of a scale model of a Viking ship to the Manx Museum from the authorities in Norway. In one particularly vigorous section he sees it as a focus to draw the ghosts of King Gorree (Orry) and his followers to set sail again.

Juan Comish
Arrane Lhong-Liauyr Ny Lochlinnee, *1939*

  XIV
  By-lesh Mannanan lhongan, v'ee 'Skeeabeyder ny Tonn,'
  Tra baillesh ish y vooadaghey, chelleeragh daase ee chionn,
  As ayns 'n aght shen yindyssagh, nee uss, Y Lhongan, gaase
  Ec aigney 'n Ree Mooar Gorree, neayr's foddey hooar eh baase.
  As jir eh rish e chaarjyn, as cuirrey 'choyrt daue neesht,
  "Tar-jee, my Heshaght Hreanagh, as lhig dooin shiaulley reesht."
  As er-y-chooyll hig adsyn, myr feeaih skibbyltagh,
  Dty cholb' y lhieeney lane, cheu-harryds lheimyragh.
  Eisht ayns e ynnyd-oayllagh, bee dagh unnane ny hoie,
  As s'leah, fo shiaull as maidjer, bee uss dy tappee roie,
  Lesh Gorree-hene dty vainshter, quoi ec vees cair ny s'cooie?
  Ayns ynnyd yn Ard-stiureyder, dty ghoaill da'n aarkey mooie.
  Eisht ersooyl lhiat 'syn aght shen hiaull 'Yn Skeeabeyder' y cheayn,
  Lesh bree ta erskyn-dooghys ny cheiltyn aynyd-hene,
  Cho seyr as geay ny marrey ta sheidey noon as noal,
  As foillanyn ta getlagh erskyn dy chooilley voayl.
  Gys Ellanyn ny Twoaie, ass puirt ny h-Ellan ain,
  Coyrt shilley er dagh valley, veih'n Thalloo-Glass gys Spaain,

As trooid Mooir Veanagh Thallooin, cha bee ayd traa dy fieau
Dy ronsagh reesht son Micklegarth, nagh dooar ad er dy rieau.

Translation
The Song of the Vikings' Long-Boat, *1939*

XIV
Mannanan had a small boat, she was 'The Wavesweeper',
When he wished to enlarge her, immediately she grew fast
And in that wonderful way, will you, O Small Boat, grow
At the will of the Great King Orry, long since that he died
And he will say to his friends, and give an invitation to them as well
"Come ye, my Heroic Company, and let us sail again"
And immediately they will come, like skipping deer
To fill your whole body, leaping into you over the side
Then in his accustomed place, each one will be seated
And soon, under sail and oar, you will be running swiftly
With Orry himself your master, who has a more appropriate right
In the place of the Chief Helmsman, taking you to the ocean outside
Then away with you in that way that 'The Sweeper' sailed the sea
With spirit that's supernatural hidden within you yourself
As free as the wind of the sea that blows hither and yon
And seagulls that fly above every place
To the Islands of the North, out of the ports of our Island
Visiting each town, from Greenland to Spain
And through the Mediterranean Sea, you'll not have time to wait
To search again for Micklegarth, that they never ever found

'Coraa Ghailckagh' also introduced the work of A S B Davies of Wales, a polyglot who translated a short story by Daniel Owen from Welsh into Manx. This, together with four other of Daniel Owen's stories, was published separately by Yn Cheshaght Ghailckagh in 1952 as 'Skeealyn Cheeil-Chiollee'. Attached to 'Skeealyn Cheeil-Chiollee' there was also a generic title, 'Lioaryn Yn Thie Thooee, Earroo 1' – 'Books of the Thatched House, Number 1'. The second book – 'Earroo 2' – came in 1954, with a further three short stories by A S B Davies, this time translated from a Scottish Gaelic source, under the title of the main story, 'Juan Doo Shiaulteyr' – 'John Black Sailor'. Here, though, is the first of the stories of A S B Davies (Art Mac Ghavid), published in 'Coraa Ghailckagh' No 4 (November 1951).

A S B Davies (Art Mac Ghavid)
Yn Edd Ec Jac, *1951*

"Cheayll oo keayrt ny ghaa dy vel ec yn aigney cooid-vooar dy phooar er slaynt ny er aslaynt y chorp, as s'feer dy-liooar shen," dooyrt ny naim Edard: shoh dhyts skeeal eisht, cho firrinagh as oddys ee ve.

Lurg dooys v'er n'aase seose my ghooinney-aeg, haink mee dy ve feer skee jeh obbyr-eirinagh, ve ny vioys ro hoccaragh dooys, as va mee er chlashtyn dy row faill vie ry-gheddyn ayns y wyllin-cadee ayns YR WYDDGRUG (balley ayns Bretin) as ersooyl lhiam dys shen dy hirrey obbyr.

Hooar mee obbyr chelleeragh, as va mee my horch dy 'er-choonee lesh ny snieuderyn as va mee feer vaynrey lesh my startey. Va dooinney-aeg elley ayns shen as eshyn mysh yn eash cheddin as mish, guilley v'er choayl 'nane jeh ny sooillyn echey, agh, ny-yeih, v'eh fakin ny smoo ass e 'nane na veagh guillyn elley fakin dy cadjinagh lesh daa hooill!

V'eh enmyssit William James, as she ny ghuilley feer vitchooragh v'eh. Haink eshyn as mish dy ve nyn gaarjyn ayns traa gerrid. Veagh William as mish goaill commeeys ayns sorch ennagh dy chluicyn gagh laa, agh ve toiggit eddyr William as mish dy row eh orrin dy ghoaill-rish yn 'oill lurg-y-cheilley, as myr shen va shin shaghney *un* smaght!

She Thomase Burgess yn dooinney va ny 'urriman 'sy chamyr-snieuee, as v'eh 'nane jeh ny fir s'dewiley as s'dwoaiagh rish ny fir-obbree honnick mee rieau. Agh va Burgess feer ghraihagh er spotcheraght as er cur-rish cluicyn brasnee noi deiney va er e churrym, as myr shen, v'eh cur foayr dy liooar er William as orrym-pene.

Va mee er lhaih boayl ennagh dy voddagh fer coyrlaghey as cur er dooinney slayntoil dy chredjal dy vel eh ching, as er dooinney ching dy chredjal dy vel eh follan, mannagh beagh y chingys echey ro hrome.

Keayrt dy row, as shinyn goaill nyn jinnair, ren mee gimraa y chooish shoh rish Thomas Burgess, as dooyrt eshyn: S'aashagh prowal y yannoo er y chooish, my yinnagh uss as Wil James cur nyn ging ry-cheilley crenaght dy yannoo eh er 'nane jeh ny fir shoh. Mannagh yarg Wil cummey red ennagh, bee yindys mooar orryms, er-yn-oyr she guilley feer schleioil t'eshyn, er-lhiams.

Loayr mee rish Wil mychione yn eie ec Burgess, as roish yn oie va cummey er n'aarlaghey ec Wil!

Va fer ny snieuderyn as yn ennym echey Jac Jones, dooinney va dy kinjagh ceau 'top-hat', as v'eh faagail eh er treiney cheu-mooie jeh'n chamyr-snieuee. Va Wil smooinaghtyn dy chiangley streng dhoo cheyl, agh lajer dy liooar, mygeayrt y mysh bun yn edd, dy jeeragh erskyn yn oirr, as dy hayrn eh stiagh mysh kerroo-oarlagh, (as ta kerroo-oarlagh ny ghaa ardvooadys, t'ou toiggal, ayns mooadys yn edd!) as eisht dy chur er Jac Jones dy chredjal dy row e chione er n'att.

'Sy voghrey, laa-ny-vairagh, cho leah as hie Jac Jones gys e obbyr, chiangl Wil y streng mygeayrt yn edd, as cordail rish y chummey, hie mish as dooyrt mee rish Jac, "John Jones, nagh vel shiu ro vie ayns slaynt moghrey jiu?" "Ta mee mie dy liooar, my ghuilley, cre'n fa t'ou briaght?" as eshyn. "Och, cha nel eh veg," dooyrt mish, "agh va mee smooinaghtyn dy vel att ennagh 'sy chione eu."

"Cha nee, ta mish ayns slaynt mie, as dy jarroo ta mee booisal er y son," dreggyr Jac.

Mysh shiaght er y chlag hie Wil huggey, as dooyrt Wil, "John Jones, cha nel shiu jeeaghyn gollriu-hene jiu, vel pian 'sy chione eu?"

"Cha nel, dy jarroo," dooyrt Jac, "agh va Ned dy jeeragh nish briaght yn red cheddin, c'red hug ort smooinaghtyn yn lheid?"

"Cha 'sayms," dooyrt Wil, "agh ta'n kione eu jeeaghyn cooid veg aitt gollrish dy row shiu er n'gheddyn builley ry-lhiattee eck. Lhig dou fakin y cheu elley. Och, cha nee, t'ad ny-neesht gollrish y cheilley, cha row mish agh sheiltyn, er-lhiam," as ersooyl lesh Wil gys e obbyr.

Mysh queig minnidyn roish traa vrishey-hroshtey hie Burgess-hene huggey as dooyrt eh, "Er-hoh uss, Jac, v'ou uss rish streeu ennagh riyr! T'ou er ve scoorit reesht, er-yn-oyr ta dty chione gollrish napin mooar cruinn! Nagh vel oo er gheddyn yn gorley-scoarnee ta goll mygeayrt ec y traa t'ayn?"

"Cha nel mee er vlastey bine beg neayr's shiaghtin, as ta my chione cho mie as kione erbee euish-hene," dreggyr Jac dy doaltattym.

"Ta mee treishteil dy vel oo ginsh yn irriney," dooyrt Burgess, as ersooyl lesh.

Tra va Jac Jones goll dys e vrishey-hroshtey, as shirrey cur e edd er e chione, cha daink eh lesh edyr. Ren eh jeeaghyn mannagh row eh er n'ghoaill edd ennagh elley, agh chooinee eh er-hene nagh row fer erbee ceau 'top-hat' agh eh-hene, as myrgeddin, va ennym scruit liorish e laue-hene ayns cheusthie yn edd. Hooar eh bayrn er eeassaght cour goll dys e lhongey, as hug eh lesh yn edd 'sy laue.

Cha daink Jac er-ash dys e obbyr lurg brishtey-hroshtey [brishey-hroshtey] ec munlaa, hug Burgess shilley er as hooar eh ayns y lhiabbee eh, surranse fo guin ghewil ayns e chione. Dooyrt Burgess rish Jac dy row eh gyn-dooyt ching nish, agh dy row lheihys ayn dy derragh couyr da chelleeragh, as dy derragh eh hene lesh yn lheihys shen huggey 'syn astyr, erreish da'n vwyllin er scuirr.

Hie Burgess as mish dy chur shilley er Jac yn oie shen as hug shin lhien cooid veg dy ooill villish ayns boteil. Choud as va Burgess as ben Jac heose 'sy chamyr-cadlee cur yn ooill er kione Jac boght, va mish heese tayrn streng jeh'n edd, as eisht, dy yeeaghyn cre cho fondagh as va'n lheiys, dooyrt Burgess rish y ven dy gholl as cur lh'ee seose huggey yn edd, as cur-my-ner! nish haink eh lesh Jac dy chur yn edd dy aashagh er e chione: dy firrinagh, liorish wheesh dy ooill as va er e chione, skyrr yn edd bunnys ro aashagh, as by-vie eh, dy row ec Jac cleayshyn mooar dy liooar dy lhiettal yn edd veih goll harrish yn eddin echey. Agh s'yindyssagh ve, ga dy row yn att er n'gholl ersooyl chelleeragh, cha scuirr yn pian cho tappee, as va Jac Jones ec y thie son shiaghtin roish hie eh reesht gys e obbyr.

Cha dooar eh fys mychione y chrout rish tree shiaghtinyn elley, as cha ren eh rieau leih dooin!

Translation
Jac's Hat, *1951*

"You heard once or twice that the will has a large stock of power over the health or unhealthiness of the body, and that's true enough," said my uncle Edward. Here for you is a story then, as true as could be.

After I had grown up as a young man, I came to be very tired of farm-work, it was too laborious a life for me, and I had heard that there was good earnings to be had in the woollen-mill in YR WYDDGRUG (a town in Wales) and away I went there to look for work.

I got work immediately, and I was a sort of helper to the spinners and I was very happy with my position. There was another young man there and him about the same age as me, a boy who had lost one of his eyes, but, nevertheless, he was seeing more out of his one than other boys would be seeing normally with two eyes!

He was called William James, and he was a very mischievous boy. He and I came to be friends in a short time. William and I would be colluding in some sort of tricks each day. But it was understood between William and myself that we had to own up to the blame one after another. Thus we avoided *one* punishment.

Thomase Burgess was the man who was the foreman in the spinning-room, and he was one of the cruellest and most detestable ones to the workmen that I ever saw. But Burgess was very fond of joking and practising provoking tricks against the men who were under his charge, and thus, he showed kindness enough to William and to me.

I had read somewhere that a person could persuade and cause a healthy man to believe that he is ill, and a sick man that he is hale, if his illness were not to serious.

Once, when we were taking our dinner, I mentioned this subject to Thomase Burgess, and he said: It's easy to make a test of the subject, if you and Wil James were to put your heads together how to do it to one of these people. If Wil devise some plan, I'll be greatly surprised, because I think that he's a very adept boy.

I spoke with Wil about Burgess's idea and before the night a plan had been made ready by Wil!

There was one of the spinners whose name was Jac Jones, a man who was always wearing a top-hat, and he was leaving it on a nail outside the spinning-room. Wil was thinking of attaching a thin black string, but strong enough, round the base of the hat, directly above the rim, and of drawing it in about a quarter of an inch, (and a quarter of an inch is two sizes, you understand, in a hat-size!) and then of getting Jac Jones to believe that his head had swollen.

In the morning the following day, as soon as Jac Jones went to his work, Wil attached the string round the hat, and as per the plan, I went and I said to Jac, "John Jones, are you not too good in health this morning?" "I'm well enough, my lad, why do you ask?" he said. "Och, it's nothing," I said, "but I think that there's some swelling in your head."

"There's not at all, I'm in good health, and indeed I'm thankful for it," replied Jac.

About seven o'clock Wil went to him, and he said: "John Jones, you're not looking yourself today, do you have a pain in your head?"

"I don't, indeed," said Jac, "but Ned was just now asking the same thing, what made you think the like?"

"I don't know," said Wil, "but your head looks a little bit strange as if you had received a blow to the side of it. Let me see the other side. Och, no, they're both the same as each other, I was just imagining it, I think," and away went Wil to his work.

About five minutes before the first breakfast time Burgess himself went to him and said, "Here you are, Jac, you were having some struggle last night! You've been drunk again, I know, because your head is like a big, round turnip! You haven't been getting the throat disease that's been going about at the present time?"

"I've not tasted a little drop for a week, and my head is as good as any head of your own," replied Jac abruptly.

"I hope that you're telling the truth," said Burgess, and away he went.

When Jac Jones was going to his lunch, and trying to put his hat on his head, he didn't succeed at all. He looked if he hadn't taken some other man's hat, but he remembered for himself that nobody wore a top-hat but himself, and as well as that, a name was written in his own hand on the inside of the hat. He borrowed a cap to go for his lunch, and he brought the hat in [his] hand.

Jac didn't come back to his work: Burgess went to see him at midday, and he found him in the bed, suffering from a severe ache in his head. Burgess said to Jac that he was undoubtedly sick now, but there was medicine to give immediate remedy, and that he would himself bring that medicine to him in the afternoon after the mill had closed.

Burgess and I went to see Jac that afternoon and we brought a small amount of sweet oil in a bottle. Whilst Burgess and Jac's wife were up in the bedroom putting the oil on poor Jac's head, I was downstairs pulling the string from the hat, and then, to show just how effective the medicine was, Burgess said to the wife to go and bring up to him the hat, and behold ye! now Jac succeeded in putting the hat easily on his head: in truth, with as much of the oil as was on his head, the hat slipped almost too easily, and it was good, that Jac had ears big enough to prevent the hat from going over his face. But it was amazing, though the swelling had gone away immediately, the pain didn't stop as quickly, and Jac Jones was at the house for a week before we went again to his work.

He didn't find out about the guile for three more weeks, and he never ever forgave us!

It was inevitable that 'Coraa Ghailckagh' should note the deaths of some of the remaining speakers of Manx. Amongst those who had met them was another Gaelic scholar, Kenneth H Jackson. In the Preface to Contributions to the Study of

Manx Phonology (1955), Jackson says that 'I owe a deep debt of gratitude to the native speakers themselves, that tiny company of guardians of the last remnants of the Manx language, once chengey ny mayrey Ellan Vannin, soon to be so no more.' His Introduction shows the reasons for his view:

> Some [of ten native speakers] ... are a good deal more fluent than others, but all have long ceased to use Manx as their daily medium of intercourse, mostly for many years, though the efforts of the new generation of Manx students have caused them to rub some of the rust off more recently. Hence they frequently forget, especially since in addition they are almost all very old, and it was often impossible therefore for me to get anything like all the words and phrases I asked for. Thus some would often know a singular but not its plural, and so on, and would be unable to give the Manx for the commonest things. In addition it is probable that their Manx pronunciations have been considerably influenced by English, as is only to be expected now that Manx is no longer used in daily conversation, and is only more or less dimly remembered by a handful of people who have regularly spoken nothing but English for years.

Nevertheless, 'Coraa Ghailckagh' continued its work. One of the contributors to four issues, including the majority of No 13 in 1956, was Frank Bell Kelly, then living in Wolverhampton. John Gell (Juan y Geill), the editor of 'Coraa Ghailckagh', also asked Kelly to provide an Introduction to his 'Conversational Manx' which was published in 1954. Kelly was a student of Irish and Scottish Gaelic as well as Manx, and this is reflected in his first published piece. It is a translation into Manx of an Irish story, and is followed by a short discussion on orthography. Kelly then renders the first part of the story in a Scottish Gaelic form. Kelly allows his knowledge of the other forms of Gaelic to adopt slightly unusual forms even in the 'standard' Manx version, such as har rish rather then harrish or Sh'immey rather than Shimmey. However, this is the opening of the story, and the alternative orthography.

Frank Bell Kelly
Yn Brack T'Ayns Yn Awin Mooar, *1952*

Oddins cur enn er yn vrack shen veih dagh ooilley vrack va rieau goit ayns poyll jeh strooan; ta tummid erskyn mooarane e chynney echey, as eash nagh vel ec lane jeu.

Agh, yn cheeayl ta 'sy chione echey! Ta eeasteyryn jeh ny shiaght skeeraghyn craidit, sproghtit er e hon fud ny bleeantyn foddey; dagh ooilley lheid y bite va currit er dooan rieau, shirragh ad, cha nee agh cur er yn mitchoor dy vrack agh gob birragh dy haih magh har rish yn clagh t'eh ny chummal fo, yn famman echey gleashagh dy craidoilagh as ersooyl lesh dy kiune.

'S fakinit veagh eh, heese voyd 'syn ushtey gial, dyn scansh erbee goaill jeeds, ny jeh yn bite ayd, kied echey aghtal yn mioleyder t'ayn. She ort-hene veagh yn treihys, as eshyn 'g irree gys eaghtyr yn ushtey dy reih carchuillagyn veagh jeh'n daah cheddin as jeh'n chaslys cheddin rish y 'nane veagh er dty ghooan hene; yn brack gastey creeney shen! Sh'immey ta'n mollaght-mynney hooar eh jeh ny eeasteyryn 'sy lhing echey.

'Nee gra rhym t'ou, by vian lhiat ve dty helgeyr, eeastagh son yn brack? Inshyms dhyt; Gow dys Ard-Magher hoshiaght, eisht jean ainjys rish eeasteyr-vrick t'ayns y voayl shid. Abbyr rish, dy dooar oo naight jeh'n vrack, as dy vel eh kiarit ayd gyn yn ard d'aagail derrey vees eh 'sy phoagey lhiat.

An Breac t'anns an Abhainn Mor (*alternative orthography*)

Fhoduins cur aithne air an bhreac sen bhoi dagh uile bhreac bha riumh gamhaite anns poil de sruan; ta tumaid airscionn moran a chinneadh aige, a's ais nagh bheil aig lan deubh.

Ach, an chial ta 'sa chion aige! Ta iastaran de na seacht scireachan craduit, sprochtuit air a shon fud ny bliantan fada; dagh uile lethid a bait bha curuit air dhubhan riumh sireach 'ad – chan 'eadh ach cur air an mitiur de bhreac ach gob biorach do shaith 'mach har rish an chlach t'e 'na chumal fo, an faman aige glaiseach creaideolach, a's airsubhal leis do ciun.

'S facuinit bheach e, shios bhoid 'san uiste geal, dun scainse air bith gamhail diots, no de'n bait aghads, cead aige achtal an mioladair t'ann. 'Se ort fhein bheach an troigheas, a's esean 'g eiridh gus uachtar an uiste do roigh carchuileagan bheach de'n dath cheadn' a's de'n chaslaios cheadn' ris an 'nan bheach air do dhubhan fhein; An breac gasta crionna sen! 'S iomadh ta'n mollacht-mionna ghuair e de na iastaran 'san linn aige.

'Ni 'g radh rium ta thu bu mhian leat bheith do shealgair, iastach son an breac? Innseams duit: gabh dus Ard-Macha thoiseacht, eisd, dean aithndeas ris iastairbhric t'anns an bhall siud. Abair ris, d'fhuair thu naidheacht de'n bhreac, a's do bheil e cairit aghad gun an ard d'fhagail daire bhios e 'san phoga leat.

Translation

The Trout That's in the Big River, *1952*

I could recognise that trout from every other trout that was ever caught in a pool of a stream; he has a bulk above most of his kind, and an age that most of them don't have.

But, the sense that's in his head! Fishermen of the seven parishes are ridiculed, made frantic for him throughout the long years; every sort of bait that was ever put on a hook, they would seek it, it only makes the rogue of a trout adopt a sharp-pointed mouth [a pout] to push out across the stone he is living under, his tail moving mockingly as away with him calmly.

It's seen he would be, down from you in the bright water, without any importance attaching to you, or of your bait, however skilful the lure. It's you yourself would have the misery, and him rising to the surface of the water to choose a fly that would be of the same colour and of the same appearance as the one that would be on your hook; that clever, wise trout! Many is the resounding curse he got from the fishermen in his time.

Are you saying to me, you would yearn to be a hunter, fishing for the trout? I'll tell you; go to Armagh first, then get acquainted with a trout-fisherman that's in the place yonder. Say to him, that you got news about the trout, and that you intend not to leave the area until it's in your pack.

As the editor of 'Coraa Ghailckagh', John Gell (1899-1983) wrote prefatory notes about the contributors and their work. His own style is that of the late native speakers whom he knew personally, and this is similar to that of the nineteenth century work of Neddy Beg Hom Ruy – full of idiom, yet in many respects setting out clauses and sentences in a similar way to English and with rare use of the included object. Gell's gift was in teaching conversational Manx, and his 'Conversational Manx' of 1954, with phonetic rendering of whole phrases of Manx, not just individual words, is his masterwork. He is rightly recognised as one of the fathers of the Manx revival. His everyday prose style is reflected in an original work (though unfinished), 'Yn Whallag'. 'Yn Whallag' digresses greatly, so the story hardly progresses in 31 foolscap pages. Its language is prosaic, despite incidents which could have been enhanced by a more exciting and direct approach. This is an example, as it appears in the foolscap manuscript (it was serialised in 'Dhooraght' a magazine adjunct to Yn Cheshaght Ghailckagh's newsletter, in 1998–99).

John Gell
Yn Whallag, *c.1950s*

Eisht dinsh Hommy dou yn aght va'n ayr echey caillt er y cheayn, tra va Hommy-hene ny ghuilley beg: Va Robin er lhong enmyssit y 'Ben Varrey', as v'ee cheet thie veih'n slyst airhey ayns Africa Sheear, agh myr v'ee shiaulley tessyn y Vaie Biscay, roie ee stiagh ayns sterrym mooar, as ny tonnyn girree myr sleityn. Va'n Ben Varrey shiaulley dy mie as ooilley yn carmeish eck kianglit coourse [sic] as sauchey, agh doaltattym heid y gaal myr dorrin agglagh, as vrish yn shiaull-mullee syrjey seyr, as va bennalt dy feie.

Chelleeragh va Robin heose er y luir-hiaull, agh huitt faarkey mooar y lhong as cheau eh ee er e lhiattee, derrey va'n lieh-latt ayns ny tonnyn, as tra va'n lhong er kiouyl corrym reesht cha row Robin ry-akin, v'eh caillt.

Translation
The Whallag, *c.1950s*

Then Tommy told me the way his father was lost at sea, when Tommy himself was a little boy: Robin was on a ship named the 'Ben Varrey' ['Woman of the Sea'], and she was coming home from the gold coast in West Africa, but as she was sailing across the Bay of Biscay, she ran into a great storm, and the waves were rising like mountains. The Ben Varrey was sailing well and all her canvas holding course (?) and safe, but suddenly the gale blew like a dreadful tempest, and the highest foresail broke free, and it was flapping wildly.

Immediately Robin was up on the yard-arm, but a great sea dropped the ship and it threw her on her side, until the yard-arm was in the waves, and when the ship was on even keel again Robin was not to be seen, he was lost.

The same straightforward style is evident in John Gell's autobiographical work published in 1977 by Yn Cheshaght Ghailckagh, 'Cooinaghtyn My Aegid as Cooinaghtyn Elley' ('Reminscences of My Youth and Further Reminiscences'). However, the final copy of 'Coraa Ghailckagh' (New Year, 1957) contains a piece of original poetry by him.

John Gell
Aalican, *1957*

My ragh shiu seose trooid Skylley Chreest,
Trooid Skylley Chairbrie as Malew,
Gys buill ny moainee, freoaie as rheeast;
Treigeil ny baljyn, seose da'n clieau,
Faagail ny raaidyn mooarey lhean
Dy hooyl ny bayryn cam as coon;
Yn boayl ta'n ushag goaill srrane [sic, for arrane]
Erskyn yn cloie as thaish y trooan,
Yn boayl ta bossan, luss as blaa
Nyn soaral millish skeaylley lhean.
Ny s'yrjey foast, ta'n aittin slaa
Lesh airhey-wuigh yn clane rheestane –
Chyndaa! As tastey 'ghoaill jeh'n reayrt
Ta sheeyney magh gys foddid reir,
Lesh daaghyn sollys skeeaylt mygeayrt
Er glion as magheryn, keayn as speyr.
Cre'n aalid, kiune as eunyssagh!
Roauil mygeayrt er feiy yn laa,
Er-lhiams dy beagh eh taitnyssagh
Ayns shoh dy vaghey son dy bra.! [sic]

Translation
Tranquility, *1957*

If you were to go up through Kirk Christ [Rushen],
Through Kirk Arbory and Malew,
To the places of the turbary, heather and moor;
Forsaking the towns, up to the mountain,
Leaving the broad high roads
To walk the twisting and narrow lanes;
The place where the bird sings
Above the playing and the murmur of the stream,
The place where the herb, plant and flower
Broadcast wide their sweet smelling.
Higher still, the gorse paints
With golden yellow the whole moorland –
Turn! And take heed of the view
That stretches out to the distance as far as possible,
With bright colours scattered about
On glen and fields, sea and sky.
What beauty, serene and delightful!
Roaming about throughout the day,
I think that it would be pleasant
To live here forever!

John Gell also undertook a translation of Tennyson's 'Morte d'Arthur' which demonstrates his ability to produce a very close paraphrase of the original. This is the opening section.

John Gell
Morte D'Arthur, *c.1960s*

Eisht feiy'n laa ren feiyr'n caggee rowl
Ny mast' ny sleityn rish y vooir gheuree,
Derrey va'n Boayrd Ree Adha, fer lurg fer,
Er duittym ayns Lyonnesse mygeayrt nyn Jiarn
Ree Adha; eisht, er-yn-oyr v'eh ny lhottey dowin,
Hrog seose dy ghastey Bedevere yn Ree,
Ard Vedevere, fer s'jerree jeh ooill' e Chrightyn,
As dymmyrk eh gys keeill eh, rish y vagher:
Va'n Charree brisht, as Crosh ny vrishey neesht,
Shassoo er meer dhoo dy halloo lhome;
Er y derrey heu faarkey, as er'y cheu elley

Hoie ushtey mooar, as va'n eayst lane.

Eisht loayr Ree Adha rish y Bedevere:
"Nee eiyrtys yn laa jiu feasley slane
Yn commeeys share jeh Crightyn ard-ghooagh
Jehsyn ta'n seihll freayll goo. Lheid y saveen
T'ad cadley, ny deiney bynney lhiam. Er-lhiam
Nagh dermayd arragh, ec traa erbee ry-heet
Taitnys da'n annym lesh taggloo jeh aghtyn ooasle,
Shooyl mygeayrt ny garaghyn as plaaseyn
Jeh Camelot, myr ayns ny laghyn roish-nish.
Ta mee stroiet liorish'n sleih ren mee croo,
Ga dy loo Merlin ddoys dy darrins er-ash
Dy reill keayrt elley; agh lhig da ve, cre vees!
Ta mish bwoailt dy dowin trooid my chione,
Dy n'egooish cooney, cha vaikyms'n irree-laa:
Er-y-fa gow uss nish yn cliwe Excalibur,
Va my voyrn, son t'ou cooinaghtyn cren aght
Ayns ny shenn laghyn, mun-laa souree, ren roih
Girree seose magh ass mean y logh
Coamrit ayns sheeidey bane, druiagh, yindyssagh,
Greimmey yn cliwe, as kys dymmyrt mee tessyn,
As ghow mee eh, as er cheau eh gollrish Ree;
As raad erbee veem inshit ayns arrane,
Ayns traa ry-heet, bee shoh neesht er ny hoiggal.
Agh nish ny jean cumrail, gow uss Excalibur
As ceau eh foddey magh ayns mean y logh:
Freill arrey gyere, as cur lhiat fockle hym."

Literal translation of the Manx
Morte D'Arthur

Then throughout the day the noise of battle rolled
Amongst the mountains by the sea of winter,
Until King Arthur's Table, one by one,
Had fallen in Lyonnesse about their Lord
King Arthur; then, because he was wounded deep,
Bedevere [sic] expertly lifted up the King,
Great Bedevere, the last one of all his Knights,
And he carried him to a church, by the field:
The Chancel was broken, and a Cross in a broken state too,
Standing on a dark piece of barren land;
On the one side an ocean, and on the other side

Sat a great water, and the moon was full.
Then spoke King Arthur to Bedevere:
"The result of this day today undo the whole
Of the best fellowship of famed Knights
Of which the world keeps word. Such the sleep
They're sleeping, the men I loved. I think
That we will never ever give, at any time to come
Pleasure to the soul with talking of worthy acts,
Walking about the gardens and palaces
Of Camelot, as in the days before now.
I am destroyed by the people I created,
Though Merlin swore to me that I would come back
To rule another time; but let it be, what will be!
I am struck deeply through my head,
That without help, I won't see the rise of day:
For which reason take you now the sword Excalibur,
That was my pride, for you remember how it was
In the old days, a summer's mid-day, an arm
Rose up out of the middle of the lake
Clothed in white silk, mystic, wonderful,
Holding the sword, and how I rowed across,
And I took it, and have worn it like a King;
And wherever I may be mentioned in a song,
In time to come, this too shall be understood.
But now don't delay, take you Excalibur
And throw it far out in the middle of the lake:
Keep sharp watch, and bring word to me."

Original poem by Tennyson
Morte D'Arthur

So all day long the noise of battle roll'd
Among the mountains by the winter sea;
Until King Arthur's table, man by man,
Had fall'n in Lyonnesse about their Lord,
King Arthur: then, because his wound was deep,
The bold Sir Bedivere uplifted him,
Sir Bedivere, the last of all his knights,
And bore him to a chapel nigh the field,
A broken chancel with a broken cross,
That stood on a dark strait of barren land.
On one side lay the Ocean, and on one
Lay a great water, and the moon was full.

> Then spake King Arthur to Sir Bedivere:
> 'The sequel of to-day unsolders all
> The goodliest fellowship of famous knights
> Whereof this world holds record. Such a sleep
> They sleep – the men I loved. I think that we
> Shall never more at any future time,
> Delight our souls with talk of knightly deeds,
> Walking about the gardens and the halls
> Of Camelot, as in the days that were.
> I perish by this people which I made, –
> Tho' Merlin sware that I should come again
> To rule once more – but let what will be, be,
> I am so deeply smitten thro' the helm
> That without help I cannot last till morn.
> Thou therefore take my brand Excalibur,
> Which was my pride: for thou rememberest how
> In those old days, one summer noon, an arm
> Rose up from out the bosom of the lake,
> Clothed in white samite, mystic, wonderful,
> Holding the sword – and how I row'd across
> And took it, and have worn it, like a king;
> And, wheresoever I am sung or told
> In aftertime, this also shall be known:
> But now delay not: take Excalibur,
> And fling him far into the middle mere:
> Watch what thou seëst, and lightly bring me word.'

Whilst John Gell's Manx espouses a conversational style of late Manx, others were studying earlier texts and making conscious efforts to adopt what came to be seen as the 'classical' Manx of the Bible and other eighteenth century texts. This is demonstrated by another contributor to 'Coraa Ghailckagh', Robert L Thomson. In the following section of a story about Auddyn, published in May 1953, the included object is a distinctive feature of Robert Thomson's style.

Robert L Thomson
Skeeal Auddyn Veih'n Neear, *1953*

Haink eh ny whaiyl stiurt yn ree Sveinn, va e ennym Aki, as hirr eh bee ersyn er e hon-hene as er son y baagh. "Ta mee kiarail," as Auddyn, "dy chur y baagh da'n Ree."

Dooyrt Aki, dy voddagh eh bee y chreck dasyn, my baillesh. Dreggyr Auddyn nagh row veg echey dy chur ayns coonrey, "Agh foast baillym," as eshyn, "aght ennagh y gheddyn dy voddins y baagh y chur lhiam gys yn Ree."

Dooyrt Aki, "Foddym bee y gheddyn dhyt as aght myr ta feme ayd er, dy yannoo quaaltys rish yn Ree, agh ayns coonrey bee yn lieh cooid jeh'n vaagh lhiam-pene. As shegin dhyt smooinaghtyn er shoh – dy vow yn baagh baase, er-y-fa dy vel feme ayd er ymmodee reddyn, as ta'n argid ayd er ny vaarail, as foddee nagh bee yn eer baagh ayd ec y jerrey."

As tra smooinnee Auddyn er shen, er-lesh dy b'egin da jannoo myr va'n stiurt er ghra rish, as choard eh dy derragh eshyn yn lieh cooid jeh'n vaagh gys Aki, as ny lurg shen yinnagh yn Ree yn slane baagh y phriseil. Haink ad ny-neesht nyn guaiyl yn Ree as hass ad kiongoyrt rish y voayrd.

Cha row fys ec yn Ree quoi veagh yn dooinney shoh, as dooyrt eh rish Auddyn, "Quoi uss?" "Ta me[e] my ghooinney veih Thalloo ny Rioee," dreggyr eh, [sic] "Ta mee nish er jeet veih'n Cheer Glass, as ny lurg shen veih Lochlinn, as chiare mee dy chur lhiam hood maghauin dy row. Chionnnee mee eh lesh ooilley ny v'aym, agh nish ta mee er jeet gys doilleeid mooar – cha nel aym agh lieh-baagh ny lomarcan" [sic] as dinsh eh da'n Ree eisht kys haghyr y chooish eddyr Auddyn as Aki, yn stiurt echey.

Denee yn Ree jeh Aki, "Nee firrinagh shoh t'eh dy insh?" "S'feer eh," as yn stiurt. "As row uss smooinaghtyn, uss ren mee dty ghooinney mooar, dy nee dty oik eh dy lhiettal dooinney va kiarail dy chur lesh hym tashtey mooar, er y hon hug eh ooilley v'echey? As by vie lesh yn Ree Harald eshyn y lhiggey voish ayns shee, as eshyn ny noid dooinyn! Smooinee nish as cho cairal as t'ou er n'obbraghey 'sy chooish shoh. Veagh eh cooie uss y ve dty choyrt gy-baase, agh cha jeanyms shen y yannoo, agh hed oo ersooyl chelleeragh ass y cheer shoh, as cha jig oo arragh er-ash reesht ayns my hilley. As dhyts Auddyn, ta mee cur lheid yn booise shen as dy derragh oo dooys yn baagh slane; jean oo tannaghtyn ayns shoh maryms?"

Hug Auddyn booise da as duirree eh marish yn Ree Sveinn son tammylt.

Translation

The Story of Auddyn from the West, *1953*

He met the steward of King Sveinn, whose name was Aki, and he sought food from him for himself and for the animal. "I intend," said Auddyn, "to give the animal to the King."

Aki said, that he could sell food to him, if he wished. Auddyn replied that he had nothing to give in exchange, "But still I would wish," he said, "to find some way that I would be able to take the animal to the King."

Aki said, "I can get food for you and a way as you have need of, to have an audience with the King, but in exchange I myself will have a half-interest of the animal. And you must think on this – if the animal dies, because you need many things, and your money has been spent, and perhaps you might not have even the bear in the end."

And when Auddyn thought about that, he thought that he had to do as the steward had said to him, and he agreed that he would give the half-interest of the animal to Aki, and after that the King would value the whole animal. They both came to meet the King and they stood before the table.

The King didn't know who might be this man, and he said to Auddyn, "Who are you?" "I'm a man from Iceland," he replied. "I have now come from Greenland, and after that from Norway, and I intended to bring to you a bear. I bought it with everything I had, but now I've come to a great difficulty – all I've got is just half an animal," and he told the King then how the situation between Auddyn and Aki, his steward, happened.

The King asked Aki, "Is this true what he's telling?" "It's true," said the steward. "And were you thinking, you whom I made a great man, that it was your office to prevent a man who was intending to bring to me a great treasure, for which he gave all he had? And King Harald was content to allow to go in peace, and him an enemy to us! Think now about how justly you have worked in this case. It would be appropriate for you to be put to death, but I won't do that, but you will go away immediately out of this land, and you will never come back again in my sight. And to you, Auddyn, I give such thanks as that as if you were to give to me the whole beast; will you stay here with me?"

Auddyn gave thanks to him and he stayed with Ree Sveinn for a while.

The secretary to Yn Cheshaght Ghailckagh in succession to the founding secretary Sophia Morrison was Mona Douglas. She had compiled the 1935 'Beginning Manx Gaelic/A Manx Primer' and 'Lessons in Manx' in 1936, based on Goodwin's 'First Lessons in Manx' (1901). A number of her Manx poems were published in 'Coraa Ghailckagh', and were subsequently reprinted in 'Manninagh', a cultural magazine which ran for three issues 1971-73, and 'The Manxman', a more general magazine which ran for thirteen issues 1975-1978. A poem which appeared only in 'Coraa Ghailckagh' (No 9, May 1954) was this one about the lexicographer, Archibald Cregeen.

Mona Douglas
Bardoonys Son Archibald Cregeen, *1954*

    Tra va shin roish nish gyn-yss jeh'n phobble-hene
    'Sjarroodagh jeh'n chenn ghlare – va Manninagh dooie
    Fuirraghtyn, tastagh, shooyl ny raaidyn mooie,
    Kinjagh ayns ashlish, myr chlashtyn kiaullee meein.
    Eisht deayrt eh'n ghlare ashoonagh ain ass-hene
    Gys mooinjerys ayns cheeraghyn elley ghooie
    Er duillag clouit; er-aght ayns Mannin Veen
    Veagh deiney ry-heet cummal seyr nyn geeayll

As goaill ayns shickyrys nyn eiraght mooar.
O, ta Cregeen er n'chur dooin gioot ny smoo!
Ta spyrryd noa ayns Mannin er ny chroo –
Ta shin goaill moyrn ayns mooinjerys nish dy-liooar,
As freayll yn Chengey Ghailckagh bio 'sy theihll.

Translation
Elegy for Archibald Cregeen, 1954

When we were before now ignorant of our own people
And forgetful of the old language – there was a true Manxman
Waiting, wise, walking the roads outside,
Always in a dream, as if hearing gentle music.
Then he poured out our national language out of himself
To a relationship in other native lands
On a page printed; so that in Dear Mannin
There would be men to come holding free their intellect
And taking confidently their great heritage.
O, Cregeen has given to us the greatest gift!
A new spirit has been created in Mannin –
We take pride enough in kinship now,
And keeping the Gaelic Tongue alive in the world.

Douglas's style might be described as 'naive', frequently subordinating grammar to the expression of sentiment. The following is another elegy as it appeared in 'Coraa Ghailckagh' No 12 (November 1955):

Mona Douglas
Bardoonys Son Illiam Dhone, 1955

Ta shin keaney treih – ochone!
T'Illiam Dhone er'n gheddyn baase;
Feagh e chadley, dowin dy-liooar,
Cha vel pooar ec Illiam nish.

Trimshey orrin, mooar as beg,
Cha vel veg dy yannoo ain;
Jiarg e 'uill er cleeau gyn chiass –
Lhiass dooin cur eh fo yn drine.

Gastey as feer doaiagh v'eh,

Shassoo dy bra son cairys mie,
Toshiaght jeh ny Manninee,
Lane dy bree ayns cooyrt ny thie.

Nish t'eh feayr as creoi, gyn bio
Agh ayns shoh dy-kinjagh t'eh,
Soilshey magh myr feniagh dooin,
Cur ardsmooinaght orrin dy-bra:

Cha vel marroo Illiam Dhone –
T'eh nyn gione, nyn laue, nyn gree:
Bio dy-bragh ayns skeeallyn t'eh,
Toshiaght jeh ny Manninee!

Translation
Elegy for Illiam Dhone, *1955*

We are lamenting sadly – ochone!
Illiam Dhone has died;
Peaceful his sleep, deep enough,
Illiam has no power now.

Sadness affects us, great and small,
There is nothing for us to do;
Red his blood on a breast without warmth –
We need to put him beneath the thornbush.

Clever and very decent he was,
Standing always for good justice,
The foremost of the Manx people,
Full of energy in court or house.

Now he is cold and stiff, without life
But here he always is,
Shining out as a hero to us,
Making us greatly to reflect always:

Illiam Dhone is not dead –
He is our head, our hand, our heart:
Alive for ever in stories he is,
Foremost of the Manx people!

'Coraa Ghailckagh' came to an end with its 14th edition at New Year 1957 because 'the income has never been sufficient to meet expenditure; the number of subscribers has fallen, many are in arrears, costs have risen, and the funds of the Society are insufficient to meet the annual deficiency.' Yn Cheshaght Ghailckagh continued to produce material to preserve and pass on the language, but its energies were boosted by the return home in 1962 of Douglas Crebbin Fargher, also widely known as Doolish y Karagher. A notable success was an edition of Edmund Goodwin's 'First Lessons in Manx' revised by Robert Thomson and published in 1965, which has remained in print ever since. Doug Fargher himself undertook the publication of a series of booklets under the generic title, 'The Manx Have A Word For It'. As he stated in one of them:

> The names have been obtained from all the available Manx sources, both written and oral, and some from Scottish and Irish Gaelic (for which I make no apology whatsoever). If Manx Gaelic names have been lost – as so many obviously have – due to neglect and to the former 'disrepute' of the language, then they must be restored if we are going to preserve the Manx Gaelic as a living language.

1968 saw a new approach to language teaching with 'Gaelg Trooid Jallooghyn', the text by Brian Stowell and line drawings by Philip Leighton Stowell. Brian Stowell has been involved from 1973 in writing articles in Manx for 'Carn', the quarterly magazine of the Celtic League, writing largely political commentary in the language. He also produced a number of courses for teaching Manx, such as 'Bunneydys', published by Yn Cheshaght Ghailckagh in 1974. We shall return to more of his work later.

By the early to mid 1970s, one of the tasks for the monthly committee meeting of Yn Cheshaght Ghailckagh was to arrange a rota for a short weekly summary of the news in Manx on Manx Radio. One person willing to contribute, but not enthused at delivering a news bulletin, was Robert Corteen Carswell. He began a series of contributions which included some news and comment, but also original short, comic vignettes based round the characters in The Goon Show. It was discovered that Manx Radio's schedule had allotted 15 minutes to a programme in Manx, so Carswell made use of the time with further original writing in comic programmes, short plays and documentaries. Carswell was joined by Peggy Carswell, Colin and Cristl Jerry and David Fisher. However, the scripts, some of which survive, have never been published.

In 1976, Yn Cheshaght Ghailckagh published 'Skeealaght', a collection of short stories and articles by four writers: Lewis y Crellin, John y Crellin, Colin y Jerree, and Shorus y Creayrie. The book was subtitled 'Shiartanse dy skeealyn ass beealarrish ny shenn Vanninee as jeh deiney elley' ('Some stories from the oral tradition of the old Manx people and from other people'). The foreword by Shorus y Creayrie sets out the intentions of the book:

Shorus y Creayrie (George Broderick)
Skeealaght – Raa-Toshee, *1976*

Foddee dy re yn lioar shoh yn chied lioar v'er ny yannoo dy bollagh ayns Gaelg rish lane bleeantyn. Er yn aght shoh she nyn aigney eh cur roish deiney as foays mie ocsyn er studeyrys ny Gaelgey lheid ny skeealyn shoh ta cooid veg anchaslagh rish ny va ry gheddyn roie. Ta shiartanse dy skeealyn aynshoh aashagh dy liooar daueyn nagh vel foast schleioil lesh y Ghaelg, as ta fir elley ayn ta gaase glioon er glioon ny s'doillee as she lheid y shoh ta er ny orraghey hug sleih ta flaoil sy Ghaelg. As s'treisht lhien dy bee ad ymmydoil da dy chooilley ghooinney s'mie lesh lhaih Gaelg chammah's taggloo sy Ghaelg.

Translation
Story-telling – Foreword, *1976*

It's possible that this book is the first book that was done wholly in Manx for many years. In this way it's our intention to place before people who appreciate the study of Manx stories the like of these that are a little bit different from what was available previously. Some of the stories here are easy enough for those who are not yet practised in Manx, and there are others that grow little by little more difficult and it's the like of these that have been aimed at people who are fluent in Manx. And we hope that they'll be useful to everybody who likes reading Manx as well as talking in Manx.

The monthly committee meeting of Yn Cheshaght Ghailckagh also arranged a rota for contributors to a column in Manx in a weekly newspaper, The Manx Star. Occasional contributions in Manx had been made under the title, 'Fockle ayns dty Chleaysh' ('A Word in your Ear') by Charles Cain under the pseudonym 'Branlaadagh' ('a raver, a person incoherent in his talk'). This appeared up until 1976. A more recent occasional Manx column in newspapers has revived the name 'Fockle ayns dty Chleaysh'.

In the 1970s, Doug Fargher had joined the newspapers advertising staff and began a weekly column in The Manx Star in 1976 under the title 'Noon as Noal' ('From here and there'), using the nickname 'Breagagh' ('Liar'). He wrote reminiscences of his time in the army and of his work in Africa and Scotland; and included translations he had made of Scottish songs. However, in view of work on his English-Manx dictionary (published 1979), he invited others to take over the task of providing material for the column. George Broderick (Shorus y Creayrie) was undertaking PhD research into Gaelic, and was able to contribute translations into Manx of stories collected in Scotland, and of Manx material from the Manx Musuem. This included songs and rhymes, and also the work of Neddy Beg Hom Ruy (Edward Fargher). He also wrote articles in Manx about his interpretation of the history of the Scandinavian period in the Island. Broderick subsequently published much of this material in academic papers.

An original voice to emerge at this time was Colin Jerry, who had been one of the four contributors of material to 'Skeealaght'. Starting in 1976, he wrote a series of stories satirising what was happening in the Island, using well-known children's stories as a basis. This is the first of them.

Colin y Jerree (Colin Jerry)
Ny Three Muckyn Beggey, 1976

Feer foddey er dy henney, roish my screeu ad sheese skeeal erbee, as tra va deiney as beiyn loayrt rish nyn geilley as baghey cooidjagh ayns shee, va ellan beg ayn. Va'n sleih va cummal er'n ellan beg shoh feer ghennal, ga dy row ad g'obbragh bunnys feiyn'n [sic] laa, as ga nagh row monney argid oc. Va nyn baitchyn slayntoil, va ny magheryn oc messoil, as va'n keayn lome lane dy eeastyn mooarey. Myr shen cha row monney oc agh cha row ad g'eearree monney as cha lhiass daue g'obbragh ro hrong.

Ayns ny laghyn v'ayn shen va three muckyn beggey baghey boayl ennagh er'n ellan, as gollrish yn sleih elley v'ad gennal dy-liooar derrey'n laa haink yn filliu dys nyn ghorrys. Cha s'aym cre voish haink eh agh t'ad gra dy daink eh voish ellan mooar elley faggys da'n ellan beg.

"S'mie lhiam yn boayl shoh," dooyrt eh rish-hene. "Er-lhiams dy voddym baghey dy-mie ayns shoh."

Hie eh lesh shilley er ny three muckyn beggey. Tra haink eh dys yn dorrys ghow ad aggle roish hoshiaght. V'ad shieltyn [sic] dy row ad er chlashtyn lhied y skeeal shoh roie.

Aghterbee, cha dooyrt yn filliu veg mychione sheidey sheese troggalyn agh dooyrt eh, "S'mie lhiam yn cummal beg shoh, as y gharey as y reayrt yindyssagh. B'vie lhiam baghey ayns shoh mee-hene. C'red ta shiu gra?"

"Cha nel reamys ain," dooyrt ny three muckyn beggey, "as myrgeddin t'ou fakin yn mooadys jeh'n gharey, ta palchey dy vee er-nyn-son hene, agh cha voddagh shin beaghey uss neesht. Ta ourys orrin neesht dy darragh drogh smooinaghtyn stiagh ayns dty chione keayrt ennagh, as beemayd eeit eu."

"Cha nel mee cheet er shen," dooyrt yn filliu. "She my yeearree eh yn cummal shoh y chionnaghey."

Ghow ny three muckyn beggey yindys er shen as loayr ad rish nyn geilley rish tammylt. Fy-yerrey dooyrt fer jeu,

"Cha nel shin lane shickyr dy voddagh shin creck nyn dhie as nyn dhalloo. S'lesh yn Ree ad as ta shin g'eeck mayl da er-nyn-son."

"C'red ta'n mayl shen my-ta?" vrie yn filliu.

"Ta shin g'eeck possan dy shuin gagh sourey da," dooyrt ad.

"Hem lesh shilley er," dooyrt yn filliu roo, "as yiowym magh dy-chooilley red mychione yn chooish," dooyrt yn filliu.

Myr shen hie eh kionefenish y Ree as vrie eh jeh shiartanse ny [dy] feyshtyn croutagh as aghtal. Erreish da clashtyn rish dooyrt yn Ree:
"S'feer dy vel mee goaill mayl son yn thalloo. Agh cha nee lhiams eh. Cha nel mee agh freayl yn thalloo ass leih yn sleih. Fod ny three muckyn beggey creck kied dy vaghey ayns nyn dhie dhyt."

Hie yn filliu er-ash dys thie ny three muckyn beggey as dinsh eh yn clane skeeal roo.

"Ta palchey dy argid aym," dooyrt eh. "C'woad ta shiu g'eearree son yn tannys?"

Hayrn eh argid magh ass e phoggaid as chum eh ny noteyn fo stroinyn ny muckyn. Cha row ad er vakin wheesh dy argid ayns nyn mea as roish my row fys oc c'red va'd jannoo va'n thie creckit as va'd nyn shassoo cheu mooie.

"C'red neemayd nish?" dooyrt ad rish nyn geilley. "Cha nel thie erbee ain nish. Lhisagh shin shirrey er fer elley."

Hooyll ad mygeayrt yn ellan feie'n laa as tra haink yn coleayrtys cha row thie erbee foast oc. Cha row thie erbee elley follym as cha jinnagh fer erbee creck thie daue er-yn-oyr dy row fys ec dy-chooilley pheiagh nagh beagh thie erbee elley rygheddyn. Yn oie shen v'ad eginit dy chadley fo'n chleigh. Er'n laa er-giyn hie ad kionefenish yn Ree as vrie ad ersyn son cooney.

"Cha nodmayds veg y yannoo," dooyrt yn Ree. "T'ou er chreck dty eiraght, as cha nel thie ny thalloo erbee elley foddym cur diu. Shegin diu goll er-ash dys yn 'illiu as briaght ersyn vel eh arryltagh dy chreck yn thie er-ash diu."

Myr shen ren ny three muckyn ny dooyrt yn Ree roo.

"Cha nel mee g'eearree shen y yannoo er chor erbee," dooyrt eh. "Inshyms treealtys noa diu. S'lhiams yn thie agh fod shiu baghey ayns my hie myr ta shiu booiagh argid son mayl y chur dou. Eeckyms mee-hene yn mayl shuinagh da'n Ree."

"Cha nel monney argid ain er-lhimmey jeh'n argid hooar shin voyd-hene," dooyrt ad. "Cre fodmayd jannoo tra ta ooilley'n argid shen ersooyl?"

"Shegin diu g'obbragh ny s'creoie 'sy gharey as creck lossreeyn, praaseyn as y lhied shen," dooyrt yn filliu. "Fod shiu cur ad ersooyl dys ardjyn elley."

Cha row red erbee elley fod ny three muckyn beggey jannoo as va'd eginit dy heet dy ve sorch dy vondaghyn 'sy cheer oc-hene. Laa ny Jees [sic] ny-sanmey va'n Ree shooyll 'syn ard-valley as haink yn filliu ny-whaiyl. Va'n filliu scryssey dy lhean.

"C'red t'ou er ve jannoo?" dooyrt yn Ree.

"Mish!" dreggyr yn filliu, "cha nel mish er ve jannoo veg. Cha nel mee agh er n'ghoaill toshiaght. Fuirree ort as jeeagh orrym!"

Translation
The Three Little Pigs, *1976*

A very long time ago, before they wrote down any story, and when men and animals spoke to each other and lived together in peace, there was a little island. The people who were living in this little island were very happy, though they were working almost right through the day, and though they didn't have much money. Their children were healthy, their fields were fruitful, and the sea was chock full of big fish. So they didn't have much but they didn't want much and they didn't have to work too hard.

In those days there were three little pigs living somewhere in the island, and like the other people they were happy enough until the day the wolf came to their door. I don't know where he came from but they say that he came from another big island near to the small island.

"I like this place," he said to himself. "I reckon that I can live well here."

He went to visit the three little pigs. When he came to the door they were afraid of him at first. They imagined that they'd heard a story like this before.

Anyway, the wolf said nothing about blowing down buildings but he said, "I like this smallholding, and the garden and the wonderful view. I'd like to live here myself. What do you say?"

"We don't have room," said the three little pigs, "and besides you see the size of the garden, there's plenty of food for our own selves, but we couldn't feed you as well. We're also suspicious that a bad thought would come into your head some time and we'd be eaten by you."

"That's not what I mean," said the wolf. "It's my wish to buy this property."

The three little pigs were surprised at that and they spoke together for a while. Eventually one of them said,

"We're not completely sure that we could sell our house and our land. They belong to the King and we pay rent to him for them."

"What's that rent, then?" asked the wolf.

"We pay a bunch of rushes each summer to him," they said.

"I'll go and see him," said the wolf to them, "and I'll find out everything about this issue," said the wolf.

So he went before the King and he asked him certain crafty and clever questions. After he had heard him the King said:

"It's true that I take rent for the land. But it's not mine. I only keep the land on behalf of the people. The three little pigs can sell you permission to live in their house."

The wolf went back to the house of the three little pigs and he told them the whole story.

"I have plenty of money," he said. "How much do you want for the tenancy?"

He pulled money out of his pocket and he held the notes under the noses of the pigs. They hadn't seen that much money in their lives and before they knew what they were doing the house was sold and they were standing outside.

"What shall we do now?" they said to each other. "We don't have a house now. We ought to look for another one."

They walked round the island throughout the day and when the gloaming came they still didn't have a house. There was no other house empty and nobody else would sell a house to them because everybody knew that there wouldn't be another house available. That night they were forced to sleep beneath the hedge. On the following day they went before the King and they besought him for help.

"We can't do anything," said the King. "You've sold your heritage, and there's no other house or land at all that I can give you. You must go back to the wolf and ask him whether he's willing to sell the house back to you."

So the three pigs did as the King said to them.

"I don't want to do that at all," he said. "I'll tell you a new proposal. The house is mine but you can live in my house as long as you're content to give money to me for rent. I myself will pay the rush rent to the King."

"We don't have much money apart from the money we got from you yourself," they said. "What can we do when all of that money is gone?"

"You must work harder in the garden and sell vegetables, potatoes and that sort of thing," said the wolf. "You can send them away to other areas."

There was nothing else the three little pigs could do and they were forced to become more or less slaves in their own country. A day or two later the King was walking in the capital and the wolf met him. The wolf was grinning widely.

"What have you been doing?" said the King.

"Me!" replied the wolf, "I've not been doing anything. I've only just started. Just wait and watch me!"

When George Broderick left the Island to further his academic career, Doug Fargher again took up the task of preparing material for 'Noon as Noal'. In particular, he wrote of meeting the native speakers of Manx. This is one of his reminiscences of the summer in 1948, when he was a 22 years old, having come to realise the importance of Manx from a Welsh-speaking friend during his three years in the army.

Doug Fargher

Gynsaghey Gaelg, *1977*

Un laa er y tourey shen va mee hene as my Yishag as my Warree goll trooid Creneash ayns gleashtan my ayrey as dooyrt my Warree, "Lhig dooin cur shilley er Plucky Ned heese ec Thie Harry Kelly, cha nel mee er n'akin Ned rish tammylt liauyr."

Va Ned as my Yishag Vooar Evan Crebbin er ve feer choardit tra v'ad shiaulley cooidjagh ayns lhongyn "Coast Lines", er y fa dy row Gaelg ec yn jees oc as erskyn shen v'ad nyn gheiney mooinjerey er y fa dy row un warree oc, enmyssit "Yn Chenn Pheiagh" as ish cummal ec Yn Owe. Shimmey skeeal cheayll mee voish Ned Maddrell ny s'anmey mychione Yn Chenn Pheiagh as y Gaelg vie eck!

Ansherbee, hie shin sheese dys Thie Harry Kelly dy akin y fer shoh va enmyssit "Plucky Ned" liorish my Warree, as hie shin stiagh 'sy thie as honnick mee dooinney gennal, red beg feagh as red beg croymm, ny hoie cooyl chiollee [for keeil chiollee], as chelleeragh ghow eshyn as my warree toshiaght dy loayrt ass y Vaarle Vanninagh, jannoo ymmyd jeh "thee" as "thou" as y lhied, myr va cliaghtey yn shenn sleih ec y traa shen ayns Mannin. Lurg tammylt hug my warree enney dou er Ned as dooyrt ee dy row eh enmyssit Mainshtyr Maddrell as dy row eh er ve shiaulley marish my yishig vooar as dy row Gaelg vie echey. Dinsh my warree da Ned dy row suim aym er y Ghaelg as va Ned jeant magh dy chlashtyn shen as dooyrt eh red ennagh dou 'sy Ghaelg agh cha hoig mee fockle jeh! Agh va mee ny s'croutee na shen son ooilley son va mee er lhaih "Coayl Yn Brig Lily" liorish Juan Nelson, tammylt roish shen as va fys aym dy row ny focklyn "Dooinney dy Yee" yn Ghaelg son "Man of God" (ta ny fockleyn shen ayns 'Coayl y Vrig", ec yn jerrey bunnys.) Quoi haink stiagh er dorrys Thie Harry Kelly ec y kiart vinnid shen agh saggyrt Sostynagh as blass feer Vaarlagh echey. Chionnee eh e higgad voish Ned (va Ned freayll rick er Thie Harry Kelly ec y traa shen ass lieh Thie Tashtee Ellan Vannin) as dooyrt mee rish Ned "Dooinney dy Yee!" Lheim Ned ass e hoiag bunnys as dooyrt eh ayns Baarle, "Ren oo gra shen gollrish Manninagh dooie, immee as ynsee Gaelg as tar er ash ayns shoh dy loayrt rhym tra vees ee ayd!"

"Neeym," dooyrt mee, "Neeym dy jarroo," as ren mee myrgeddin. Tra va shin faagail Thie Harry Kelly honnick mee yn eayst girree 'syn aer harrish Cronk yn Arrey as va fys aym dy row "eayst" yn Ghaelg son "moon" as vrie mee jeh Ned, tra va shin er chee goll, "Cre'n aght ta shiu fockley magh 'eayst'," as dinsh eh dou.

Ymmodee keayrtyn neayr's yn laa shen ta Ned as mee hene er ve garaghtee mychione yn chied laa hie mee dy akin eh ayns Creneash, as ny s'anmey tra va Gaelg flaaoil aym yiarragh eh rhym "Ta'n Ghaelg ayds ny share na'n Ghaelg v'ec dty Yishag Vooar nish," as va mee gollrish moddey as daa amman echey tra va mee clashtyn Ned gra shen rhym."

Translation
Learning Manx, 1977

One day that summer I myself and my Father and my Grandmother were going through Cregneish in my father's car and my Grandmother said, "Let's go and see Plucky Ned down at Harry Kelly's Cottage, I haven't seen Ned for a long time."

Ned and my Great Grandfather Evan Crebbin had been very chummy when they were sailing together in the "Coast Lines" vessels, because they both had Manx and on top of that they were related because they had the same grandmother, called "The Old Person" who lived at The Howe. Many a story I heard from Ned Maddrell later about The Old Person and the good Manx she had!

Anyway, we went down to Harry Kelly's Cottage to see this person who was called "Plucky Ned" by my Grandmother, and we went into the house and I saw a pleasant man, a bit quiet and a bit stooped, seated at the fire side, and immediately he and my grandmother started to talk Manx English dialect, using "thee" and "thou" and the like, as was the custom of the old people at that time in Man. After a while my grandmother introduced me to Ned and she said that he was called Mr Maddrell and that he'd been sailing with my great grandfather and that he had good Manx. My grandmother told Ned that I had an interest in Manx and Ned was delighted to hear that and he said something to me in Manx but I didn't understand a word of it! But I was craftier than that for all because I'd been reading "The Loss of the Brig Lily" by John Nelson, a while before that and I knew that the words "Dooinney dy Yee" were the Manx for "Man of God" (those words are in "The Loss of the Brig", almost at the end.) Who came in at the door of Harry Kelly's Cottage at that very minute but an English clergyman with a very English accent. He bought his ticket from Ned (Ned was looking after Harry Kelly's Cottage at that time on behalf of the Manx Museum) and I said to Ned "Dooinney dy Yee!" Ned almost jumped out of his seat and he said in English, "You said that like a true Manxman, go and learn Manx and come back here to talk with me when you have it!"

"I will," I said, "I will indeed," and I did too. When we were leaving Harry Kelly's Cottage I saw the moon rising in the sky over Cronk yn Arrey and I knew that "eayst" was the Manx for "moon" and I asked Ned, when we were about to go, "How do you pronounce 'eayst'," and he told me.

Many times since that day have Ned and myself been laughing about the first day I went to see him in Cregneish, and later when I had fluent Manx he would say to me, "Your Manx is better than the Manx that your Great Grandfather had now," and I was like a dog with two tails when I heard Ned say that to me.

Doug Fargher joined a small body of young language enthusiasts in visiting native speakers of Manx and recording them, thanks to money put up to buy a tape recorder by John Gell. As Doug wrote in 'Noon as Noal', 'Lhisagh Juan y Geill er ve chebbit yn Chrosh Cheltiagh (airh) dy beagh yn lhied ayn' – 'John Gell ought to have been offered the Celtic Cross (gold) if there was the like.' Doug's own reminscences triggered a series of contributions from some of those other enthusiasts, particularly Mark Braide, Charles Craine and Leslie Quirk.

Mark Braide describes the result of a cycle ride from Douglas to meet a friend in Port St Mary and then to go up to Cregneish in search of Manx speakers:

Mark Braide
Harry Kelly, *1977*

"Vel peiagh erbee ayns y valley beg shoh ta taggloo Gaelg?"

Cha row sheean ry chlashtyn. Hrog Thobm e volleeyn (as molleeyn chiu doo v'ad) as loayr eh ny goan cheddin dy meeley myr rish hene, eisht hyndaa eh gys e heshaghyn as vrie eh jeu. Yeeagh ad yn derrey yeh er y jeh elley, as eisht, lesh un aigney, chrie ad nyn ging. Hyndaa Thobm Kelly rooin. "Cha nel," dooyrt eh, "cha nel Gaelg erbee loayrit ayns shoh nish, shirr jee ayns Purt Noo Moirrey." Va shoh naight trimshagh as bunnys erskyn credjue agh son shoh as ooilley va ourys aym dy row eh ginsh breag.

Lurg faagail yn tholtan, as gennaghtyn mollit, veeit shin rish dooinney coamrit myr saggyrt ny hassoo ec giat cheu mooie jeh thie thooit. Va ennym "Cummal beg" scruit erskyn dorrys y hie as va shoh leshtal dooin dy stappal as taggloo rish, jannoo imraa jeh'n eilkin ain. Va'n ennym echey Cooke as dooyrt eh rooin ayns aght fastagh dy row eh yn cliaghtey echey dy lhaih y Vible Manninagh gagh laa.

"Dy jarroo," dooyrt mee, "ta shen yindyssagh son ta mee credjal dy vel oo dty Hostynagh liorish dty hengey. Va shin jerkal dy chlashtyn Gaelg goll er loayrt ayns shoh agh dinsh ad dooin nagh vel pyagh taggloo Gaelg nish."

Ren eh gearey choud as v'eh jeeaghyn cour y tholtan. "Vel oo fakin y shenn ghooinney ayns shen? Ta Gaelg flaaoil echey," dooyrt eh. "T'eh goaill aggle mooar roish joarreeyn, agh trooid marym, as hee mayd, son bee eh red scammyltagh myr ta shiu er jeet voish Doolish dy gholl ersooyl dyn clashtyn fockle erbee." Hie shin marish sheese y bayr beg, raad, ec oirr y bayr, va'n shenn ghooinney croymmit sheese ec niee e laueyn ayns ammair chloaie.

"Harry," dooyrt nyn garrey noa, "ta'n dooinney aeg shoh er jeet voish Doolish dy chlashtyn paart dy Ghaelg: son shickyr cha jean shiu eh y hyndaa ersooyl mollit."

"Aw," dooyrt Harry, "cha s'ayms." Eisht hass eh seose chirrymaghey e laueyn er lhiatteeyn e vreechyn as yeeagh eh dy gyere orrym. "Cha nel agh paart dy focklyn ayms – te bunnys ooilley jarroodit ayms. Er aght erbee shegin dou goll thie dy yannoo aarloo cappan dy hey son Juan as Thobm nish."

"Cum ort, Harry," dooyrt nyn garrey. "Cre'n driss t'ort? Abbyr red ennagh ta mee guee orts rish y dooinney aeg."

Duirree Harry as dooyrt eh, "As ta shiu er jeet voish Doolish, ghooinney aeg? Oh m'arrane – ta shen raad liauyr – agh cre'd t'ou laccal clashtyn?"

"Red erbee, sailliu," dooyrt mish.

"Eaisht jee, eisht," dooyrt eh, as loayr eh Padjer y Chiarn 'sy Ghaelg. Cre cha yindyssagh va dy chlashtyn yn Ghaelg firrinagh son y chied cheayrt.

Translation
Harry Kelly, 1977

"Is there anyone in this village that speaks Manx?"

There wasn't a sound to be heard. Tom raised his eyebrows (and thick black eyebrows they were) and he spoke the same words softly as though to himself, then he turned to his fellows and he asked them. They looked from one to another, and then, with one accord, they shook their heads. Tom Kelly turned to us. "There isn't," he said, "there's no Manx spoken here now, look in Port St Mary." This was sad news and almost beyond belief but for this and all I suspected that he was telling a lie.

After leaving the tholtan, and feeling disappointed, we met a man dressed like a clergyman standing at a gate outside a thatched house. The name "Cummal beg" was written above the door of the house and this was an excuse for us to stop and talk to him, making reference to our mission. His name was Cooke and he said to us in a serious manner that it was his custom to read the Manx Bible every day.

"Indeed," I said, "that's wonderful because I believe that you're an Englishman by your accent [tongue]. We were expecting to hear Manx being spoken here but they said to us that nobody talks Manx now."

He laughed as he was looking towards the tholtan. "Do you see the old man there? He has fluent Manx," he said. "He's greatly afraid of strangers, but come with me, and we'll see, because it would be a scandalous thing as you've come from Douglas to go away without a single word." We went with him down the little road, where, at the edge of the road, the old man was bended down washing his hands in a stone channel.

"Harry," said our new friend, "this young man has come from Douglas to hear some Manx: you surely can't turn him away disappointed."

"Aw," said Harry, "I don't know." Then he stood up drying his hands on the sides of his trousers and he looked sharply at me. "I only have a few words –I've forgotten nearly all of it. Anyway I have to go home to get a cup of tea ready for John and Tom now."

"Hold on, Harry," said our friend. "What's the hurry on you. Say something for the young man, I'm begging you."

Harry paused and he said, "And you've come from Douglas, young man? Upon my soul – that's a long way – but what do you want to hear?"

"Anything at all, please," I said.

"Listen then," he said, and he recited the Lord's Prayer in Manx. How wonderful it was to hear the true Manx for the first time.

Harry Kelly's name remains well-known because Harry Kelly's Cottage is an important part of Manx National Heritage's Cregneish village museum. As Mark Braide wrote of that cottage,

"Ta enney ec dy chooilley lhaihder er Thie Harry Kelly, as cha nhyrrys. Ta co-caslysyn jee ry-akin er Lioaryn-Imbee, caartyn yn Nollick as er nyn gloughyn-phost, agh var-a-mish cha beagh enney ec Harry er e hie hene ec y laa t'ayn jiu. T'ee er ve caghlaait ass towse ..."

"Every reader knows Harry Kelly's Cottage, and it's not surprising. There are photographs of it to be seen on Calendars, Christmas cards and on our postage stamps, but I'll warrant that Harry wouldn't recognize his own house in this day and age. It's changed beyond measure ..."

Mark went on to visit Harry many times and to learn Manx from him. Charles Craine's main teacher, however, is scarcely known. Charles tells of discovering him as a Manx speaker in Peel.

Chalse y Craayne (Charles Craine)
Phillie Mac Y Phaill, *1976*

... smooinnee mee dy lhisin screeu fockle ny ghaa mychione my henn charrey as fer-ynsee Phillie Mac y Phaill voish Purt ny h-Inshey. Hooar Phillie baase roish yn Nah Chaggey as er y fa shen cha bee enney er eer yn ennym echey ec monney sleih nish.

Haink mee ny whail ayns aght quaagh. Ayns y vlein 1933 ny 1934 va nane jeh my chaarjyn feer ching lesh chiassagh as v'eh, marish e huyr, ren geddyn baase veih'n doghan shen, currit dys yn Thie Lheeys ec yn ... White Hoe ec yn traa shen freilt son sleih surranse voish chiassaghyn ny lomarcan.

Fastyr Jedoonee dy row hug mee lhiams moir adsyn va ching dys Doolish dy chur shilley orroo – as shen va kied ayn dy yannoo, trooid yn uinnag. Er yn raad erash dy valley vrie y ven my oddin goll trooid Purt ny h-Inshey dy insh da ny fir-vooinjey eck ayns shen kys va ny paitchyn eck goll er. Dooyrt mee dy raghin agh gowyms rish nish nagh ren mee shen y yannoo yn laa shen.

Aghterbee, fy-yerrey chossyn shin rish 4 Straid Vona ayns Ard-valley Purt ny h-Inshey as ayns shen va shenn ghooinney as e ven as yn 'neen echey. Va'n troor dy vraane taggloo ny mast'oc hene as va mish loayrt rish y shenn ghooinney. Va lioar kiongoyrt rish er y voayrd as, ga dy row ee bun-ry-skyn dooys, v'ee jeeaghyn neu-chadjin gollrish Bible. S'cooin lhiam gra rhym-pene, "Shegin da ve feer chrauee as shegin dooys ve feer chiaralagh dyn dy yannoo ymmyd jeh fockleyn erbee gweeagh." Ooilley yn traa va shin loayrt ry-cheilley cha dod mee goaill my hooillyn ersooyl veih'n lioar son va mee shickyr nagh row yn ghlare ayn v'ee scruit Baarle. Cha smooinee mee ec yn traa shoh dy row peiagh erbee faagit 'sy theihll va lhaih Bible Ghailckagh. Fy-yerrey dooyrt mee rish. "Vel shen y Vible t'ou lhaih, Vainshter?"

"Ta," dansoor eh.
"Cha nel ee Bible Vaarleagh noidyr?"
"Cha nel."
"Nee Bible Ghailckagh t'ayn?"
"She, Bible Ghailckagh."
"As vel oo son lhaih ee?"
"Oh, ta. Cha nel mee rieau lhaih Bible erbee elley!"

Eisht dinsh mee dy row mee er ve goaill foddeeaght d'ynsaghey yn Ghailck ooilley laghyn my vea er y fa row my yishag feer flaaoil aynjee agh cha row caa aym dy ynsaghey veihsyn er yn oyr dy dooar eh baase roish my row mee daa vlein dy eash. Va mee er n'ynsaghey kuse dy ockleyn voish shenn sleih ayns laghyn m'aegid as va mee er n'gholl dys brastyl cummit ayns Doolish ec Mnr H.P. Kelly ayns y gheurey roish yn traa shen. Vrie eh jeem foddym taggloo Gailck as dooyrt mee agh beggan beg. As dooyrt eshyn, "My jig oo dys shoh nee'ms gynsaghey dhyts ooilley yn Ghailck ny t'ayms." Ren eh jannoo e chooid share as v'eh ny fer-ynsee yindyssagh as hie mee dy chur shilley er dy chooilley fastyr Jedoonee veih'n laa dy vaik mee eh son yn chied cheayrt derrey hooar eh baase. Shee dy row er yn annym echey.

Translation
Phillie Quayle, *1976*

... I thought that I ought to write a word or two about my old friend and teacher Phillie Quayle from Peel. Phillie died before the Second War and because of that not many people will recognise even his name now.

I met him in a strange manner. In the year 1933 or 1934 one of my friends was very ill with fever and he, with his sister, who died from that disease, was put to the Hospital at the White Hoe at that time reserved for people suffering from fevers alone.

One Sunday afternoon I took the mother of those who were sick to Douglas to visit them – and that there was permission to do, through the window. On the way back home the woman asked if I could go through Peel to tell her relatives there how her children were going on. I said I could go that way but I will admit now that I didn't do that on that day.

Anyway, finally we made it to 4 Mona Street in the City of Peel and there was an old man and his wife and his daughter. The three women were talking amongst themselves and I was talking to the old man. There was a book in front of him on the table and, although it was upside-down to me, it appeared uncommon like a Bible. I remember saying to myself, "He must be very religious and I must be very careful not to use any swear words." All the time we were talking together I couldn't take my eyes off the book because I was certain that the language it was written in wasn't English. I didn't think at this time that there was anyone left in the world that was reading a Manx Bible. Eventually I said to him, "Is that the Bible you're reading, Master?"

"Yes," he answered.

"It's not an English Bible either?"

"It's not."

"Is it a Manx Bible?"

"It is, a Manx Bible."

"And are you for reading it?"

"Oh, yes. I never read any other Bible!"

Then I told [him] that I had been longing to learn Manx all the days of my life because my father was very fluent in it but I didn't have an opportunity to learn from him because he died before I was two years of age. I'd learnt several words from old people in my young days and I'd gone to a class held in Douglas by Mr H P Kelly in the winter preceding that time. He asked me can I speak Manx and I said only a little bit. And he said, "If you come here I'll teach you all the Manx that I have." He did his utmost and he was a wonderful teacher and I went to visit him every Sunday afternoon from the day that I saw him for the first time until he died. May there be peace on his soul.

Though this extract from one of Leslie Quirk's articles is nominally about Caesar Cashin, it tells us more about Charles Craine's mentor, Phillie Quayle.

Leslie Quirk
Caesar Cashin, *c.1977*

Er hoh dhyt ny cooinaghtyn ayms jeh Caesar Cashin. S'feer eh dy jarroo dy row Gaelg ry-ynsaghey ayns ny brastyllyn va goll er cummal tra va mee aeg ayns Purt ny Hinshey. By chliaghtey ain son y chooid smoo lhaih ass y Lioar Chasherick agh va caa ain dy chlashtyn rish blass Caesar hene. 'Sy vlein 1932 hie yn "Kione Doo" (my vraar Walter) as mee hene as Noreen (my huyr) gys y vrastyl va goll er cummal ec y traa shen ayns Offish Vainshtyr ny Purt ayns Purt ny Hinshey ayns Straid yn Attey. Hie shin stiagh as hoie shin sheese as yeeagh mee er dagh oltey y vrastyl as va enney mie ayms er y chooid smoo j'eu. Ny vud oc va shenn dooinney ennagh as faasaag liauyr lheeah echey as smooinee mee rhym pene, "Cre'n fa ta'n shenn dooinney shen shirrey Gaelg y ynsaghey as lhied yn eash ersyn?" Cha dooar mee freggyrt da m'eysht yn oie shen agh hooar mee eh tammylt beg ny lurg. Quoi v'ayn agh Philly Quayle, yn dooinney ooasle hene, as eshyn lum-lane dy Gaelg feer vie, agh ghow eh yindys ersyn hene doaltattym nagh dod eh ee y lhaih er chor erbee! Shoh dooyrt eh rhym pene un oie, "Va mee ronsaghey ayns kishtey ennagh as hooar mee Bible Ghaelgagh, doshil mee ee as haink fys hym nagh dod mee ee y lhaih er chor erbee as ta shen y oyr dy daink mee da'n vrastyl." Son shickyrys cha row eh feer foddey derrey va'n dooinney ooasle lhaih y Ghaelg dy flaaoil! Hie kuse j'in oie elley dys brastyl ayns thie ennagh elley fo currym Philly as va ymmodee skeealyn mie ry-chlashtyn ayns shen! Oddagh lioar ve er ny screeu mychione skeealyn Philly ...

Va Caesar Cashin gyn ourys "Ayr ny Gaelgey" ayns Purt ny Hinshey ayns ny laghyn shen. Va Gaelg feer vie echey as Gaelg yindyssagh ry-chlashtyn ec y vrastyl echey. Shegin dou gra, ny yei, dy row Gaelg foddey ny share ry-chlashtyn voish yn moghey 'sy voghrey taaley ass e veeal, tra v'eh skeeabey magh e happ as "Yn Kione Doo" as mee hene cur y bainney stiagh dasyn.

Translation
Caesar Cashin, *c.1977*

Here for you are my memories of Caesar Cashin. It's true indeed that Manx was being taught in the classes that were being held when I was young in Peel. It was our practice for the most part to read from the Holy Book but we had an opportunity to hear the accent of Caesar himself. In the year 1932 the "Kione Doo" (my brother Walter) and myself and Noreen (my sister) went to the class that was being held at that time in the Harbour Master's Office in Peel in Crown Street. We went in and sat down and I looked at each member of the class and I knew the most part of them well. Amongst them was some old man with a long, grey beard and I thought to myself, "Why is that old man trying to learn Manx when he's as old as that?" I didn't get an answer to my question that night but I got it a little while later. Who was it but Philly Quayle, the great man himself, who was full of excellent Manx, but it suddenly struck him that he couldn't read it at all. This is what he said to myself one night, "I was investigating some box and I found a Manx Bible, I opened it and it occurred to me that I couldn't read it at all and that's the reason that I came to the class." It certainly wasn't long until the great man was reading Manx fluently! Some of us went on another night to a class in some other premises under Philly's charge and there many good stories to be heard there! A book could have been written about Philly's stories ...

Caesar Cashin was without doubt the 'Father of Manx' in Peel in those days. He had very good Manx and there was wonderful Manx to be heard at his class. I have to say, for all that, that there was far better Manx to be heard from him early in the morning flowing from his mouth, when he was sweeping out his shop and "Yn Kione Doo" and myself taking the milk in to him.

'Noon as Noa' went on to include articles by younger Manx speakers, including news items, reports of events, translations of folk stories and reminiscences. Brian Stowell was determined to demonstrate that Manx was capable of dealing with a complete range of subjects in the modern world. He contributed a series of articles explaining about nuclear physics, of which these are two extracts.

Brian Stowell
Pooar Veih Chesh-Vean Vreneen: Cre Cho Gaueagh? *1977*

Ta mee er screeu mychione yn aght ta bun-stooghyn myr urraniu as raadiu spreih magh scellyn-alpha, beta as gamma. She ny chesh-veanyn jeh ny breneenyn shoh ta ceau magh ny scellyn: ny lectraneyn ta goll mygeayrt y chesh-vean, cha nel ad jannoo veg sy chooish shoh. Nish, ta breneen jeh sorch erbee cho beg as nagh vod-mayd eh y akin. Dy jarroo, cha jeanmayd dy bragh breneen erbee y "akin" lesh nyn sooillyn, ga dy vodmayd soilshaghey dy vel breneenyn ayn lesh greienyn (cha nel skeeal ny chrout!). My s'beg yn breneen, sloo foast yn chesh-vean. Lurg y Chied Chaggey va fys ec fishigee dy vel corpeenyn enmyssit "protaneyn" ayns y chesh-vean jeh gagh breneen. Ta'n protane mysh daa housane cheayrt ny strimmey na'n lectrane. Ta lught lectragh ec yn phrotane as ec y lectrane neesht: lught shickyr ec yn phrotane, as lught obballagh ec yn lectrane.

Va dy liooar jeu [fishigee] er vleaystaney urraaniu lesh naeearaneyn as er scoltey chesh-veanyn urraniu dyn yss daue. Agh roish foddey va fys ec sleih dy row red yindyssagh taghyrt: va fys oc dy row ad abyl chesh-vean y scoltey dy jinnagh ad "shottal" ny chesh-veanyn shen jannoo ymmyd jeh naeearaneyn myr bulladyn beggey. Ny sodjey na shen, deayshil gagh scoltey bree feer vooar – va chiass as scel-lyn er nyn veaysley. Ny sodjey na shen foast, deayshil gagh scoltey tooilley naeearaneyn as va ny naeearaneyn abyl tooilley scoltaghyn y yannoo. Dy jinnagh ny scoltaghyn goll er as er, veagh bree ass towse er ny feaysley. Dy chelleeragh, hoig ny fishigee dy row scansh vooar ec y chooish shoh. Oddagh bleaystan agglagh erskyn smooinaghtyn ve jeant myr shoh. Dy jarroo, sy toshiaght heill sleih ennagh dy beagh y slane seihll er ny heidey seose er y fa dy jinnagh yn aa-vuilley-driaght goll er gyn scuirr!

Translation

Power From an Atom's Nucleus: Just How Dangerous? *1977*

I've written about the way that elements like uranium and radium radiate alpha, beta and gamma rays. It's the nuclei of these atoms that throw out the rays: the electrons which go round the nucleus don't contribute anything towards this process. Now, an atom of any sort is so small that we can't see it. Indeed, we'll never "see" any atom with our eyes, though we can demonstrate that atoms exist with machines (it's not a matter of a trick!). As small as is an atom, smaller still is the nucleus. After the First War, physicists knew that there were particles called "protons" in the nucleus of each atom. The proton is about two thousand times heavier than the electron. Protons have an electrical charge, and electrons do as well: protons with a positive charge, and a negative charge in electrons.

Plenty of them [physicists] had bombarded uranium with neutrons and had split uranium nuclei without realizing it. But before long people knew that something amazing was happening: they knew that they were able to split the nuclei if they were to "shoot" the nuclei using neutrons as little bullets. Further than that, each split released tremendous energy – heat and rays were released. Further than that again, each split released more neutrons, and the neutrons were able to cause further splits. If the splits were to go on and on, there would be energy beyond measure released. Immediately, the physicists understood that there was great importance attached to this subject. A bomb terrifying beyond comprehension could be made like this. Indeed, in the beginning some people supposed that the whole world would be blown up because the chain reaction would continue without cessation!

From being a small column of perhaps 500 words, the column frequently expanded to fill, with illustrations, a good half-page of a broadsheet newspaper. An example is the 1,600 words of a piece of original writing in Manx of this period. It came in January 1978 with the first part of a story called 'Ersooyl myr Scadoo' by Robart Carsalagh (Robard y Charsalagh, Robert Corteen Carswell). The story was subsequently to peter out and remained unfinished after about a dozen episodes. However, the opening part, 'Trimshey ny hOie', was strong and dramatic. This first episode was intended to form a unified whole, which was not the case with later episodes, written on a more ad hoc basis. The first part is, therefore, given in full.

Robard y Charsalagh
Ersooyl Myr Scadoo, *1978*

Trimshey ny hoie.

V'ee screeagh choud's v'ee tuittym sheese gys y laare. Woaill ee e kione noi leac y chiollagh. Cha row sheean erbee ry-chlashtyn ny lurg shen.
    Yeeagh eh urree. V'ee feer feagh as tostagh nish. V'eh ny hassoo aynshen, jus jeeaghyn urree rish lieh vinnid, foddee, gyn ennaghtyn erbee 'sy cheeayle echey. Va'n chorree ersooyl voish nish - dy jarroo, v'ee ersooyl voish cho leah's ren eh bwoailley ee. V'eh jus jeeaghyn urree. Va kesh jiarg cloie mygeayrt folt y ven aeg: folt fynn v'eh, agh nish v'eh daahit hoal as wass. Va poyll dorraghey skeayley harrish y laare crayee. Cha dug eh tastey da'n fuill. Fy yerrey hoal, haink paart dy ennaghtyn er. Doaltattym va slane fys echey er y red agglagh shoh va jeant echey. Haink ny sooillyn echey dy ve keoie reesht, agh cha nee er coontey jeh corree shoh – nish v'eh fo aggle feer dowin.
    "Yee Ooilley-niartal," as eshyn, as cha row e choraa agh sannish, "Yee Ooilley-niartal, jean myghin orrym." Va reean 'sy chleeau echey. Hug eh shilley urree nish dy gyere, as va jeir ayns e hooillyn. Honnick eh yn fuill eck foast goll er lhiggey harrish laare y thie vooar as harrish leac y chiollagh myrgeddin. Honnick eh broo jiarg er y lieckan eck, as va fys mie echey dy dug eshyn y broo shen jee. Cha baillish jeeaghyn urree arragh. Hyndaa eh e ghreeym, as ren eh snapperal gys y dorrys, raad v'eh ny hassoo vaidjyn, meekey veih soilshey ny greiney as ny jeir echey.
    Cha row fer erbee ry-akin er y chassan cheumooie jeh'n thie. Va'n thie faggys da crosh-raad beg, raad raink y cassan shoh bayr beg. Cha row fer erbee ry-akin er y raad shoh noadyr. Va corp ny ben aeg waagh ny chooyl echey ayns dorraghys y thie, agh va eshyn ny hassoo cheumooie, as va'n ghrian soilshean er. Haink croutid er. Cha row fer erbee ry-akin – kiart dy liooar, eisht: cha row eshyn ry-akin liorish fer erbee noadyr.
    Hug eh shilley er y chrosh-raad mysh jeih stundayrt voish er y cheu-yesh.
    Doaltattym, roie eh gys y chrosh-raad. Er cheu elley y vayr lheim eh seose er y chleigh ai[t]tnit. Va barney beg eddyr ny thammagyn. Chroym eh sheese er mullagh y chleigh, er yn oyr nagh beagh e chione ry-akin er-skyn jeh kione yn aittin. Cha scuirr eh nish er chor erbee, as roie eh roish ry-lhiattee jeh'n chleigh. Va fys mie echey er y cheer mygeayrt y mysh, as tra v'eh faggys da balley-hallooin, hie eh er raad sliurey ooilley mygeayrt. Cha scuirr eh derrey raink eh bayr mooar. Ren eh peeikearagh hoshiaght, roish my roie eh harrish y vayr shoh. Ny lurg shen, ersooyl lesh reesht, tessyn ny magheryn er yn aght cheddin as roie.
    Fy yerrey, v'eh ayns y ghlion, mastey ny biljyn. V'eh pandoogh, as yn ennal echey croo bodjalyn baney 'syn aer. Ga dy row eh cliaghtey shooyl y cheer shoh,

nish v'eh skee erreish da roie, as v'eh gollish. Va ennaghtyn dowin echey nish. Eish[t], hooar eh toshiaght er feddal.

"C'raad ta'n guilley shen?" as y dooinney mooar.

"S'cocoylagh [S'cosoylagh] eh dy vel eh hoal-wass 'sy ghlion reesht," as e ven, Ealish. "S'mennick t'eh aynshen."

"Shee Yee orrym, Ealish," as Ned. "Ta dty voir dy kinjagh ec y chenn cheeill, ta nyn mac dy kinjagh 'sy ghlion chaglym stoo er-e-son – cha nel mee goaill yindys dy vel sleih loayrt my-nyn-gione." Hug Ealish shilley gyere er. Loayr Ned reesht.

"S'cooin lhiam," as eshyn, "keayrt dy row ayns my skeerey hene ..."

"Nagh vel shen oyr elley?" vrie Ealish. Chum Ned e hengey. Va Ned Bridson ny ghooinney tholleee as lajer, lesh folt fynn as faasaag liauyr. Va skeerey ny mayrey echey er y Twoaie Vooar, as dy jarroo v'eh jeeaghyn gollrish Loghlinagh. Cha row yn sleih 'syn ard shoh soiaghey monney jeh'n joarree shoh voish skeerey elley, agh cha row sleih 'syn ard shen soiaghey monney jeh lught-thie Ealish noadyr. Va palchey dy 'leih cliaghtey goll gys Doolish voish yn ard shoh cour y vargey, agh yinnagh Ealish shooyl y raad ny lomarcan. Haink Ned ny quail er y raad keayrt dy row shiaght bleeaney jeig er dy henney. Ren ad taggloo rish y cheilley er y raad as ayns Doolish. Ny lurg shen, yinnagh Ned cur shilley urree dagh keayrt va margey goll er cummal. Ec jerrey'n tourey ren ad poosey.

Shen myr v'eh. Va fys ec Ned dy row eshyn ny yoarree ayns y skeerey shoh, as gyn ourys yinnagh yn sleih loayrt my-e-chione, as foddee eer noi echey – agh cha dooyrt peiagh erbee veg as eshyn kionefenish!

Hie Ned nish gys y dorrys. Yeeagh eh my-hiar, as honnick eh e vac shooyl y raad garroo faggys da'n awin. "Shoh eshyn," dooyrt eh, "ta Illiam cheet nish." Haink e ven gys y dorrys as v'ad jeeaghyn er nyn mac choud's v'eh drappal seose voish yn awin 'sy choan, jannoo ymmyd jeh cassan trooid y rhenniagh gys y chroit er yn ughtagh. V'eh ny ghuilley cho fynn as yn ayr echey, as v'eh cheet dy ve ny ghooinney cho mooar as Ned myrgeddin, ga nagh row eh agh queig bleeaney jeig dy eash.

"Fastyr mie, my ghooinney-seyr," as Ealish, "as c'red ta shen?" V'ee jeeaghyn er poagey beg v'echey.

"Oh, jus tooilley stoo son my warree – lossreeyn as y lheid," dreggyr Illiam. Hie ad ooilley stiagh 'sy thie vooar, raad va aile dy voain cloie ayns y chiollagh. Hug Illiam y poagey er y voayrd.

"V'ou uss 'sy ghlion feiy'n 'astyr shoh, eisht?" as Ealish.

"Oh, va, va," dreggyr y guilley, agh haink yn eddin echey dy ve red beg bane. "Va, va, dy jarroo."

"C'red ta jannoo ort, Illiam? Vel oo ching?" Va Ned briaght jeh.

"Cha nel, yeyd – cha nel veg jannoo orrym er chor erbee," dooyrt Illiam, "agh gyn breag erbee, ta accrys orrym!" She breag v'ayn.

"Shen yn aght lesh guillyn," as Ealish, "accryssagh dy kinjagh!"

Va Illiam ny lhie 'sy lhiabbee echey, agh cha daink cadley er. V'eh smooinaghtyn.

Cha by vie lesh lhiassaghey rish e voir as ayr. Cha row agh un c[h]arrey elley echey – bare da'n lught-thie echey ve nyn gaarjyn, myr v'eh. Nagh row sluight Chirree Corkish eh?

V'eh smooinaghtyn nish mychione y 'neen. V'eshyn ny lhie ayns chiass ny lhiabbee echey – as ish? V'eh coe ayns y dorraghys. Hooar eh nearey nish, jeh'n aght ren eh gearey 'sy ghlion. Cha row eh shickyr mychione e ennaghtyn hene. Aynshen, 'sy ghlion, v'eh slane jeant magh nagh row eh goit – nagh row eh eer fakinit – ec peiagh erbee. Eer aynshen v'eh foast fo aggle mooar; v'eh pandoogh as gollish; va reean ayns e chleeau reesht. Agh v'eh foast seyr – shen y fa ren eh gearey. Nish, ayns e lhiabbee, haink ny jeir reesht. Dy jarroo, v'eh ayns y doo as ny jeirree.

Smooinee eh er y ven aeg reesht. Smooinee eh er yn aght yeeagh ee er dy jeeragh 'sy cheeill Jedoonee. Cha nee shilley bieau fastagh v'eh – ren ee jeeaghyn er dy daaney, as she shilley ... well, shilley cuirrey v'eh. Dy mennick cheayll eh guillyn elley loayrt mychione yn aght ren ee jeeaghyn orroosyn – as ny by vie lhieusyn jannoo. As nish, yeeagh ee ersyn.

Hooar e moir baase bleeantyn er dy henney. Va fys ec Illiam nagh row yn ayr eck sthie tra hie eh gys e thie. Ren eh crankal er y dorrys.

"Trooid stiagh," as ish. "Illiam Bridson! C'red t'ou jannoo aynshoh?" V'ee loayrt rish myr ben-seyr rish guilley beg. Ren Illiam jiargaghey.

"Well," dooyrt eh, "ren uss jeeaghyn orrym 'sy cheeill jea, as ..."

"Va mee jeeaghyn er muc ayns muclagh jea – vel eshyn mayrts neesht?"

"Agh smooinee mee ..." as Illiam, agh loayr y ven aeg reesht:

"Smooinee uss? Ren uss smooinaghtyn, ghuilley beg?" Haink Illiam dy ve red beg corree.

"Cha nee uss agh shey bleeaney jeig dy eash," as eshyn, "as cha nel uss dty ven-seyr noadyr!"

"As cre'n aght ta fys ayds er mraane-seyrey?" dreggyr y ven aeg. "Er-lhiams dy vel uss dty vuc veih'n vuclagh shen!"

"Cum dty hengey! Bannee mee, va mee smooinaghtyn dy row us feer aalin ..."

"Oh," as y ven aeg, as nish ren ee loayrt ayns coraa s'inshley as s'caarjyssee, "er-lhiats dy vel mee feer aalin. Gur eh mie ayd."

"Aalin dy jarroo," as Illiam, shirrey fockleyn kenjal elley, "as smooinee mee dy ren uss cur cuirrey dou dy heet lesh shilley ort."

Ren y ven aeg mongey. "Cuirrey dhyts?" dooyrt ee, as ren ee mongey reesht. Ren Illiam mongey myrgeddin, goaill boggey jeh e coraa millish as eddin waagh. "Cuirrey dhyts?" as y ven aeg reesht. Eisht loayr ee ayns coraa ard as mooaralagh:

"Dhyts? Cha nel uss agh dty ghuilley beg boght, as mac y joarree myrgeddin. Ersooyl lhiat gys dty vuclagh, vuc!"

Nish va Illiam slane mollit, as corree dy jarroo. "As quoi uss, eisht?" dyllee eh. "T'ou uss cho boght as mish. Cha nee agh branlaadagh uss, yah!"

"Agh cha nee sluight Chirree Corkish mish," deam y ven aeg.

"Well?" as Illiam. "Well? Cha nee peccah shen!"

"She sluight Verree Dhone uss," deie yn ven aeg.

"C'red va shen?" as Illiam, as v'eh bane-c[h]orree nish. "C'red va shen?"
"Sluight Verree Dhone, sluight Verree Dhone!" ren ee floutyraght, as yn eddin as y c[h[oraa eck jannoo faghid jeh.
Woaill eh e lieckan lesh e vass. Ren ee loagan, as v'ee currit jeh cormid. Screeagh ee. V'ee screeagh choud's v'ee tuittym sheese gys y laare. Woaill ee e kione noi leac y chiollagh. Cha row sheean erbee ry-chlashtyn ny lurg shen.
Va cooinaght mie ec Illiam er y loght shoh as eshyn ny lhie 'sy lhiabbee echey. V'eh coe ayns y dorraghys. She trimshey ny hoie v'ayn.

Translation

Away Like a Shadow, *1978*

The dead of night (literally, 'Sadness of the night')

She was screaming as she was falling down to the floor. She struck her head against the hearth slab. There wasn't any sound to be heard after that.

He looked at her. She was very still and silent now. He was standing there, just looking at her for half a minute, perhaps, without any emotions in his mind. His anger was gone from him now – indeed, it was gone from him as soon as he hit her. He was just looking at her. A red froth was bubbling about the young woman's hair: blonde hair it was, but now it was stained here and there. A dark pool was spreading across the clay floor. He paid no attention to the blood. At long last, he experienced some emotion. Suddenly he knew full well what an awful thing he'd done. His eyes became wild again, but this was not because of anger – now he was very deeply scared.

"God Almighty," he said, and his voice only a whisper, "God Almighty, have mercy on me." There was a tightness in his chest. He looked at her now sharply, and there were tears in his eyes. He saw her blood still continuing to run across the floor of the kitchen and across the hearth slab as well. He saw the red bruise on her cheek, and he knew very well that he gave that bruise to her. He didn't want to look at her any more. He turned his back, and he staggered to the door, where he was standing for a short time, blinking from the sunlight and his tears.

There was nobody to be seen on the path outside the house. The house was near to a small crossroad, where this path reached a small road. There was nobody to be seen on this road either. The body of the beautiful young woman was behind him in the darkness of the house, but he was standing outside, and the sun was shining on him. Cunning came to him. There was nobody to be seen – very well, then: he wasn't to be seen by anybody either.

He cast a glance at the crossroad about ten yards from him on the right. Suddenly, he ran to the crossroad. On the other side of the road he jumped up on the gorse-clad hedge. There was a little gap between the bushes. He bent down on top of the hedge, so that his head would not be seen above the top of the gorse. He didn't stop now at all, and he ran on alongside the hedge. He knew the country round about him very well, and when he was near to a farm, he went on a longer route all around it. He didn't stop until he reached a large road. He peeped out first, before he ran across this road. After that, away he went again across the fields in the same manner as before.

Eventually, he was in the glen, amongst the trees. He was panting, and his breath was creating white clouds in the air. Though he was used to walking this country, now he was tired after running, and he was sweating. He sat down and leaned his back against a tree. His emotion was deep now. Then, he began to shake with laughter.

"Where's that boy?" said the big man.

"He's probably down there in the glen again," said his wife Ealish. "He's often there."

"For God's sake, Ealish," said Ned. "Your mother is always at the old keeill, our son is always in the glen gathering stuff for her – I'm not surprised that people talk about us." Ealish gave him a sharp look. Ned spoke again.

"I remember," he said, "once upon a time in my own parish ..."

"Isn't that another reason?" asked Ealish. Ned held his tongue. Ned Bridson was a robust and strong man, with blonde hair and a long beard. His native parish was on the north, and indeed he looked like a Viking. People in that area didn't much accept this stranger from another parish, but people in that area didn't much accept Ealish's family either. There were plenty of people accustomed to going to Douglas from this area for the market, but Ealish would walk the road alone. Ned met her on the road once upon a time seventeen years ago. They spoke to each other on the road and in Douglas. After that, Ned would call on her each time a market was being held. At the end of the summer they married. That's how it was. Ned knew that he was a stranger in this parish, and doubtless the people would talk about him, and perhaps even against him – but nobody said anything when in his presence!

Now Ned went to the door. He looked eastward, and he saw his son walking the rough road near to the river. "Here he is," he said, "Illiam is coming now." His wife came to the door and they watched their son whilst he climbed up from the river in the valley, using the path through the bracken to the croft on the upslope. He was a boy as blonde as his father, and he was becoming a man as big as Ned as well, though he was only fifteen years of age.

"Good afternoon, my good sir," as Ealish, "and what's that?" She was looking at a small bag he had.

"Oh, just more stuff for my grandmother – herbs and the like," replied Illiam. They all went into the kitchen, where the turf fire was playing in the hearth. Illiam put the bag on the table.

"You were in the glen throughout the afternoon, then?" said Ealish.

"Oh, yes, yes," replied the boy, but his face became rather white. "Yes, yes, indeed."

"What's wrong with you, Illiam? Are you ill?" Ned was asking him.

"I'm not, Dad – there's nothing wrong with me at all," said Illiam, "but without a word of a lie, I'm hungry!" It was a lie.

"That's the way with lads," said Ealish, "always hungry!"

Illiam was lying in his bed, but sleep didn't come to him. He was thinking. He didn't like lying to his mother and father. He only had one friend – it would be better for his family to be friends, as it were. Was he not a descendent of Kirree Corkish?

He was thinking now about the girl. He was lying in the warmth of his bed – and her? He was weeping in the darkness. He was ashamed now of the way he laughed in the glen. He was uncertain about his own emotion. There, in the glen, he was completely overjoyed that he wasn't caught – that he wasn't even seen – by anyone. Even there he was still greatly afraid; he was panting and sweating; there was a tightness in his chest again. But he was still free – that's the reason he laughed. Now, in his bed, the tears came again. Indeed, he was in the blackness of tears.

He thought of the young woman again. He thought of the way she looked directly at him in the church on Sunday. It wasn't a quick, modest look – she looked at him boldly, and it was a look ... well, a look of invitation. He often heard other boys talk about the way she looked at them – and what they'd like to do. And now, she looked at him.

Her mother died years ago. Illiam knew that her father wasn't home when he went to the house. He knocked on the door.

"Come in," she said. "Illiam Bridson! What are you doing here?" She was talking like a lady to a little boy. Illiam blushed.

"Well," he said, "you looked at me in the church yesterday, and ..."

"I was looking at a pig in a pigsty yesterday – is it with you as well?"

"But I thought ..." said Illiam, but the young woman spoke again:

"You thought? Did you think, little boy?" Illiam became rather angry.

"You're only sixteen years old," he said, "and you're no lady either!"

"And how do you know about ladies?" replied the young woman. "I think you're the pig from that pigsty!"

"Hold your tongue! Bless me, I was thinking that you were very beautiful ..."

"Oh," said the young woman, and now she spoke in a lower and more friendly voice, "you think that I'm very beautiful. Thank you."

"Beautiful indeed," said Illiam, looking for more kind words, "and I thought that you gave me an invitation to come and see you." The young woman smiled.

"An invitation to you?" she said, and she smiled again. William smiled as well, enjoying the sweet voice and attractive face. "An invitation to you?" said the young woman again. Then she spoke in a voice high and haughty:

"To you? You're nothing but a little poor boy, and the son of a stranger too. Away with you to your pigsty, pig!"

Now Illiam was completely confounded, and angry indeed. "And who are you, then?" he shouted. "You're as poor as I am. You're raving, girl!"

"But I'm not a descendent of Kirree Corkish," shouted the young woman.

"Well?" said Illiam. "Well, that's not a sin!"

"You're a witch's get," [literally, the issue of Berree Dhone, a name associated with a witch in Maughold parish] yelled the young woman.

"What was that?" said Illiam, and he was furious now. "What was that?"

"Witch's get! Witch's get!" she said contemptuously, and her face and her voice mocked him.

He struck her cheek with the flat of his hand. She tottered, and she lost her balance. She screamed. She was screaming as she was falling to the floor. She struck her head against the slab of the hearth. There wasn't a sound to be heard after that.

Illiam well-remembered this crime as he lay in his bed. He was weeping in the darkness. It was the dead of night.

Up to the late 1970s, the only book of music associated with the Island that was readily available was 'Manx National Songs', in print since 1896. Since the mid 1970s, Colin Jerry had sought out original songs in Manx. Aware that they were of interest to others, he decided to issue them in a form which gave the bare melody and the Manx words. In some cases, he was able to pair up a song from one source with words from another. An original booklet called 'Kiaull ny Manninee' ('Music of the Manx People') was produced for a Board of Education local studies seminar in 1976. This was subsequently expanded by Jerry into 'Kiaull yn Theay' ('Music of the Folk'), published by Yn Cheshaght Ghailckagh in an inexpensive but attractive format, hand written (including the staves and music) by Jerry. This was quickly adopted by schools, and was followed by 'Kiaull yn Theay 2'. Even the titles of tunes not accompanied by words are in Manx, with very few exceptions. The result is that, within a generation, schoolchildren have gone from recognizing the English titles and words bestowed upon material in 'Manx National Songs' to recognizing and referring to the material by their titles in Manx. Songs are, more often than not, sung in Manx from 'Kiaull yn Theay'. 'Kiaull yn Theay' is an important Manx language resource in itself, and has been invaluable in bringing Manx to public notice and use through the titles of the pieces, even for those who have hesitated to sing the Manx lyrics.

Another welcome development in 1979 was the publication by Shearwater Press of a facsimile edition of the 1819 Manx Bible with added prefatory material and art work under the title 'Bible Chasherick yn Lught Thie – The Manx Family Bible'. The following text is from Robert Thomson's Introduction.

Robert Thomson
Bible Chasherick Yn Lught Thie, *1979*

Lhaih-jee yn lioar yindyssagh shoh. Lhig da feallagh elley ee y chionnaghey as y chur er y skelloo myr red coayr as quaagh, fooillagh ny eashyn t'er ngholl shaghey, agh jean-jee shiuish yn lioar shoh y chionnaghey as y lhaih. Nee lhaih yn lioar shoh jeeaghyn diu glare ny Manninee ec yn yrjid eck, roish my dooar y Baarle laue yn eaghtyr urree, ga dy vel soar baarlaghys urree ny cheayrtyn; nee'n lioar shoh fosley diu tashtey mooar dy skeeallyn, as creenaght, as arraneyn, gyn imraa y yannoo jeh'n vondeish spyrrydoil dauesyn ta lhaih lesh credjue. Lhaih-jee ee l'hee hene, as nee shiu jiole stiagh ayndiu hene thooilley dy'n Ghailck share as s'dooghyssee oddys shiu y gheddyn; lhaih-jee ee marish y Vible Vaarlagh as gowee shiu yindys kinjagh cre cha schleioil as v'adsyn ren ee y hyndaa gys Gailck, as gynsaghey dy yannoo yn red cheddin. Cha nod glare myr y Ghailck, va keayrt dy row bunnys marroo, ve bio reesht as bishaghey mannagh dayrn ee bea as niart veih ny shenn fraueyn eck. Shoh farrane y vea: dagh unnane ta paagh, tar-jee gys ny ushtaghyn.

Translation
The Family Holy Bible, *1979*

Read this wonderful book. Let other people buy it and put it on the shelf as an odd and strange thing, the fragments of an age gone by, but you particularly buy it and read it. This book will show you the language of the Manx people at its height, before English got the upper hand over it, though there is a whiff of anglicization about it sometimes; this book will open to you a great store of stories, and wisdom, and songs, without making mention of the spiritual advantage to those who read with belief. Read it for itself, and you will soak up into yourselves a flood of the best and most natural Manx you could find; read it with the English Bible and you will always be surprised just how skilful were those who translated it to Manx, and learned to do that same thing. A language like Manx, that was once almost dead, cannot be living again and on the increase unless it drew life and strength from its old roots. This is a well of life: each one who thirsts, come to the waters.

A further great fillip for the Manx language was the publication in 1979 of 'Fargher's English-Manx Dictionary', also by Shearwater Press. Doug Fargher wrote in the Preface, of which the following is part.

Doug Fargher
Preface to English-Manx Dictionary, *1979*

The vocabulary of a living language is constantly changing and extending. It borrows extensively from other languages. In this dictionary I have tried to give new connotations to old Manx words and have borrowed unashamedly from our Gaelic cousins. Loan words are not easily recognised except by the expert and hundreds of Irishisms and Scotticisms are now a vital part of the living Manx Gaelic of the late twentieth century, or 'Neo-Manx' as the scholars would have it, our last native speaker, my cousin Ned Maddrell, having died in 1974.

The aim of this dictionary is purely practical. It is largely a prescriptive work and not a descriptive one, that is to say, it does not aim to be a record pure and simple of the language as it was spoken at any time during its history, but tries to provide some sort of basic standard upon which to build the modern Manx langauge of today and tomorrow, in order that those who feel the need to express themselves in Manx may here find the necessary means to do so.

...

I make no apology whatsoever for attempting to restore to the Manx language mutations, genders and certain other characteristics of Gaelic which without doubt existed in pre-literary and classical Manx but which had already disappeared before the final demise of the native speakers, owing to the havoc wrought on the language by English.

...

In spite of the enforced anglicisation of the Manx people since the 1872 Education Act, the anglo-americanisation of the Island in our own times and the present day influx of thousands of new residents, there has been a great revival of Manx national consciousness over the past fifteen years since the formation of the first nationalist political movement, which has led to a much greater interest in and use of the native tongue, especially among the younger people of the Island. It is to them, yn feallagh aegey, that I leave this dictionary in the hope that Manx will survive as a living language into the next century and beyond. I also hope that the book will serve as a memorial to the wonderful old Manx men and women who taught me Chengey ny Mayrey Ellan Vannin when I was a young man and who transformed me from being culturally a West Briton into a Manxman. Without the living reality of the spoken language which was passed on by them to my generation and which we in our turn have handed on, we might as well (as the old Manx would have said) "Took our Manx books and hoove them on the back of the fire".

Contributers to 'Noon as Noal' were able to use the dictionary to extend the vocabulary used in translating stories and writing articles, though it was sometimes necessary either to gloss unfamiliar words and phrases or preferably to make the context for their use very clear so as to make the meaning obvious. In 1991, 'Fockleyr Gailck-Baarle' ('Manx-English Dictionary') a reverse of Fargher's dictionary was published by Phil Kelly, who has published a lot of other useful material in hard copy and on the world wide web. These include an extensive series of reprints of articles which had appeared in 'Noon as Noal', many of them under the imprimatur of 'Rannag Ghoo' ('Black Frog').

In 1982, it was thought that the newspaper was to bring 'Noon as Noal' to an end. In order to have a weekly Manx column in at least one newspaper, permission was obtained for a column under the name 'Cree ny Cooish' ('The Heart of the Matter') to appear in the Isle of Man Weekly Times. For a time, both 'Noon as Noal' and 'Cree ny Cooish' appeared. However, 'Noon as Noal' came to an end, whilst 'Cree ny Cooish' appeared from 1982 to 1984. Most of the contributions for 'Cree ny Cooish' were by Carswell. They consisted of translations of stories, official notices, jokes, magazine and encyclopaedia articles, covering a range of subjects and registers, plus historic material. However, there was little original material. A reprint of this material in bound, A4 photocopied format was made available in the 1990s. Carswell had also begun to make a similar mix of material available through a magazine called 'FRITLAG', which ran for 14 editions from 1983 to 1987. The magazine included illustrations and maps with captions and legends in Manx.

The main focus for the production of original material in Manx was an annual arts festival, revived in 1978 by Mona Douglas, and called 'Yn Chruinnaght' ('The Gathering'). Yn Chruinnaght had classes for an original poem and an original song in Manx. Robert Carswell entered work in these classes, over a number of years, often as the sole contributor. Some of these were published in 'FRITLAG', such as this one, based on a traditional pattern:

Robard y Charsalagh (Robert Corteen Carswell)
Ny Tree Reayrtyn S'Aaley, *1983*

> 1. Ny tree reayrtyn s'aaley, rere rouailtagh reagh –
> Lhie-ghreiney aahoilshaghey er glionney dy lhune;
> Irree ny greiney lurg oie dy chiaull as rinkey;
> As soilshey gastey gial ayns sooillyn graih my chree.
>
> 2. Ny tree reayrtyn s'aaley, rere Manninagh moyrnagh –
> Lhie-ghreiney my-heear harrish Nherin ny nooghyn;
> Irree ny greiney harrish Sostyn ny seihltee;
> As mish aynshoh lesh shilley er'n Ellan Sheeant.
>
> 3. Ny tree reayrtyn s'aaley, rere yn dooinney jeeragh –
> Lhie-ghreiney Oie'll Voirrey bannit ayns y Nollick;
> Irree ny greiney Laa Caisht, tra dirree nyn Jiarn;
> As graih erreeishagh meen ayns eddin Yeesey Creest.

Translation
The Three Most Beautiful Sights, *1983*

> 1. The three most beautiful sights, according to the lusty rambler –
> Sunset reflecting on a glass of ale;

Sunrise after a night of music and dance;
And a bright, lively light in the eyes of the love of my heart.

2. The three most beautiful sights, according to a proud Manxman –
Sunset westwards over Ireland of the saints;
Sunrise over England of the worldly people;
And me here with a view of the Blessed Isle.

3. The three most beautiful sights, according to the religious man –
Sunset on the blessed Eve of Mary in the Christmas time;
Sunrise on Easter Day, when our Lord arose;
And gentle, compassionate love in the face of Jesus Christ.

George Broderick had continued to send pieces for inclusion in 'Noon as Noal', and one of them was an original song composed by him five years after the disasterous fire in 1973 which destroyed Summerland, a modern holiday facility in Douglas, and after the findings of an inquiry into it had been released. It was his intention to show that Manx could deal with an unpleasant and contentious modern subject, as well as plain narrative and whimsy, and is a powerful piece of writing. However, only a shortened version had been published in 'Noon as Noal' in 1978, omitting graphic detail. The full song did not appear until 1987 in issue 13 of 'FRITLAG'. Perhaps to make the subject-matter more acceptable, the construction of the song follows that of some carvals and folk songs.

Shorus y Creayrie (George Broderick)
Arrane Mysh Aile Y Ghrianane, *1987*

Eaisht-jee rhyms, my chaarjyn
As gowyms diu nish arrane
Mychione yn aile mooar atchimagh
Ren lostey'n Grianane
Cha bione dooin rieau y lheid shoh
Cha nod mayd insh gyn pian
Mysh lieh-cheead sleih va marrooit
She, deiney 's cloan as mraane

Ve fastyr braew as aalin
Mysh kerroo oor dys hoght
Va daa housane dy leih sy voayl
'Sbeg eie v'oc er y chragh
Va paitchyn cloie dy maynrey
Ny jishagyn giu jough

Ny mummigyn goaill soylley jeh
Fir-giense as spotchyn v'oc

Ny lossagyn, rere y skeeal
Goaill toshiaght ayns cabbane
Ass ymmyd as ny lhie cheu-mooie
Ry-lhiattee'n Ghrianane
Tree guillyn aeg voish Lerpool
Lesh foaddanyn v'ad cloie
T'ad gra dy doad ad aile beg ayn
'S magh ass dy ren ad roie

V'eh lostey 'shen rish tammylt beg
Gyn yss da peiagh erbee
Doaltattym bleaystey orroo shen
Voish woalley as voish clea
Ass Oroglas ve ooilley jeant
Ve shilley blugganyn-aile
As tuittym gollrish fliaghey
Er deiney 's mraane gyn reih

V'ad jannoo lesh ny dorryssyn
Yn chragh shoh y aagail
Lesh geulaghyn va paart oc jeiht
Nagh voddagh ad scapail
Va mustheyr mooar ny mast'oc
Ayns siyr roie noon as noal
As stampey er-y-cheilley
Nyn mioys son dy choayl

Va paart cheet neose ny greeishyn
As lossaghyn [sic] cheet nyn aare
Agh greimit ec yn aile dy chionn
Rish radlingyn v'ad thaait
Paart elley plooghit ec y yaagh
Va cheet veih lostey'n terr
Lieeney trooid y slane voayl
Faagail veg daue agh baase

Cheu-sthie jeih minnidyn, t'ad gra
V'aile ayn voish kione gy kione
Brooightoil bodjally[n] dhoo dy yaagh
Sy speyr as seose gys niau

Cha jeean yn chiass ry ghennaghtyn
Voish kerroo meeill' ersooyl
Myr coirrey aileagh-loshtee
Dy jeeragh roish nyn sooill

Ayns yindys as thanvaneys
Hass chionnal mooar dy leih
Lane fys oc er yn torchagh
Va taghyrt daue cheu-sthie
Cha dod ad veg y yannoo roo
Agh geaishtagh rish nyn eie
As blakey er glout jiar[g] dy aile
Nyn gree oc trimshagh, treih

Tra haink ad laa ny vairagh
Dy ronsaghey mygeayrt
Feer atchimagh yn shilley
Feer foudagh yn reayrt
Convayrtyn losht as lheamysagh
Gyn cass, gyn roih, gyn kione
Gyn enn currit orroo shen
Agh rish fainey er y laue

As lurg yn chragh ve shaghey
Bing vooar va curt er bun
Yn obbyr oc dy feddyn magh
Cre'n aght haink aile 've ayn
Cha row eh orroo shirrey magh
Quoi s'lesh y foill son shoh
"No villains" chord eh roo dy ghra
Lurg taggloo tammylt mooar

Feer danjeyragh p[a]art dy stoo
Va ymmydit 'sy voayl
Beoyn er Oroglas rish aile
Agh cha ghow ad raaue ny coyrle
Va reilyn currit gys y cheu
Son argid dy hauail
Rolaueid-aile cha row rieau ayn
Y lhied nagh vod shiu credjal

As nish te traa, my chaarjyn
'Chur jerrey er m'arrane

Mychione lieh-cheead dy gheiney
Va losht 'sy Ghrianane
S'goan vees mayd abyl y yarrood
Cre'n arcys as cre'n scoagh
S'cooin lhien yn chragh cho atchimagh
Huitt er ny deiney boght'.

Translation

A Song About the Summerland Fire, *1987*

Listen to me, my friends
And I'll now sing you a song
About the awful, large fire
That burnt Summerland
We never knew the like before
We cannot tell without pain
About fifty people who were killed
Yes, men and children and women

It was a fine and beautiful evening
About a quarter-to-eight
There were two thousand people in the place
They had little inkling of the disaster
There were children playing happily
The dads drinking beer
The mums enjoying
The entertainers and their jokes

The flames, according to the report
Started in a cabin
Out of use and lying outside
To the side of Summerland
Three young boys from Liverpool
Were playing with matches
They say that they lit a little fire in it
And that they ran out of there

It was burning there for a little while
Without anyone's knowledge
Suddenly bursting on those people
From wall and from roof
It was all made out of Oroglas
It was shedding balls of fire

And dropping like rain
On men and women indiscriminately

They were making for the doors
To leave the carnage
With chains some of them were shut
So that they couldn't escape
There was great confusion amongst them
In haste running hither and thither
And trampling each other
So as to lose their lives

There were some coming down the stairs
And flames coming near them
But held tightly by the fire
They were fused to the rails
Some others were suffocated by the smoke
That was coming from the burning of the tar
Filling throughout the whole place
Leaving nothing for them but death

Inside of ten minutes, they say
The fire covered from end to end
Belching black clouds of smoke
In the air and up to heaven
So keenly was the heat to be felt
From a quarter of a mile away
Like a blazing, fiery furnace
Directly before their eyes

In wonder and astonishment
A large throng of people stood
Fully aware of the torment
That was happening to those inside
There was nothing they could do for them
But listen to their cry
And stare at the red mass of fire
Their hearts sorrowful and sad

When they came on the following day
To search about
The sight was absolutely awful
The scene was wholly morbid

Dead bodies burnt and blemished
Without a foot, without an arm, without a head
They were only identified
By a ring on their hand

And after the carnage was over
A large committee was established
Their work to find out
How the fire came to happen
It wasn't their responsibility seeking out
Who bore the responsibility for this
"No villains" it suited them to say
After talking for a long while

Very dangerous some of the material
That was used in the place
Oroglas was flammable
But they heeded no warning or advice
Rules were put to the side
In order to save money
There were never any fire precautions
You couldn't believe the like

And now it's time, my friends
To put an end to my song
About the fifty people
Who were burnt in Summerland
Scarce may we be able to forget
Such calamity and such horror
We remember such an awful disaster
Befell the poor people

'FRITLAG' also published some rhymes for children. In 1983 a Manx playgroup had been set up under the title 'Beeal Arrish' ('Mouth Mimicking' – 'Oral Tradition'). In addition to traditional Manx rhymes, some Irish children's rhymes were adapted by Peggy and Robert Carswell for use in the playgroup, and books for young children were translated into Manx. Particular favourites were Eric Hill's books for Ventura Publishing Ltd about the puppy, Spot. In 1986 Yn Cheshaght Ghailckagh published Manx versions of two of Eric Hill's books, in which 'Spot' became 'Breck' in Manx. These were 'Car ny Bleeaney marish Breck' ('Through the Year with Spot') and 'Ta Breck gynsaghey coontey' ('Spot learns to count'). Yn

Cheshaght Ghailckagh also undertook the printing of a Manx version of Usborne's popular 'The First Thousand Words' by Heather Amery and Stephen Cartwright. This has proved very popular, and has been followed by 'First Hundred Words in Manx' and 'Everday Words in Manx'

A translation on a more extensive scale was Brian Stowell's Manx version of Lewis Carroll's 'The Adventures of Alice In Wonderland' ('Contoyrtyssyn Ealish ayns Cheer ny Yindyssyn' - 1990). This was first made available in an A4 photo-copied format, but has subsequently been reissued in 2006 by Yn Cheshaght Ghailckagh in a full-colour commercial edition by Brimax Books with illustrations by Eric Kincaid.

Brian Stowell
Faaie-Croquet Y Venrein, *1990*

Heill Ealish nagh row ee rieau er nakin faaie-croquet cho quaagh sy vea eck: va oirragyn as creaghyn ass towse ayn: she arkanyn-sonney bio va ny bluckanyn-croquet, as she lossyraneyn bio va ny thornaneyn, as beign da ny sidooryn ad hene y ghoobley as shassoo er nyn laueyn as cassyn, dy yannoo ny h-aaeghyn.

Hoshiaght, y chied doilleeid ec Ealish, va shen cur smaght er y lossyrane eck: haink eh lhee cur e chorp, aashagh dy liooar, fo'n roih eck, as e lurgaghyn croghey sheese, agh, dy cliaghtagh, kiart myr va'n mwannal echey er ny yeeraghey eck as v'ee er chee bwoalley yn arkan sonney lesh e chione, veagh eh cassey eh hene mygeayrt as jeeaghyn seose ayns e h-eddin er aght cho boirit as nagh dod ee jannoo fegooish tuittym er garaghtee; as tra veagh e chione currit sheese eck reesht, as veagh ee er chee goaill toshiaght reesht, veagh ee brasnit dy mooar dy 'eddyn magh dy beagh yn arkan sonney neu-rowlit as er chee snaue ersooyl: as, ny sodjey na shoh, dy cliaghtagh veagh oirrag ny creagh raad erbee veagh ee laccal cur yn arkan sonney huggey, as, myr veagh ny sidooryn dooblit kinjagh girree seose as shooyl gys buill elley er y faaie, hoig Ealish feer tappee dy nee gamman feer doillee v'ayn dy jarroo.

Va ny cloideryn ooilley cloie ec yn un cheayrt, gyn fuirraghtyn rish shayllyn, as ad tuittym magh car y traa, as jannoo caggey son ny h-arkanyn sonney; ayns traa feer gherrid, va eulys agglagh er y Venrein, va stampey mygeayrt as gyllagh magh "Ersooyl lesh e chione!" ny "Ersooyl lesh e kione!" red goll rish un cheayrt gagh minnid.

Va imnea mooar cheet er Ealish: son shickyrys, cha row ee er duittym magh lesh y Venrein foast, agh va fys eck dy noddagh eh taghyrt ec traa erbee, "as eisht," smooinee ish, "cre'n erree harragh orrym? T'ad feer ghraihagh er giarrey ny king jeh sleih ayns shoh: t'eh ny yindys mooar dy vel peiagh erbee faagit bio!"

Translation

The Queen's Croquet-Ground, *1990*

Alice thought she had never seen such a curious croquet-ground in her life; it was all ridges and furrows; the balls were live hedgehogs, the mallets live flamingoes, and the soldiers had to double themselves up and to stand on their hands and feet, to make the arches.

The chief difficulty Alice found at first was in managing her flamingo: she succeeded in getting its body tucked away, comfortably enough, under her arm, with its legs hanging down, but generally, just as she had got its neck nicely straightened out, and was going to give the hedgehog a blow with its head, it would twist itself round and look up in her face, with such a puzzled expression that she could not help bursting out laughing: and when she had got its head down, and was going to begin again, it was very provoking to find that the hedgehog had unrolled itself, and was in the act of crawling away: besides all this, there was generally a ridge or furrow in the way wherever she wanted to send the hedgehog to, and, as the doubled-up soldiers were always getting up and walking off to other parts of the ground, Alice soon came to the conclusion that it was a very difficult game indeed.

The players all played at once without waiting for turns, quarrelling all the while, and fighting for the hedgehogs; and in a very short time the Queen was in a furious passion, and went stamping about, and shouting "Off with his head!" or "Off with her head!" about once in a minute.

Alice began to feel very uneasy: to be sure, she had not as yet had any dispute with the Queen, but she knew that it might happen any minute, "and then," thought she, "what would become of me? They're dreadfully fond of beheading people here; the great wonder is, that there's any one left alive!"

Brian Stowell was appointed as the first Manx Language Officer to the Isle of Man Government in 1992. He and a team of two peripetetic Manx teachers developed a Manx course for use in schools. The Government had been taken aback at the extremely positive response when it offered children an opportunity to take optional Manx lessons. The number of children who have received a foundation in speaking and reading and writing Manx now forms a substantial percentage of the younger generation. Interestingly, children now correct their parents' pronounciation of words which are to be seen increasingly in the names of buildings, official letterheads, road signs and shop signs.

Though 'FRITLAG' had ceased publication as a magazine in 1987, Robert Carswell collected material that he had written mainly during the 1980s and published them under the imprimatur of 'FRITLAG' during the 1990s. In 1994, a collection of poems (some in English) was published under the title 'Shelg yn Drane'. The title is a pun on the name of the custom of 'Hunting the Wren' – in Manx, 'Shelg yn Drean'. The collection's title, 'Shelg yn Drane' translates as 'Hunt the

Rhyme'. In the following two poems from the collection, the rhymes are internal, through assonance and consonance.

Robard y Charsalagh (Robert Corteen Carswell)
Er y Cheer 'Sy Cheeiragh, *1994*

> Er y cheer 'sy cheeiragh, ta sheean cheet 'syn aer –
> Maaley ny kirree aegey, tayrit ec onnaneyn ta gaase
> Myr faal: eayin veggey geamagh magh ec dagh gass birragh,
> Choud's t'ad shirrey bayr dy hooyl gyn gortey,
> Geiyrt er y cheilley trooid y gharee gharroo.
> Sharroo ta'n seihll shoh: s'trimshagh ta ny trughanee
> Ta maaley dy ve seyr: ard-choraa as beggan keeayle.
> Ayns y voghrey, hig yn goayr.

Translation
In the Countryside in the Gloaming, *1994*

> In the countryside in the gloaming, there's a sound coming in the air –
> Bleating of the little sheep, caught in the thistles that grow
> Like a fence: little lambs calling out at each sharp shoot,
> Whilst they seek a path to walk without wound,
> Following one another through the rough moorland.
> Bitter is this world: so sad are those complainers
> Who are bleating to be free: a loud voice and little wit.
> In the morning, the goat will come.

Robard y Charsalagh (Robert Corteen Carswell)
Foillycan Ec Yn Uinnag, *1994*

> Nagh re er yn uinnag woaill skianyn dy baanrit,
> Cretoor boght cleaynit ec chiass ny greiney?
> Oranj, bwee, jiarg as bane, myr lossagyn dy ghaaghyn bio
> Ec glonney ghaait.
> Nagh re er nyn inchyn ta'n jesh-chliaghtey jannoo
> Ec traa malaineagh?
> Cre'n annym nagh vel laccal scapail?
> Leoie gys leoie, agh lhig da'n annym irree,
> Myr phoenix gaavioghey reesht.
> Agh foast ta coraa fer fockley-magh ayns yn 'aasagh,
> "Cha nel mee credjal".

Livrey shin veih mee-chredjue as far-hreisht.
Livrey shin veih'n theihll shoh dy jesh, as,
Rish y choold elley, dy glen –
Joan gys joan, smooinaghtyn gys smooidraght,
Tra ta ny chaghteryn lectragh
Ta goll mygeayrt nyn gorys nearag
Scuirr.
Atreih, my 'oillycan beg, cho beg as uss my smooinaghtyn
Va cur ort annym beayn.
Uss cretoor giare-heiltagh, gollrhympene.
Nee nyn n'yoan covestey roish y gheay.
Uss, t'ou laccal scapail yn uinnag;
Mish, y ghlonney ghaait.

Translation

Butterfly at the Window, *1994*

Is it not on the window that wings beat wildly,
A poor creature attracted by the heat of the sun?
Orange, yellow, red and white, like flames of living colour
At the stained glass.
Is it not our minds that the ceremony affects
At a maudlin time?
What soul doesn't want to escape?
Ashes to ashes, but let the spirit rise,
Like a phoenix reviving again.
But still there's the voice of one crying out in the wilderness,
"I don't believe".
Deliver us from superstition and false hope.
Deliver us from this world neatly, and,
Taking one thing with another, cleanly –
Dust to dust, thought to a smidgin,
When the electrical messages
That go round our nervous system
Stop.
Alas, my little butterfly, as small as you is my thought
That makes you an eternal soul.
You're an ephemeral creature, like myself.
Our dust will coalesce before the wind.
You, you want to escape the window;
Me, the stained glass.

This was followed in 1996 by 'Arraneyn 'sy Ghaelg' ('Songs in Manx'), which included some material dating back to 1975. This is a song which was also submitted for a class in Yn Chruinnaght in the 1980s:

Robard y Charsalagh (Robert Corteen Carswell)
Irree Ny Greiney, *1996*

    1. Irree ny greiney harrish y vooir.
    Shoh yn oor ta'n laa cheet rish.
    Skellyn skeaylley harrish y cheayn.
    Foddey as lhean ta'n soilshey nish.
    Lurg goullyn gial y vadran glass,
    Ta'n ghrian soilshean, cur lhee e chiass.
    Irree ny greiney harrish y vooir.
    Shoh yn oor ta'n laa cheet rish.

    2. Irree ny greiney harrish y cheer.
    Sheeyney my-heear ta soilshey'n laa.
    Druight er duillag as dossan y drine:
    Shimmey bine t'er gass as blaa.
    Ta'n ollagh doostey ayns yn 'aaie.
    Jeh'n ushtey oor t'ad giu nyn saie.
    Irree ny greiney harrish y cheer,
    Sheeyney my-heear ta soilshey'n laa.

    3. Chiassid ny greiney ayns Mannin veg veen.
    Ta'n cheer as y cheayn nyn lhie ec fea.
    Tashid y voghree vees girree myr gaal,
    As jannoo craa-skell ayns chiass vunlaa.
    Cho souyr ta'n Ellan 'syn 'astyr mie.
    Ta'n Sourey cheet gys cheer my ghraih.
    Chiassid ny greiney ayns Mannin veg veen.
    Ta'n cheer as y cheayn nyn lhie ec fea.

Translation
Sunrise, *1996*

    1. Sunrise across the sea.
    This is the hour the day appears.
    Beams spreading across the sea.
    Far and wide is the light now.
    After the bright rays of the grey dawn,

The sun is shining, bringing its heat.
Sunrise across the sea.
This is the hour the day appears.

2. Sunrise across the land.
Stretching westward is the light of the day.
Dew on the leaf and the cluster of the thorn tree:
Many a drop is on stem and flower.
The cattle awaken in the meadow.
Of the fresh water they drink their fill.
Sunrise across the land.
Stretching westward is the light of the day.

3. The warmth of the sun in dear little Mannin.
The land and the sea are lying at rest.
The dampness of the morning is rising as a vapour,
And causing a shimmer in the noon heat.
So comfortable is the Island in the fine afternoon.
The Summer is coming to the land I love.
The warmth of the sun in dear little Mannin.
The land and the sea are lying at rest.

1996 was also the year in which another extensive translation project was published. This was Joan Caine's version of Agatha Christie's 'Murder on the Orient Express'. This is how 'Dunverys er Traen-Tappee yn Niar' opens.

Joan Caine
Dunverys er Traen-Tappee yn Niar, *1996*

CABDIL 1 Troailtagh Scanshoil er Traen-Tappee Taurus

V'eh queig er y chlag moghrey geuree dy row, ayns Syria.
   Va'n traen, va'd gra Yn Traen-Tappee Taurus rish ayns lioaryn-oayllys yn raad yiarn, ny hassoo liorish yn ardan ec Aleppo. V'eh goaill stiagh carriads-aarlee as bee, carriads-cadlee as daa charriads ynnydagh.
   Va aachaptan Frangagh aeg ny hassoo rish yn ghreeish va leeideil seose stiagh 'sy charriads-cadlee, ceau cullee stoamey, coloayrt rish dooinney beg, va coodit dy mie seose dys ny cleayshyn echey. Cha row veg jeh ry-akin agh baare bane-jiarg jeh stroin as yn daa vaare jeh far-veeal cassit seose.
   V'eh feayr agglagh, as cha beagh fer erbee trooagh mychione faagail bannaght er joarree ooasle, agh ren Aachaptan Dubosc yn currym echey dy dunnal. Huitt raaghyn graysoil veih e veillyn ayns Frangish flaaoil. Agh cha row fys echey er cre

mychione v'eh. Son shickyrys, va fouaghyn er ve ayn, myr dy cliaghtagh ayns lheid ny cooishyn.

Va tappey yn Chionfenee – yn kionfenee echeysyn – er jeet dy ve ny s'messey as ny s'messey. Eisht va'n joarree Belgagh shen er jeet, voish Sostyn va'd gra. Va shiaghtin chionn, quaagh er ve ayn. Eisht va reddyn ennagh er daghyrt. Ren offishear ooasle dy row marroo eh-hene; ren fer elley girree ass e obbyr; ren eddinyn imneagh coayl yn imnea oc doaltattym; va roie-arraghyn sidooragh dy row er nyn lhaggaghey. As doaltattym va'n kionfenee – kionfenee er-lheh aachaptan Dubosc – er n'yeeaghyn dy ve jeih bleeaney ny s'aa.

Va Dubosc er far-chlashtyn paart jeh coloayrtys eddyr yn chionfenee as yn joarree. "Ta shiu er hauail shin, *mon cher*," dooyrt yn kionfenee dy toghtagh, as yn far-veeal mooar bane echey craa myr v'eh loayrt. "Ta shiu er hauail onnor yn armee Frangagh – ta shiu er haghney mooarane fuillaghtys. Cre'n aght foddym cur bwooise diu son coardail rish my yeearree? Ta shiu er jeet foddey …"

Va'n joarree (er ennym M. Hercule Poirot) er chur freggyrt traaoil da shen, va goaill stiagh yn raa "Agh dy jarroo nagh vel cooinaght aym dy ren shiu sauail yn vioys aym keayrt dy row?"

Eisht va'n kionfenee er chur freggyrt traaoil elley da shen, gobbal toilchinys erbee son y chirveish shaghey shen, as lesh imraaghyn elley jeh'n Rank, jeh'n Velg, jeh gloyr, jeh onnor as jeh lheid ny reddyn elley, va'd er chlamey ry-cheilley dy creeoil, as haink yn coloayrtys gy-kione.

Cha row fys erbee foast ec Aachaptan Dubosc er cre mychione v'eh, agh va'n currym ersyn d'aagail bannaghtyn er M. Poirot tra daag eh er Traen-Tappee Taurus, as v'eh jannoo shen lesh ooilley'n yeeanid va cooie da offishear aeg as coorse gialdynagh roish.

Agatha Christie
Murder on the Orient Express

CHAPTER 1– An Important Traveller on the Taurus Express (literal translation)

It was five o'clock on a winter's morning, in Syria.

The train, which they call the Taurus Express in the railway guide books, was standing alongside the platform at Aleppo. It included a kitchen- and food-wagon, a sleeping car and two local carriages.

A young French lieutenant was standing by the step that led up into the sleeping-car, wearing a smart uniform, talking with a small man, who was well covered up to his ears. There was nothing of him to be seen but the pink tip of a nose and the two tips of a twirled up moustache.

It was dreadfully cold, and nobody would be envious about giving a farewell to an esteemed stranger, but Lieutenant Dubosc bravely carried out his responsibility. Gracious phrases fell from his lips in fluent French. But he didn't know what it was all about. Certainly, there had been rumours, as usual in such affairs.

The General's temper – his own general – had become worse and worse. Then that Belgian stranger had come, from England they were saying. There had been a strange, tense week. Then some things had happened. A certain illustrious officer had killed himself; another one had resigned from his job; anxious faces suddenly lost their anxiety; certain military precautions had been relaxed. And suddenly the general – particularly the lieutenant Dubosc's general –had looked to be ten years younger.

Dubosc had imperfectly heard part of a conversation between the gneral and the stranger. "You have saved us, *mon cher*," said the general emotionally, his great white moustache quivering as he spoke. "You have saved the honour of the French army – you have avoided much bloodshed. How can I thank you for complying with my request? You have come far ..."

The stranger (by the name of M. Hercule Poirot) had given an appropriate reply to that, which included the phrase "But of course am I not mindful that you saved my life once upon a time?"

Then the general had given an appropriate reply to that, denying any merit for that past service, and with other references to France, to Belgium, to glory, to honour and other things of that sort, they had embraced heartily, and the conversation came to an end.

Lieutenant Dubosc still didn't know what it was about, but his duty was to bid farewell to M. Poirot when he left on the Taurus Express, and he was doing that with all the enthusiasm that was appropriate to a young officer with a promising career ahead of him.

The Twenty-first Century

Like many small-scale publications in the 1980s and 1990s, 'Dunverys er Traen-Tappee yn Niar' was in bound, A4 photocopy format. The umbrella organisation, 'Caarjyn ny Gaelgey' ('Friends of Manx') also made booklets of other material available in this format. Similarly, Phil Kelly had made available articles reprinted from 'Noon as Noal' and 'Carn', had published the reverse of Fargher's dictionary and also published a guide to placenames. He had undertaken a considerable amount of work exploring how technology as it became available could provide support for Manx, and making this and other material available on the world wide web. He was involved with Dr J F Craine in setting up an online dictionary through the auspices of 'Undinys Eiraght Vannin ('Manx Heritage Foundation') ... In 2005, again through 'Undinys Eiraght Vannin', Dr Craine's expertise led to the development of a searchable electronic edition of the 1819 Bible.

The publications for use in school by the Manx peripetetic teachers from 1992 were in bound, A4 photocopied format. The Manx unit also created courses for 'Teisht Chadjin Ghaelgagh' ('The Ordinary Manx Certificate'), a GCSE equivalent (from 1997), and for 'Ard-Teisht Ghaelgagh' ('High Certificate of Manx'), an 'A' level equivalent (from 2002). Both involved the production of course material, and much was supplied by Brian Stowell. He had also been contributing short sections of an original story to a newspaper together with explanations of the Manx phrases and grammar used in it. In 2005, this story became the first full-length novel in Manx,'Dunveryssyn yn Tooder-Folley' ('The Vampire Murders'), a murder mystery which also satirized certain elements of Manx society. The following passage is from the opening of the book.

Brian Stowell
Dunveryssyn Yn Tooder-Folley, *2005*

CABDIL 1

Hooar ad y corp marroo ec lieh-oor lurg nuy sy voghrey. Va ben y thie boirit nagh row Mnr Jones er jeet neose dy gheddyn anjeeal sy thie-goaldee. V'ee crankal as crankal er dorrys yn chamyr-lhiabbagh, agh cha row freggyrt ry gheddyn. Fy yerrey, ren ee feddyn magh nagh row yn dorrys glast as ren ee fosley eh. Cho leah's honnick ben y thie yn dooinney ny lhie sy lhiabbee, ren ee toiggal dy row red ennagh agglagh er daghyrt.

Va Mnr Jones ny lhie er y dreeym echey, jeeaghyn er y far-voalley lesh sooillyn lhean, blakey. Agh cha row eh fakin veg er y fa dy row eh marroo. Va brelleein harrish y chooid smoo jeh'n chorp echey, agh va'n eddin as mwannal echey ry akin as v'ad cho bane as sniaghtey. Va daa howl beg sy wannal echey.

Cha dod ben y thie, Bnr Quilleash, ve shickyr, agh foddee dy row yn corp marroo mongey. Hooar ee rey rish y smooinaght as haink corree urree, beggan: c'red v'eh jannoo, geddyn baase sy thie ecksh? As c'raad va'n ven aeg shen ren cheet marish Mnr Jones dy hannaghtyn sy thie-aaght? 'Mnr as Bnr Jones'? Insh dou skeeal elley. Eisht haink aggle er Bnr Quilleash. C'red v'ee jannoo? Va dooinney marroo ny lhie sy thie-aaght eck as v'ee smooinaghtyn ny reddyn shoh.

Agh ny yei shen as ooilley … Bare jee gyn loaghtey red erbee sy chamyr. Nagh bane va'n eddin ec y fer marroo! V'eh jeeaghyn dy row eh rooisht. Son shickyrys, v'eh mongey. Baase maynrey? Va'n eaddagh echey fillit dy jesh er caair faggys da'n lhiabbee – erreish jee v'er ceau yn argid shen er pressyn-eadee. Cullee-eaddee jesh as costal. Braagyn costal currit dy jesh er y laare faggys da'n lhiabbee. Ooilley eaddagh fyrryn: dyn eaddagh bwoirryn erbee.

Eisht honnick Bnr Quilleash y poodyr bane er meer dy phabyr er y voayrd beg ec y lhiabbee. Va pioban beg ayns shen neesht. 'Stoo anleighagh' sy thie-aaght eck? Cha nee flooyr v'ayn son shickyrys. Cho leah's v'ee er nakin yn cubbyl shen v'ee smooinaghtyn dy row red ennagh quaagh fo raad. Y ven aeg aalin as yn shenn dooinney. Cre hon reih ad y thie-aaght ecksh? Yee ooilley-niartal.

Ren ee jeeaghyn er y chorp marroo reesht. Va mysh queig kentimeadar eddyr y daa howl sy wannal. She tuill ghlenney v'ayn. V'eh quaagh agglagh. Eisht smooinee ee dy bare jee cur fys er ny meoiryn-shee as ren ee goll sheese ny greeishyn dy tappee gys y chellvane syn offish veg eck. Ren ee jeeley nuy-nuy-nuy dy kiarailagh. Cre'n shirveish v'ee geearree? Ny meoiryn-shee, gyn ourys. V'ee loayrt dy meeley er aggle dy beagh ny goaldee sy chamyr-yinnairagh clashtyn.

Translation
The Vampire Murders, *2005*

CHAPTER 1
They found the dead body at half-past nine in the morning. The landlady was worried that Mr Jones hadn't come down to get breakfast in the guest house. She was knocking and knocking at the bedroom door, but there was no reply to be had. Eventually, she found out that the door wasn't locked and she opened it. As soon as the landlady saw the man lying in the bed, she understood that something dreadful had happened.

Mr Jones was lying on his back, looking at the ceiling with wide eyes, staring. But he wasn't seeing anything because he was dead. A sheet was over the most part of this body, but his face and neck were visible and they were as white as snow. There were two small holes in his neck.

The landlady, Mrs Quilleash, couldn't be sure, but perhaps the dead body was smiling. She got rid of the thought and she got angry, a little: what was he doing, dying in her house? And where was that young woman who came with Mr Jones to stay in the hotel? 'Mr and Mrs Jones'? Tell me another. Then Mrs Quilleash became frightened. What was she doing? There was a dead man lying in her hotel and she was thinking these things.

But for all that … It would be better for her not to touch anything in the room. Wasn't the dead one's face white! He appeared to be naked. For sure, he was smiling. A happy death? His clothing was folded neatly on a chair near to the bed – after she'd spent that money on wardrobes. A smart and expensive suit. Expensive shoes placed neatly on the floor near to the bed. All men's clothes: no women's clothing at all.

Then Mrs Quilliam saw the white powder on a piece of paper on the little table at the bedside. There was a little pipe there as well. 'Illegal substances' in her hotel? It certainly wasn't flour. As soon as she'd seen that couple she was thinking that there was something strange going on. The beautiful, young woman and the old man. Why had they chosen her hotel? God almighty!

She looked at the dead body again. There were about five centimetres between the two holes in the neck. They were clean holes. It was awfully strange. Then she thought that she'd better let the police know and she quickly went down the stairs to the telephone in her little office. She dialled nine-nine-nine carefully. What service did she want? The police, without a doubt. She was speaking softly, afraid that the visitors in the dining room would be hearing.

The fact that this was produced in the format of a conventional novel of 279 pages with an attractive cover demonstrates a new confidence in Manx. There is now a large enough Manx-reading public to buy such books, to make their production feasible. Other reference books have also been produced in a similarly professional format, building on Doug Fargher's 'The Manx Have a Word For It' series of the late 1960s and early 1970s. 'Manks Flora' by John "Dog" Callister and Chris Sheard (2007) contains plant names in Manx as well as English and Latin. 'Eeanlee Vannin' ('Birds of Man') by Paul Rogers (2008) is in similar format.

At the same time as Yn Cheshaght Ghailckagh published Brian Stowell's original story, it also published, in a similar confident and ambitious format, his translation of a book for younger readers in Irish by Cathal O Sandair, 'Reks Carlo ayns Mannin' ('Reics Carlo ar Oilean Mhanann' – 'Rex Carlo in the Isle of Man'). Books for younger readers have been translated for use in Manx-medium playgroups and schools since the inception in 1983 of the 'Beeal Arrish' playgroup. This was followed later by a playgroup called 'Yn Chied Chesmad' ('The First Step') and then the founding of an organisation called 'Mooinjer Veggey' ('Little People') which continues to run playgroups. Mooinjer Veggey also set up a Manx-medium class which has since developed into a Manx-medium primary school. Translation of stories for use in these playgroups and schools had been undertaken on an ad hoc basis by teachers and enthusiasts. In 2006 Robert Carswell began working at the Bunscoill Ghaelgagh (Manx-medium primary school), translating material for children from age 5 years to 11 years of age, including books and posters covering all subject areas of the curriculum. With children having left the Bunscoill Ghaelgagh to go on to secondary education, secondary course resources in Manx have also been translated for history, geography, religious studies and computer/media studies.

Another new voice appeared in 2005, when Graham Naylor published his own collection of short stories and other writings in hardback under the title 'Te Scruit' ('It is written'). The major part of the stories draw on his personal experience of working in and visiting hospitals, as in the following extrract.

Graham Naylor
Goll Er Oai, *2005*

Dy kinjagh t'eh jeeaghyn dou dy ve feer trimshagh dy vel boandyryn as fir lhee ta cliaghtey ve kenjal as co-ennaghtagh, gaghtey cho bolveanagh as cho ard-wannalagh tra t'ad ceau cullee-chadjinit. T'ad cheet dy ve nyn ayrnyn gyn persoonid ayns jeshaght vooar neuphersoonagh. Foddee dy vel y corys jannoo jeshaghtyn jin ooilley. Ansherbee va stoo-lheeys currit da my voir, morfeen tilgit stiagh fo chrackanagh as va'n eiyrtys mianit er ny chosney. Haink e eddin dy ve lhiaggit, haink ee dy ve feagh as yeeagh ee dy ve ny cadley dy sheeoil reesht.

Nish, she trimshey ny h-oie v'ayn. Va shin nyn soie, cummal greim er laue my voir as gra fockle ny ghaa blandeyragh ree, nish as reesht. Reesht ghow shin tastey jeh ny sheeanyn ayns y ward. Son y chooid smoo, she sheeanyn dy chadley v'ayn; tayrn ennal dy trome, strinnooghyn. Nish as reesht v'ad nyn sheeanyn neusmaghtit jeh shenn vraane; breim sheeynt ny brooighe feiyragh. Ny yei, ny smoo lhiantynagh va ny meeryn dy choloayrtys, mectullagh voish bleeantyn er dy henney, va er nyn vockley magh liorish shenn vraane rouaillagh.

"Immee as jeeagh quoi shen ec y dorrys! Vel Ealish ayn?"
"Cur lhiat cappan dy hey er my hon, Horys!"
"Ny jean jarrood dy 'ollmaghey yn crockan-mooyn, Hom."
"Immee as jeeagh quoi shen ec y dorrys! Vel Ealish ayn?"

Va'n ward ny host reesht. Dooyrt shin beggan dy 'ocklyn rish y cheilley agh son y chooid smoo va shin nyn dost er lhimmey jeh tallaghey dy blandeyragh rish my voir.

Translation

Going Ahead, *2005*

It always appears to me to be very sad that nurses and doctors who are usually kind and sympathetic, act so foolishly and stiff-necked when they wear uniforms. They become personality-free parts of a great, impersonal machine. Perhaps the system makes machines of us all. Anyway medicine was given to my mother, morphine injected subcutaneously, and the desired effect achieved. Her face became slackened, she became quiet and she appeared to be sleeping peacefully again.

Now, it was the dead of night. We were sitting, keeping hold of my mother's hand and saying a soothing word or two to her, now and then. Again we noticed the sounds in the ward. For the most part, it was the sounds of sleeping; heavy drawing of breath, snoring. Now and again they were the uncontrolled sounds from old women; a drawn out fart or a noisy belch. For all that, the most haunting were the scraps of conversation, echoes from years ago, that were declaimed by rambling old women.

"Go and see who's at the door! Is Ealish in?"
"Fetch a cup of tea for me, Shorys!"
"Don't forget to empty the piss-pot, Tom."
"Go and see who's at the door! Is Ealish in?"

The ward was silent again. We said a small amount of words to each other but for the most part we were silent except for murmering soothingly to my mother.

The advent of a young voice is a further welcome development, arising from the availability of Manx in schools, the Teisht Chadjin Ghailckagh and the Ard-Teisht Ghailckagh. In 2007, Yn Cheshaght Ghailckagh published an original story of 18,500 words by Christopher Lewin together with other translations and pieces written by him, under the title, 'Jough-laanee Aegid as Skeealyn Elley' ('Elixir of Youth and Other Stories'). As Christopher Lewin wrote in his foreword:

> Ny-yei, choud's va mee screeu, as kiartaghey, ny skeealyn shoh, hooar mee magh ram mynphointyn jeh'n ghrammeydys as yn ymmyd jeh'n chengey nagh bione dou roie, as haink mee er palchey feyshtyn doillee nagh vel

Gaelgeyryn ooilley ayns coardailys my-nyn-gione.

[Nevertheless, whilst I was writing, and correcting, these stories, I found out many details of the grammar and the use of the language that I didn't know before, and I came across many difficult questions that not all Manx speakers agree about.]

The production of a number of books in recent years has underlined this. It is perhaps the case that, in trying to develop new literature, authors seek to develop new ways of saying things, combining elements of conventional grammar and idioms in new forms outside established conventions. However, Christopher Lewin has tried to ensure that the novelty is in his stories rather than in the grammar and idioms in which he tells them. The following is an extract from the title story.

Christopher Lewin
Jough-Laanee Aegid, *2007*

Ny s'anmagh yn oie shen, foddey lurg da Judy as ny paitchyn gimman thie, tra va Ealish goll dy lhie, doshil ee yn vynjeig dy vedshin lesh farrym bog jeh'n phabyr bane. Haink ny milljanyn cliaghtagh magh, as y stoo noa; as eisht, tra v'ee er-chee yn poagey-pabyr y cheau ersooyl, ren boteil veg elley surlley magh. Huitt ee er y laare, agh cha row ee brisht, booise da Jee.

As ee troggal seose y voteil, smooinee Ealish ree-hene, "Shoh quaagh! C'red t'ayn? Nee marran ren ad ec y chapp?" Va'n stoo ayns y voteil cho sullyr as crystal; she fliughid v'ayn dy jarroo, cha nee milljanyn ny syrup chiu. "Oddagh eh ve ushtey," dooyrt Ealish er ard, "ga s'cosoylagh dy nee drug feer niartal t'ayn. Cha beagh fys aym's er y lheid!" Lurg grig ny ghaa dy resooney, dooyrt ee: "Ny foddee dy nee nane jeh ny 'medshinyn elley' shid t'ayn. Red ennagh myr y red shid ... s'mie lesh y Phrinse Chalse eh ... cre'n ennym t'er? ... homeopatee, ennym ennagh myr shen."

Va lipaid laue-screeuit er y voteil, agh va'n screeu feer veg as doillee ry lhaih. V'eh screeuit lesh penn jiarg, hug Ealish my-ner, as smooinee ee dy row shen quaagh neesht, er yn oyr dy row fys eck dy vel potecareeyn cliaghtey goaill ymmyd jeh pennyn glassey. Hrog ee seose y voteil gys y toilshey dy voddagh ee yn lipaid y lhaih.

Lhaih ee dy kiarailagh:
Jough-laanee Aegid.
Ny gow rour ec yn un traa, as ny gow tooilley derrey lurg da goll er scryssey magh assyd. Bee beggan palchey. Myr shinney t'ou nish, saa hig oo dy ve. Nee yn eiyrtys farraghtyn kiare ooryn as feed.

"Graih veen, shoh quaagh dy jarroo!" docklee Ealish magh. "Jough-laanee! Ta shen sheeanal folliaghtagh! Agh gyn ourys cha nee agh stoo ennagh t'ayn son mraane ta jeih bleeaney as feed d'eash ry-hoi geddyn rey rish 'craplagyn'," dooyrt ee dy granganagh. Ren ee gearey. "Vel fys ec lheid ny mraane shid cre ta craplag?"

Yeeagh ee er y voteil reesht. Dy doaltattym ren ee gennaghtyn egin agglagh dy ghoaill bine jeh'n jough-laanee. Cha voddagh eh jannoo jeeyl erbee urree, voddagh? Cha nee mannagh nee agh stoo ry-hoi leodaghey craplagyn v'ayn? (Ga dy row ourys er Ealish dy voddagh red erbee leodaghey ny craplagyn ecksh.)

Agh ny-yei shen as ooilley, va'n slane red sheiltyn dy ve ro whaagh da Ealish. Va'n folt er e mwannal girree tra v'ee jeeaghyn er y voteil shen. Oddagh y stoo ve anleighalagh!

Chrie ee e kione, as deab ee dy yarrood y jough-laanee as ee goll gys y chamyr-oonlee dy ghlenney ny feeacklyn eck. Agh cha dod ee gimman eh magh ass e haigney; as tra haink ee er ash dy lhie sheese dy chadley, ren ee deayrtey bine beg jeh'n jough-laanee sheese e scoarnagh. Ren ee gennaghtyn oolagh chelleeragh ny lurg, agh smooinee ee dy cadlagh. "Oh well, ta mee gaase shenn. My yioym baase noght, bee bea lane er ve aym. Cha nel mee geddyn baase aeg. S'cummey…"

Translation

Elixir of Youth, *2007*

Later that night, long after Judy and the children had driven home, when Ealish was going to bed, she opened the parcel of medicine with a soft rustle from the white paper. The usual tablets came out, and the new stuff; and then, when she was about to throw the paper-bag away, a little bottle tumbled out. It fell on the floor, but it wasn't broken, thank God.

As she picked up the bottle, Ealish thought to herself, "This is strange! What is it? Is it a mistake they made at the shop?" The stuff in the bottle was as clear as crystal; it was indeed a liquid, not tablets or a thick syrup. "It could be water," said Ealish out loud, "though probably it's a very powerful drug. I wouldn't know about the like!" After a moment or two of weighing it up, she said: "Or perhaps it's one of those 'alternative medicines' yonder. Something like yonder thing … Prince Charles likes it … what's the name of it? … homeopathy, some name like that."

There was a hand-written label on the bottle, but the writing was very small and difficult to read. It was written with a red pen, Ealish beheld, and she thought that that was strange as well, becuase she knew that pharmacists customarily used green pens. She lifted up the bottle to the light so that she could read the label.

She read carefully:

Elixir of Youth
Do not take too much at any one time, and do not take more until it has worn off out of you. A little will be plenty. The older you are, the younger you will become. The effect will last twenty-four hours.

"Goodness gracious, this is indeed strange!" declared Ealish. "Elixir! That sounds mysterious! But no doubt it's only some stuff for women who are thirty years old in order to get rid of 'wrinkles'," she said grumpily. She laughed. "Do the like of yonder women know what a wrinkle is?"

She looked at the bottle again. Suddenly she felt a dreadful compulsion to take a drop of the elixir. It couldn't do any harm to her, could it? Not if it was only stuff to reduce wrinkles? (Though Ealish doubted that anything could reduce her wrinkles.)

But for all that, the whole thing seemed to be too odd to Ealish. The hair on her neck rose when she looked at that bottle. Could the stuff be illegal!

She shook her head, and she tried to forget the elixir whilst she went to the bathroom to clean her teeth. But she couldn't drive it out of her mind; and when she came back to lie down and go to sleep, she poured a little drop of the elixir down her throat. She felt guilty immediately after, but she thought sleepily, "Oh well, I'm growing old. If I die tonight, I'll have had a full life. I'm not dying young. It doesn't matter ..."

The years 2007 and 2008 brought two books of short stories translated into Manx by R W K Teare. The first was 'Jeih Skeealyn Scaanjoon – Liorish Koizumi Yakumo' ('Ten Ghost Stories – By Koizumi Yakumo'). This is part of a story concerning an old tree-cutter, Mosaku, and his eighteen-year-old apprentice, Minokichi.

R W K Teare
Yuki Onna, *2007*

Haink cadley dy tappee er y chenn dooinney, agh ren y scollag lhie as ny sooillyn echey feayn foshlit, geaishtagh rish y gheay agglagh as y sniaghtey goll er imman noi'n woalley.

Va'n awin freayney as va leaystey as jeestyrnee ec y waane gollrish junkey er yn 'aarkey mooar. V'eh sterrym atchimagh as dagh minnid haink yn aer dy ve smoo as smoo feayr.

Heid y gheay yn sniaghtey ny heebey noi'n woalley. Agh, fy yerrey, ga dy row eh feer feayr, haink cadley er neesht. Eisht, dy doaltattym, huitt sniaghtey kiart er e eddin, as ren eh moostey. Va dorrys y waane er ny 'osley lesh hene, as ayns soilshey y sniaghtey (yuki-akari), honnick eh ben 'sy chamyr, as cullee vane urree. V'ee sheidey yn ennal eck huggey, as yn ennal jeeaghyn gollrish jaagh gial bane.

Bunnys 'sy challid cheddin, hyndaa ee e kione, yeeagh ee er as haink ee er-e-skyn.

Ren eh e chooid share dy eamagh agh hooar eh nagh dod eh cur magh veg.

Ren ee croymmey er-e-skyn as haink ee ny s'inshley as ny s'inshley gys va nyn n-eddinyn bunnys bentyn ry cheilley. Honnick eh dy row ee feer aalin, ga dy row ny sooillyn eck cur aggle er.

Ren ee blakey er rish tammylt beg, eisht vynghear ee as dooyrt ee myr sannish; "smooinee mee dy jinnin y red cheddin dhyt as ren mee da'n dooinney elley, agh cha noddym agh goaill kuse dy erreeish ort, saa uss, as t'ou dty ghuilley bwaagh. Minokichi; cha jeanym skielley dhyt nish. Agh, dy beagh oo ginsh da fer erbee mychione ny reddyn t'ou er vakin noght, eer dty voir hene, hig fys hym as bee'm dty varroo. Cooinee ny focklyn aym!" Lurg jee gra shen, hyndaa ee veih as hie ee magh ass y dorrys.

From the Japansese of Koizumi Yakumo
Yuki Onna

Sleep came quickly to the old man, but the youth lay with his eyes wide open, listening to the dreadful wind and the snow being driven against the wall.

The river was heaving and the hut was swaying and creaking like a junk on the ocean. It was an awful storm and each minute the air became colder and colder.

The wind blew the snow into a drift against the wall. But, finally, though it was very cold, sleep came to him as well. Then, suddenly, snow fell right on his face, and he wakened suddenly. The door of the hut was opening by itself, and in the light of the snow (yuki-akari), he saw a woman in the room, wearing a white suit. She was blowing her breath towards him, and the breath looked like bright, white smoke.

Almost in the same second, she turned her head, she looked at him and she came above him.

He did his best to shout but he found that he couldn't produce anything.

She bent down above him and she came lower and lower until their faces were almost touching together. He saw that she was very beautiful, though her eyes frightened him.

She stared at him for a little while, then she smiled and she said in a whisper; "I thought that I would do the same to you as I did to the other man, but I can only feel some sympathy for you, young as you are, and you are a handsome boy, Minokichi; I will do you no harm now. But, if you were to tell anyone about the things you've seen tonight, even your own mother, I'll know and I'll be killing you. Remember my words!" After she had said that, she turned and she went out of the door.

Short stories in Irish by Ray Lawless (Re O Laighleis) under the title 'Ecstasy and Other Stories' were published in 1994. A translation into Scottish Gaelic had been published in 2004. It was with an eye to this latter source that R W K Teare made a translation of these stories as 'Ecstasy as Skeealyn Elley' ('Ecstasy and Other Stories') in 2008. This is the opening of one of the stories.

R W K Teare
Creeaght, *2008*

Lhie eh er e ghreeym as yeeagh eh er far-voalley y chamyr. By haittin daah geayney y pheint lesh, ga dy row eh fo vullagh thie ny hasslayntee. She sorch dy ghlass-jade v'ayn – daah graysoil. V'eh cur yindys er dy by haittin lesh eh – she daah v'ayn veagh cur jiarg-ghrayn er beggan dy vleeantyn er-ash. S'yindyssagh, smooinee eh, yn aght ta'n baght ec sleih caghlaa ec traaghyn doillee; myr s'mooar lhiat red tra ta gaue ayn dy bee eh goit voyd. As ec yn am shoh, va un red shickyr, she shen dy ragh ad er goaill veih: yn daah geayney, y bane, y buigh, yn jiarg – dy chooilley assee bentyn rish daaghyn; dy chooilley horch dy bollagh. Y baase. Tree mee, foddee; tree shiaghtin, tree laa – cha nod eh goll er gra lesh shickyrys. Cha row shickyrys ayn agh dy daghyragh eh dy doaltattym.

Va eddinyn cheet rish nish reesht – cheet veih traa ry hraa dy 'eddyn magh kanys va inchyn Eamon. Rock Hudson, Magic Johnson, Freddie Mercury, Arthur Ashe. Deiney mooarey. Deiney va er n'yannoo red ennagh mooar nyn mea; deiney as va'n ardghoo oc ayns beeal y cleih feiy'n teihll. Agh eshyn, Eamon Kelly, nagh dooar caa echey ard-ghoo y chosney foast! Cre'n fa eshyn? Ec eash nuy bleeaney jeig! Cre'n chaghteraght, cre'n chreenaght, cre'n choyrle veagh echeysyn dy 'aagail da'n teihll? Cre'n raaue ymmyrkagh eshyn da'n teihll mychione AIDS? Quoi ghoghe sym ayns ny veagh echey dy raa?

Translation

Courage, *2008*

He lay on his back and looked at the ceiling of the room. He approved of the green colour of the paint, though he was under the roof of the house of the sick. It was a sort of jade green – a graceful colour. It surprised him that he approved of it – it was a colour that would have raised in him an unremitting loathing a few years ago. It's wonderful, he thought, the way that people's opinion changed at difficult times; like when you make much of a thing when there's a danger that it'll be taken away: the colour green, white, yellow, red – every mischief to do with colours; every sort altogether. Death. Three months, perhaps; three weeks, three days – it couldn't be said for certain. There was no certainty except that it would happen suddenly.

Faces appeared now and again – coming from time to time to find out how was Eamon's mind. Rock Hudson, Magic Johnson, Freddie Mercury, Arthur Ashe. Great men. Men who'd done something great [in] their life; men whose repute was in the mouth of the people throughout the world. But he, Eamon Kelly, who didn't get his chance to gain repute yet! Why him? At the age of nineteen! What message, what wisdom, what advice would he have to leave to the world? What warning would he bear to the world about AIDS? Who would be interested in what he would have to say?

Following his book of short stories, Graham Naylor published a full-length novel called 'Brann Foillycan' ('A Butterfly's Dream') about global warming in 2008.

Graham Naylor
Brann Foillycan, *2008*

1

Keayrt dy row va'n foillycan hene er ve ny phraddag. Cha nee yn sorch ta dhone as geayshteenagh ta ratchal mygeayrt. Cha nee, er chor erbee. V'eh ny sorch litcheragh ta bog as geayney as bwoyagh, yn sorch ta guillyn cur stiagh ayns costrayl lesh duillag ny ghaa as eisht lhiggey da geddyn baase. Cha by chooinee lesh ve ny phraddag. Neayr as yn traa shen v'eh er ve aa-hroggit as er ny chlaaraghey dy noa; dy insh yn irriney, v'eh er ve jeant ass y noa. V'eh gee duillagyn agh nish, as eshyn ny 'oillycan, va'n beaghey echey naghtyr, jough ny Jeeghyn.

Cha row ennym er yn 'oillycan as s'liklee nagh vel ennym er foillycan erbee. Atreih t'eh er foillycanyn dy ve er mayrn as adsyn gyn bashtey. Ny yei, va ny foillycanyn elley gra rish ayns glare oillycanagh, "Ya-nn-ta-na," ta shen dy ghra ayns y Ghaelg, "yn fer ta dy kinjagh shirrey," er yn oyr dy row yn foillycan shoh dy kinjagh shirrey jough ny Jeeghyn.

Lurg lheid y laa, va'n foillycan skee as cheh. Hoie eh sheese ayns goal billagh, erskyn yn chayt. Yeeagh eh mygeayrt y mysh dy hickyraghey nagh beagh eh fo baggyrtys, as ren eh dy kiarailagh ny skianyn echey y 'illey as chaddil eh. Tra ren eh doostey v'eh ayns boayl feiyragh.

Lheie yn musthaa ersooyl as ghow yn caarliagh toshiaght, "Vraane as Gheiney Seyrey, surrys enn hannah dy atchimagh ta stayd y theihll as t'eh orrin dy reih yn aght share dy gholl er nyn doshiaght veih yn traa shoh magh. Ry-hoi red ennagh y yannoo, shen yn oyr ta shin er nyn jaglym cooidjagh jiu; son roud ta shin er loayrt fegooish coardail. Shegin dooin cur stap er anvea; nish t'eh orrin dy aghtey." Va cauaig voish yn chaglym as yllagh ny ghaa dy choardail. Hie yn caarliagh er, "Hoshiaght, eiym er scruderyn ny fo-vingyn dy chur giare-choontaghyn jeh'n chooish."

Yn halley, ayn va Coonceil y Theihll chaglym, v'eh mooar as souyr as lung lane dy leih y laa v'ayn. Son y chooid smoo va sleih ceau eaddeeyn va cosoylagh rish ny eaddeeyn jeh dagh peiagh elley as va sorch dy Vaarle ec dy chooilley pheiagh, row yn crackan oc bane ny dhone ny doo ny bwee. Va sleih neufeagh; ren ad foostyrey as tallaghey.

"Scrudeyr Bing yn Chymmyltaght!"

"Gura mie ayd, Y Chaarliagh. Nee'm lhaih voish giare-choontaghyn Chaglym y Ving, hie er cummal yn wheiggoo laa jeig jeh Mee Vayrnt, mleeaney, daa villey keead as queig-jeig as treefeed."

Translation
A Butterfly's Dream, *2008*

1
Once upon a time the butterfly itself had been a caterpillar. Not the sort that's brown and hairy that races around. No, not at all. It was the lazy sort that's soft and green and attractive, the sort that boys put in a jar with a leaf or two and allow it to die. It had no recollection of being a caterpillar. Since that time it had been rebuilt and programmed anew; to tell the truth, it had been made afresh. It used to eat leaves but now, with its being a butterfly, its nourishment was nectar, the drink of the Gods.

The butterfly didn't have a name and it's likely that no butterly has a name. Unfortunately it's the lot of butterflies to remain unbaptised. Nevertheless, the other butterflies called it in the butterfly tongue, "Ya-nn-ta-na", which is to say in Manx, "the one that's always seeking," because this butterfly was constantly seeking the drink of the Gods.

After such a day, the butterfly was tired and hot. It sat down in the fork of a tree, above the cat. It looked about it to make sure that it wouldn't be threatened, and it carefully folded its wings and it slept. When it awoke it was in a noisy place.

The turmoil died away and the chairman began, "Ladies and Gentlemen, the state of the world is already awfully well-known and we have to choose the best way to go forward from this time on. In order to do something, that's the reason we've gathered together today; for too long we have spoken without agreement. We must put an end to strife; now we have to act." There was a murmur from the meeting and a cry or two of agreement. The chairman went on, "First, I'll call on the secretaries of the sub-committees to give their summaries of the situation."

The hall in which the Council of the World was meeting was big and comfortable and absolutely full of people that day. For the most part people were wearing clothes that were similar to each other's clothes and everbody spoke a sort of English, whether their skin was white, brown, black or yellow. People were uneasy; they fidgeted and murmered.

"The Secretary of the Environment Committee!"

"Thank you, Chairman. I'll read from the minutes of the Committee's Meeting, which was held on the fifteenth of March, this year, 2175."

From a text taking us into the future, we turn finally to a text with links to the distant past. Sophia Morrison's 'Manx Fairy Tales' was published originally in 1911. One story had been written in Manx with an English translation and there was a short rhyme in Manx, also with English translation. There were also six verses in Manx without translation of The Traditionary Ballad. The most part of the book, though, was in English. Peddyr Shimmin and Chris Sheard made a translation of this work. Through the Manx Heritage Foundation they published 'Skeealyn

Mooinjer Veggey Vannin' in 2008. One of the shorter tales embroiders The Traditional Ballad, returning us to our starting point – Manannan Beg Mac y Leirr, Little Manannan Son of Leirr:

Peddyr Shimmin and Chris Sheard
Manannan Mac Y Leirr, *2008*

She Manannan Mac y Leirr, Mac ny Marrey, va'n chied ree va reill ayns Mannin. V'eh ny 'er obbee mooar, as v'eh cho pooaral dy row sleih haink ny yei credjal dy row eh ny yee. Va doon cloaie mooar echey er Inish Pherick, as dod eh jannoo un dooinney ny hassoo er e voallaghyn caggee jeeaghyn gollrish keead. Tra honnick eh lhongyn e noidyn shiaulley, chloagagh eh yn ellan mygeayrt lesh kay argid nagh row eh ry akin; as mannagh row shoh speeideilagh as haink e noidyn faggys da, cheauagh eh speiltyn stiagh syn ushtey as hyndaagh eh dys lhongyn ad. Laa dy row v'eh mooie shooyl er Barrool, tra honnick eh dy row lhongyn caggee ny Loghlynnee ayns baie Phurt ny h-Inshey. Er shen hyndaa eh eh hene dys cummey tree cassagh as rowl eh myr queeyl neose voish mullagh y clieau cho tappee as y gheay. She traa yn vooir-hraie v'ayn sy phurt bunnys, as va strooan dy ushtey glistragh roie magh dys y cheayn. Va brooinyn claddee ec y trooan raad va duillagyn glassey lhean yn chiast gaase. Myr shen, ren Manannan baatyn beggey ass y chiast, ymmodee jeu, as hiauill eh e vaatyn sy trooan. As tra hiauill yn lhuingys veg magh ass y phurt, hug eh orroo jeeaghyn myr dy row ad nyn lhongyn caggee mooarey as lane skimmee caggee oc. Eisht huitt atchim er ny Loghlynnee tra honnick ad yn lhuingys Vanninagh, as yiar ad nyn deaddyn, hrog ad nyn shiaullyn, as hie ad roue cho tappee as dod ad, as hie Manannan as e ellan er faagail ayns shee. Myr shoh v'eh freayll Mannin, as cha nee lesh e chliwe, ny lesh e vhow as e hideyn.

Va halley fleah mooar sy doon echey, raad veagh guillyn braew cloie kiaull bing, as gammanyn roortagh dy hoilshaghey magh y treanid as niart oc. Va cabbyl echey enmyssit Enbarr yn Wing Liauyr, dod troailt myr y gheay chammah harrish keayn as thalloo. V'echey myrgeddin coyin bieau dod goaill greim er baagh oaldey erbee, as cliwe enmyssit Yn Freggyrtagh, va'n lhott echey dy kinjagh marrooagh, as e Vanglane Obbee, as e vaatey yindyssagh, Skeab ny Tonnyn.

V'eh reill Mannin dy mie rish ymmodee bleeantyn as v'eh dellal rish ny Manninee dy kiart as corrym. Son mayl cha row eh shirrey er dagh nane jeu agh bart dy leaghyryn glassey va orroo cur lhieu huggey er Barrool Jiass dagh Oie'll Eoin. Va'n ellan ny voayl maynrey as grianagh lane dy reddyn taitnyssagh, as cha row peiagh erbee ayns shen shenn ny skee ny trimshagh.

Cha row Manannan rieau jarroodit ec ny Manninee, as rish thousane blein va nyn eeasteyryn goaill yn arrane shoh cheet, choud's v'ad goll magh er y cheayn. Eer gys lhing nyn ayraghyn v'ad jannoo ymmyd j'ee:
Manannan Beg Mac y Leirr,
Bannee orrin as nyn maatey,

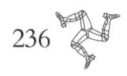

Mie goll magh as ny share cheet stiagh,
Lesh ny bioee as ny merriu aynjee.

Translation

Manannan Son of Leirr [the Sea], *2008*

It's Manannan Mac y Leirr, Son of the Sea, who was the first king that ruled in Man. He was a great wizard, and he was so powerful that people who came after him believed that he was a god. He had a great stone castle on St Patrick's Isle, and he could make one man standing on the battlements look like a hundred. When he saw his enemies' ships under sail, he would cloak the island around with a silver mist so that it couldn't be seen; and if this wasn't successful and his enemies came near to it, he would throw chips of wood into the water and he would turn them into ships. One day he was out walking on Barrule when he saw that there were Viking warships in Peel bay. With that he turned himself into a three-legged shape and he rolled like a wheel down from the top of the mountain as swift as the wind. It was almost the time of the low tide in the harbour, and there was a glittering stream of water running out to the sea. There were marshy banks to the stream where the wide green leaves of the sedge were growing. So, Manannan made little boats out of the sedge, lots of them, and he sailed his boats in the stream. And when the little fleet sailed out of the harbour, he made them appear as if they were great warships with full warrior crews. Then dread fell on the Vikings when they saw the Manx fleet, and they cut their ropes, they raised their sails, and away they went as quickly as they could, and Manannan and his island remained in peace. Thus he was keeping Man, and not with his sword, or with his bow and his arrows.

There was a great banquet hall in his fortress, where fine lads would be playing sweet music, and athletic games to demonstrate their heroism and strength. He had a horse called Enbarr of the Long Mane, that could travel like the wind both over sea and land. He also had swift hounds that could catch hold of any wild beast, and a sword called The Answerer, the wound from which was always mortal, and his Magic Branch, and his wonderful boat, Wave Sweeper.

He was ruling Man well for many years and he dealt with the Manx people rightly and properly. For rent he only sought from each of them a bundle of green rushes that they had to take to him on South Barrule on each St John's Eve. The island was a happy place and sunny, full of pleasant things, and there wasn't anybody there who was old or tired or sad.

Manannan was never forgotten by the Manx people, and for a thousand years the fishermen used to sing this following song, whilst they were going out on the sea. Even down to our father's time they were using it:

Little Manannan Son of Leirr [the Sea]
Bless us and our ship,
Good going out and better coming in,
With the living and the dead in her.

Bibliography

Books

Anon, 1829, *Coontey jeh Saggyrt William Tyndall* [An Account of the Priest William Tyndall], Sheshaght ec Bristol jeh Agglish Hostyn [The Society at Bristol of the Church of England], Bristol.

Anon, 1840, *The Book of Common Prayer, and administration of The Sacraments, and other Rites and Ceremonies of the Church according to the use of the United Church of England and Ireland: together with the Psalter or Psalms of David, pointed as they are to be sung or said in churches. Translated into Manks for the use of the Diocese of Man*, Fifth edition, Society for Promoting Christian Knowledge, London.

Anon, 1846, *Lioar dy Hymnyn As Arraneyn Spyrrydoil, chyndait gys Gailck veih lioaryn Wesley as Watt, &c* [A Book of Hymns and Spiritual Songs, translated into Manx from the books of Wesley and Watts, &c], M A Quiggin, Douglas.

Anon, 1891, *Carvalyn Gailckagh, Chyndaait ayns Baarl, Marish Goan-Foshlee Giare – Manx Carols, Translated into English, With a Short Preface*, John Christian Fargher, Douglas.

Anon, 1939, 'In Memoriam: John Joseph Kneen', in W Cubbon (ed), *The Journal of the Manx Museum* Vol IV, No 58, March 1939, Manx Museum, Douglas.

Bible Chasherick yn Lught-Thie – The Manx Family Bible,1819 reprinted 1979, Shearwater Press, Douglas.

Borrow, George, 1857, Advertisement for an intended publication, 'Wanderings in Quest of Manx Literature', quoted in A W Moore's 'Introduction' to Anonymous, 1891, *Carvalyn Gailckagh – Manx Carols*, John Christian Fargher, Douglas.

Brady, Rev James and Tate, Rev Nahum, 1692; 2006 printed on demand copy of a 1751 edition (original work 1692), *A New Version of the Psalms of David, Fitted to the Tunes Used in Church*, Kessinger Publishing, Whitefish.

Bridson, Joseph (as Joe Vreejey), 1760, *Coontey Ghiare jeh Ellan Vannin ayns Gailck* [A Short Account of the Isle of Man in Manx], in Paul Bridson Hon Secretary, 1872, *Manx Miscellanies* Vol I, Vol XX, The Manx Society, Douglas.

Broderick, George (as Shorus y Creayrie), (ed), 1976, 'Skeealaght' [Storytelling], *Yn Cheshaght Ghailckagh*, Douglas.

Broderick, George, 1981, 'Baase Illiam Dhone' [The Death of Illiam Dhone], in Brian O Cuiv (ed), *Celtica*, Vol XIV, Instituid Ard-Leinn Bhaile Atha Cliath, Dublin.

Broderick, George, 1982, 'Manx Stories and Reminiscences of Neddy Beg Hom Ruy', *Zeitschrift fur Celtische Philologie*, Band 38 & 39, Max Niemeyer Verlag, Tubingen.

Broderick, George, 1984, 'Ny Kirree Fo Niaghtey' [The Sheep Under the Snow], in Brian O Cuiv (ed), *Celtica*, Vol XIV, Instituid Ard-Leinn Bhaile Atha Cliath, Dublin.

Broderick, George, 1984, *A Handbook of Late Spoken Manx*, 3 volumes, Max Niemeyer Verlag, Tubingen.

Broderick, George, 1999, *Language Death in the Isle of Man – An investigation into the decline and extinction of Manx Gaelic as a community language in the Isle of Man*, Max Niemeyer Verlag, Tubingen.

Caine, Joan, 1996, *Dunverys er Traen-Tappee yn Niar – liorish Agatha Christie – er ny hyndaa ayns Gailck* [Murder on the Orient Express – by Agatha Christie – having been translated into Manx], Caarjyn ny Gaelgey, St John's.

Caine, Philip W, 1920, 'Manx Carols and Their Writers' in P G Ralfe (ed), 1926, *Proceedings*, Vol II, No 4', The Isle of Man Antiquarian and Natural History Society, Douglas.

Callister, John 'Dog' and Sheard, Chris, 2007, *Manks Flora*, Moddey Publications, Kirk Michael.

Carswell, Robert Corteen (ed), 1983-1987, FRITLAG [A Rag], 14 issues, FRITLAG, Douglas.

Carswell, Robert Corteen, 1994, *Shelg yn Drean* [Hunt the Rhyme], FRITLAG, Douglas.

Carswell, Robert Corteen, 1996, *Arraneyn 'sy Ghaelg* [Songs in Manx], FRITLAG, Douglas.

Chalenor, James, 1656, 'A Short Treatise of the Isle of Man', in Rev J G Cumming (ed), 1864, *Chalenor's Treatise – Isle of Man*, Vol X, The Manx Society, Douglas.

Christian, Thomas, 'Pargys Caillit' [Paradise Lost] in R L Thomson (ed), 1995, *Pargys Caillit/An abridgment of John Milton's/Paradise Lost/By Thomas Christian/with the anonymous translation of/Thomas Parnell's/The Hermit, Centre for Manx Studies Research Report 3*, Centre for Manx Studies, Douglas.

Cregeen, Archibald, 1984 facsimile of 1910 revised reprint of original dated 1835, *Fockleyr ny Gaelgey – Chaglit Liorish Archibald Cregeen* [Dictionary of Manx – Compiled By Archibald Cregeen], Yn Cheshaght Ghailckagh, Douglas.

Crellin, Lewis, 2006, *Skeealyn Lewis Crellin* [The Stories of Lewis Crellin], The Manx Heritage Foundation, Douglas.
Cubbon, William (comp and ed), 1939, *A Biographical Account of Works Relating to the Isle of Man* (Two volumes), Oxford University Press, London.
Curghey, Rev Matthias and Wilks, Rev James, 1761, reprinted 1819, 'The Psalms of David', in Anonymous, 1840, *The Book of Common Prayer, and administration of The Sacraments, and other Rites and Ceremonies of the Church according to the use of the United Church of England and Ireland : together with the Psalter or Psalms of David, pointed as they are to be sung or said in churches. Translated into Manks for the use of the Diocese of Man*, Fifth edition, Society for Promoting Christian Knowledge, London.
Draskau, Jennifer Kewley, 2006, *Account of the Isle of Man in Song*, Centre for Manx Studies, Douglas.
Draskau, Jennifer Kewley, 2008, *Practical Manx*, Liverpool University Press, Liverpool.
Fargher, Douglas C, c.1966–c.1972, *The Manx Have A Word For It*, 5 volumes, D C Fargher, Port Erin.
Fargher, Douglas C, 1979, *Fargher's English-Manx Dictionary*, Shearwater Press, Douglas.
Fargher, John Christian publ, 1891, *Carvalyn Gailckagh – Manx Carols*, John Christian Fargher, Douglas.
Farquar, Edward, 1901, republished 1994, *Skeealyn Aesop* [Aesop's Fables'], P J Kelly, Kirk Michael.
Feltham, John, 1798, 'A Tour Through the Island of Mann in 1797 and 1798', in Rev Robert Airey (ed), *Feltham's Tour*, Vol VI, The Manx Society, Dogulas.
Fitzgerald, Edward, 1964, *The Rubaiyat of Omar Khayyam, Rendered into English Verse by Edward Fitgerald*, John Baker for the Richards Press, London.
Gell, John (as Juan y Geill), (ed), 1951-1957, *Coraa Ghailckagh* [Manx Voice], 14 issues, Yn Cheshaght Ghailckagh, Isle of Man.
Gell, John (as Juan y Geill), 1977, *Cooinaghtyn my Aegid as Cooinaghtyn Elley* [Recollections of my Youth and Other Recollections], Yn Cheshaght Ghailckagh, Isle of Man.
Gell, John, 1981 published 1996, 'Morte d'Arthur' in Phil Gawne (ed), *Dhooraght*, Nos 3 and 4, Yn Cheshaght Ghailckagh, Isle of Man.
Gell, John, no date published 1998-9, 'Yn Whallag' in Phil Gawne (ed), *Dhooraght*, Nos 10, 11 and 12 (1998) and Nos 13 and 14 (1999), Yn Cheshaght Ghailckagh, Isle of Man.
Gill, Rev William (ed), 1859, 'Editor's Introduction', in *The Manx Grammar*, Vol II, The Manx Society, Douglas.
Gill, W H, 1896, *Manx National Songs with English words, selected from the MS. Collection s of The Deemster Gil, Dr. J. Clague and W.H. Gill*, Boosey & Co, London.

Goodwin, Edmund, 1901 (corrected, enlarged and revised by Robert Thomson 1966), *First Lessons In Manx*, Yn Cheshaght Ghailckagh, Douglas.
Gregor, D.B., 1980, *Celtic – A Comparative Study*, The Oleander Press, Cambridge, England and New York, N.Y.
Harrison, William (ed), 1869, *Mona Miscellany*, Second Series, Vol XVI, The Manx Society, Douglas.
Harrison, William (ed), 1873, *Mona Miscellany*, Vol XXI, The Manx Society, Douglas.
Jerry, Colin, 1978, *Kiaull yn Theay* [The Music of the People], Yn Cheshaght Ghailckagh, Isle of Man.
Jerry, Colin, 1979, *Kiaull yn Theay 2*, Yn Cheshaght Ghailckagh, Isle of Man.
Jerry, Colin, 1989, *Ny Tree Muckyn Beggey* [The Three Little Pigs], privately published, Isle of Man.
Jerry, Colin, 1996, *Shey Skeealyn Jeig* [Nineteen Stories], privately published, Isle of Man.
Kelly, P J ed no date, Series of reprints of material first printed in *Noon as Noal* [From Here and From There], *Rannag Ghoo* [Black Frog], Kirk Michael.
Kermode, P M C, 1907, *Manx Crosses, reprinted 1994 with an Introduction by David M Wilson and appendices*, The Pinkfoot Press, Balgavies, Angus.
Kneen, J J, 1934, 'Rubaiyat Omar Khayyam Chyndaait ayns Gailck' [The Rubaiyat of Omar Khayyam Translated into Manx], in *The Journal of the Manx Museum*, Vol. II –Nos. 38, 39, 40, 41, The Manx Museum, Douglas.
Kneen, J J, 1936, 'Cheer nyn Aeg' [The Country of the Young] in *Lessons in Manx – Part 2*, Yn Cheshaght Ghailckagh, Douglas.
Lewin, Christopher, 2007, *Jough-laanee Aegid as Skeealyn Elley* [The Elixir of Youth and Other Stories], Yn Cheshaght Ghailckagh, St Jude's.
Marstrander, Carl J S, 1929, 'Dagbok – Appendix A' in George Broderick, 1999, *Language Death in the Isle of Man*, Max Niemayer Verlag, Tubingen.
Moore, A W (ed), 1885-1887, *The Manx Note Book – 3 volumes*, G H Johnson, Douglas.
Moore, A W, 1896, *Manx Ballads and Music*, G & R Johnson, Douglas.
Naylor, Graham, 2007, *Te Scruit* [It is Written], *Fedjag Screeuee Vannin* [Manx Quill], Isle of Man.
Naylor, Graham, 2008, *Brann Foillycan* [The Butterfly's Dream], *Fedjag Screeuee Vannin*, Isle of Man.
O'Rahilley, T F, 1932, *Preface to Irish dialects past and present*, Browne and Nolan, Dublin.
Paton, Cyril I, 1925, 'Manx Carvals and Carval Books, With Notes on Some of the MSS.' in P G Ralfe (ed), 1926, *Proceedings*, Vol II, No 4, The Isle of Man Natural History and Antiquarian Society, Douglas.
Phillips, Bishop John, c 1610, in A W Moore ed assisted by Professor John Rhys, 1893 and 1894, *The Book of Common Prayer in Manx Gaelic* Vols I and II Vols XXXII and XXXIII, The Manx Society, Douglas.

Rogers, Paul, 2008, *Eeanlee Vannin – Birds of Mann*, Yn Cheshaght Ghailckagh, Isle of Man.

Rhys, Professor John, 1894, 'Preface to The Phonology of Manx Gaelic' in A W Moore ed assisted by Professor John Rhys, 1893, *The Book of Common Prayer in Manx Gaelic* Vol II, Vol XXXIII, The Manx Society, Douglas.

Sacheverell, William, 1688, 'An Account of the Isle of Man' in Rev J G Cumming (ed), 1859, *Sacheverell's Survey of the Isle of Man*, Vol I, The Manx Society, Douglas.

Sheard, Chris as Shimmin, Peddyr, 2008, *Skeealyn Mooinjer Veggey Vannin – Sophia Morrison* [Manx Fairy Tales – Sophia Morrison], Manx Heritage Foundation, Douglas.

Speed, John, 1611, 1614, 1627, 'Speed's History', in William Harrison (ed), 1871, *The Old Historians of the Isle of Man*, Vol XVIII, The Manx Society, Douglas.

Stowell, Brian 1990 republished 2006, *Ealish ayns Cheer ny Yindyssyn* [Alice in Wonderland], Yn Cheshaght Ghailckagh, St Jude's.

Stowell, Brian, 2005, *Dunveryssyn yn Tooder Folley* [The Vampire Murders], Yn Cheshaght Ghailckagh, Douglas.

Stowell, Brian, 2005, *Reks Carlo ayns Mannin – Liorish Cathal O Sandair* [Rex Carlo in Mann – By Cathal O Sandair], Yn Cheshaght Ghailckagh, Douglas.

Teare, R W K, 2007, *Jeih Skeealyn Scaanjoon – Liorish Koizumi Yakumo* [Ten Ghost Stories – By Koizumi Yakumo], Yn Cheshaght Ghailckagh, St Jude's.

Teare, R W K, 2008, *Ecstasy as skeealyn elley – Re O Laighleis* [Ecstasy and other stories – Ray Lawless], Yn Cheshaght Ghailckagh, St Jude's.

Thomson, Robert L, 1981, *Lessoonyn Sodjey 'Sy Ghailck Vanninagh* [Further Lessons in Manx Gaelic], Yn Cheshaght Ghailckagh, Doolish.

Thomson, Robert L, 1983, 'The Continuity of Manx', in Christine Fell et al (ed), *The Viking Age in the Isle of Man*, Viking Society for Northern Research, University College, London, pp.169-174.

Thomson, R L and Pilgrim, A J, no date, *Outline of Manx Language and Literature*, Yn Cheshaght Ghailckagh, Isle of Man.

Thomson, R L, 1979, 'Introduction' in 1819 reprinted 1979, *Bible Chasherick yn Lught-Thie* [The Family Holy Bible], Shearwater Press, Douglas.

Thomson, R L, (ed), 1997, *Paart dy Homileeyn ny Sharmaneyn Oikoil Agglish Hostyn* [Some Homilies or Official Sermons of the Church of England], Yn Cheshaght Ghailckagh, Douglas.

Thomson, R L, (ed), *1998, Yn Fer-raauee Creestee – The Christian Monitor*, Yn Cheshaght Ghailckagh, Douglas.

Waldron, George, 1731, 'A Description of the Isle of Man', William Harrison (ed), 1865, *Waldron's Isle of Man – 1726*, Vol XI, The Manx Society, Douglas.

Walker, William, 1748, *Yn Sushtal Scruit liorish yn Noo Mian* [The Gospel Written by St Matthew], printed for Bishop Thomas Wilson, Bishopscourt.

Wilson, Thomas, 1707, facsimile edition 1972, *The Principles and Duties of Christianity*, The Scolar Press Limited, Menston, Yorkshire, England.

Wood, G W, 1911, 'Manx Language Literature', in *Manx Quarterly*, No 10, S K Broadbent, Douglas.

Websites

http://www.gaelg.iofm.net/
http://www.isle-of-man.com/manxnotebook/
http://www.learnmanx.com/
http://www.mannin.info/MHF/index2.htm
http://www.mannin.info/MHF/index3.htm